QUEST FOR A STAR

QUEST *for a* STAR

THE CIVIL WAR LETTERS AND DIARIES OF COLONEL FRANCIS T. SHERMAN OF THE 88TH ILLINOIS

Edited, with Commentary, by
C. KNIGHT ALDRICH

Voices of the Civil War
Frank L. Byrne
Series Editor

The University of Tennessee Press / Knoxville

The Voices of the Civil War series makes available a variety of primary source materials that illuminate issues on the battlefield, the homefront, and the western front, as well as other aspects of this historic era. The series contextualizes the personal accounts within the framework of the latest scholarship and expands established knowledge by offering new perspectives, new materials, and new voices.

Frontispiece: Col. Francis Trowbridge Sherman. Courtesy of Library of Congress.

The paper used in this book meets the minimum requirements of ANSI/NISO Z39.48-1992 (R 1997) (Permanence of Paper). The binding materials have been chosen for strength and durability. Printed on recycled paper.

LIBRARY OF CONGRESS CATALOGING-IN-PUBLICATION DATA

Sherman, Francis Trowbridge, 1825–1905.
Quest for a star : the Civil War letters and diaries of Colonel Francis T. Sherman of the 88th Illinois / edited with Commentary by C. Knight Aldrich. — 1st ed.
p. cm. — (Voices of the Civil War)

ISBN 1-57233-064-3 (cl.: alk. paper)
1. Sherman, Francis Trowbridge, 1825–1905—Correspondence. 2. United States. Army. Illinois Infantry Regiment, 88th (1862–1865). 3. United States—History—Civil War, 1861–1865—Personal narratives. 4. Illinois—History—Civil War, 1861–1865. 5. Soldiers—Illinois—Correspondence. I. Aldrich, C. Knight (Clarence Knight), 1914–. II. United States. Army. Illinois Infantry Regiment, 88th (1862–1865). III. Title. IV. Series: Voices of the Civil War series.
E505.5 88th .S48 2000
973.7'473'092—dc21
[B]
99-6507

To eight of Colonel Sherman's great-great-great grandchildren:
David, Katie, Drew, Brian, Matt, Jenny, Dan, and Adam

CONTENTS

ILLUSTRATIONS

Figures

Maps

FOREWORD

The *Voices of the Civil War* series, in which this work is the eleventh volume, has brought to light a rich array of previously unpublished source material. Its soldier writers have come from both North and South and have included officers and enlisted men. While some fought in the eastern theater, many served in the more neglected West. One voice was that of an African American and one that of a white woman, but most have belonged to white males of varying backgrounds.

Francis Trowbridge Sherman, whose *Quest for a Star* (a general's insignia) is the present volume, was unlike the numerous participants in the Civil War who hailed from rural areas and small towns. He came from the city of Chicago and was colonel of the 88th Illinois, raised there. His letters and diaries, carefully edited by Dr. C. Knight Aldrich, tell something of the unit's history and its service with the Army of the Cumberland. Thus there is much about campaigning in Kentucky and Tennessee, with good descriptions of the battles of Perryville and Stones River and an especially graphic account of the attack on Missionary Ridge. While Sherman sometimes commanded a brigade, his most important service was as a staff officer. The latter post entailed exposure that resulted in his capture and imprisonment for three months. Readers are likely to be interested in his account of prison conditions and the exchange process. Especially informative is his diary of service as a member of General Sheridan's staff with the Army of the Shenandoah in the war's last months.

Besides strictly military matters, Sherman's papers illustrate how all aspects of the war were entwined with politics. Sherman's status as a prominent "War Democrat" both advanced and hindered his army career. His father, to whom many of his letters were addressed, was a Chicago hotel keeper and political leader associated with the Peace Democrats. His son's comments reveal much about wartime political emotions and also about the politics of army promotions.

As was the case with several other books in this series, the editing of *Quest* by one of the writer's descendants gives this Voice a tone of profound familial pride.

Frank L. Byrne
Kent State University

PREFACE

I first heard that I had a great-grandfather who fought in the Civil War when I was ten or eleven years old. At that time his son-in-law, my grandfather, was living at the Union League Club in Chicago. Grandfather was a tall, handsome, imperious, retired politician, given to dramatic pronouncements. He usually came to our home in the northern suburbs for Sunday dinner, after which we would drive him back in our 1924 Lexington touring car.

While we drove down Sheridan Road one Sunday afternoon, my grandfather was haranguing my father, as he often did, about his lack of interest in our family's part in the early history and politics of Chicago. Just as we entered Lincoln Park, my grandfather admonished my father, "You care so little about what's important to our family that I suppose you don't even know the name of that *horse!*" With a sweeping gesture, he leveled his forefinger at the equestrian statue of Gen. Philip Sheridan. My father gritted his teeth and said nothing, whereupon my grandfather, with a deep sigh, turned to me in the back seat and explained that at the end of the war—the Civil War—his father-in-law had offered to put Sheridan's favorite horse out to pasture on his downstate farm. The horse, which had been given to Sheridan following a skirmish in Mississippi in August 1861, was named Rienzi after the site of the skirmish, which in turn had been named after the Italian patriot. Sheridan rode Rienzi through forty-five engagements, nineteen of which were pitched battles. In one of the latter, in October 1864, the general galloped from "Winchester, twenty miles away,"[1] to rally his troops at Cedar Creek and turn defeat into victory. Rienzi, renamed Winchester, remained with Sheridan throughout the war, enjoyed a long and peaceful retirement on our family farm, died in 1878 at the age of nineteen, and now can be seen, stuffed, in the National Museum of American History in Washington, D.C.

My grandfather evidently expected that I would pick up where my father had failed. I have, but it has taken longer than he had hoped. My grandfather's papers, including his father-in-law's Civil War diaries and his letters home, lay dormant for fifty years after his death, until 1984, when I retired from the medical school faculty in Charlottesville, Virginia. Retirement gave me leisure to read some of my great-grandfather's papers. Using his diary as a guide, I followed his path with the Army of the Cumberland from Louisville through Tennessee to Atlanta, and through Charlottesville near the end of the war on his way to Appomattox. In tracing the long marches and in walking the battlefields, I was stirred by the hardihood and the commitment of the men who slogged through

Sheridan Statue, by Gutzon Borglum, in Lincoln Park. Chicago Park District, Special Collections.

such difficult terrain and fought so courageously. It seemed incredible, for example, that anyone could have scaled Missionary Ridge at the spot where he and his troops attacked—even under the best of circumstances, let alone under enemy fire.

I have based this book on my great-grandfather's letters and parts of his diaries. His full name was Francis Trowbridge Sherman. Most of his letters were written to his father, Chicago Mayor Francis Cornwall Sherman. In them, and in his diaries, he described many of the Civil War operations of the Army of the Cumberland from the time the 88th Illinois regiment joined it in September 1862 until it moved into position for the Battle of Atlanta in July 1864. He missed that battle because he was captured just before it started. He spent three months in Confederate prisons before he was exchanged; later he served on General Sheridan's staff during the last few months of the war.

The Army of the Cumberland and the Tennessee campaigns have been overshadowed by the struggle in the East for Washington and Richmond. The Tennessee campaigns began the task of cutting the Confederacy in two and made it possible for Gen. William T. Sherman to finish the job with his march through Georgia. The division of the Confederacy occurred at a time when the Union was tired of war and disappointed that the victories at Gettysburg and Vicksburg had not brought instant peace. It was a great accomplishment—one that restored confidence in the Union Army and in the Lincoln administration just in time for the 1864 election.

Colonel Sherman's letters and diaries provide a running account of these crucial military operations by a private citizen who rapidly became a competent officer. He had strong opinions about the war and about its politics, and he stated them vigorously. Paralleling his account of the campaign and his concern about his father's political associates is his preoccupation with promotion; for over two years he believed that he was entitled to be promoted to the rank of brigadier general, but he did not receive his star until after the war was over. His letters portray a bright, capable, ambitious, self-trained officer who was sometimes moralistic, often contentious, and always impatient with incompetence. His impatience and contentiousness occasionally got him in trouble; as he once wrote, "I cannot truckle and play the courtier; it is not in my nature."

Only one photograph shows him during his military career (fig. 2). The only description of his appearance that I can find comes from the memoirs of Charles Lewis Francis, a private in Colonel Sherman's 88th Illinois Infantry until his capture at Stones River. Francis, evidently no fan of his colonel, described him: "In person he was tall and slim.[2] He had a darkish red face and prominent features, suggestive of a tincture of Indian blood. Both in his face and temperament he was decidedly biliously inclined. Perhaps I would be better understood if I said that his countenance was Cassius-like . . . although I saw him every day for nearly five months I rarely saw him smile."[3]

Colonel Sherman indeed lacked the light touch (his rare attempts at humor were heavy-handed), and his letters suggest that he was sometimes depressed as well as frustrated. His most persistent source of frustration was being deprived of the recognition that, with some justification, he believed he deserved. Although he frequently commanded a brigade, he remained a colonel from 1862 until the war was over. Despite having little formal military training himself, he did not hesitate, in letters to his father, to criticize Gen. Don Carlos Buell and others among his superiors whom he considered incompetent and to complain, often bitterly, about the way the war was being waged. (On the other hand, he consistently—and sometimes unrealistically—commended the officers and men who served under him.) He was even more critical of his father's politics, particularly his father's association with "Peace Democrats."

Although his father had been a strong antislavery Democrat before the war, he never had been an abolitionist, and his politics seemed tied more closely to strengthening Chicago business than to questions about slavery. He had no problem abandoning his antislavery position when it became politically expedient to do so;[4] as the war went on, he became increasingly sympathetic to the Peace Democrats. The son remained a War Democrat whose motivation to fight against the South seems to have been primarily to preserve the Union; in his letters he mentioned the slavery issue only once, four months after the Emancipation Proclamation.

Whenever he wrote home, Colonel Sherman was articulate, long-winded, and often flowery, in accord with the style of the times; to a modern reader he may seem platitudinous.[5] He liked complicated words; in one letter to his mother he used *ubiquitous* and *incubus* in the same sentence. His diary notations, on the other hand, usually were limited to terse, factual reports of daily activities. For the most part, he wrote letters while in camp and diary entries when on the move; there are few diary notations on days he was in camp.

The colonel complained frequently of the paucity of letters from home;[6] unfortunately I have been unable to find any letters to him from either his wife or his parents. Some of the content of Mayor Sherman's response to his son's criticism of his politics can be inferred from Colonel Sherman's subsequent letters; the camps and marches of the Army of the Cumberland, however, did not make it easy for soldiers to save letters from home.

No 1862 diary is available. After the battle of Stones River, Colonel Sherman wrote that Rebel cavalry had captured his wagon on December 31, 1862, and had destroyed his personal belongings, including his papers. The 1862 diary and perhaps a new 1863 diary may have been among the destroyed papers. It is also possible that there never was an 1862 diary and that he did not decide to write one until the summer of 1863—the first diary entries for 1863 are in June.

He wrote frequent letters in 1862 and 1863; in 1864 and 1865, there are fewer letters but many diary entries. The letters give fuller accounts; therefore, on the rare occasions when both letters and diary describe the same events, I have relied on the letters.[7]

Fortunately the colonel's penmanship was excellent, with few words indecipherable. Although he had a hard time with the spelling of personal names,[8] his spelling otherwise was almost perfect. Except for periods and an occasional comma, he did not bother much with punctuation, and paragraphing did not concern him. In the interest of readability, I have done some minor editing in these areas, such as substituting semicolons for commas.

As a psychiatrist, I recognize the risks of diagnosing anyone—even, or perhaps especially, a family member—without having examined that person. However, I cannot resist inserting in this preface a few speculations about my ancestor's psychodynamics.

Frank's life story and the harsh criticism he directed toward both his father and certain superiors suggest that he retained a fair amount of unresolved and frustrated competitiveness with his father, which he transferred to various father figures. At the same time, he seems to have been more dependent on his father than he would have liked to be.

In civilian life Frank was always in his father's shadow, usually working either for him or in positions his father obtained for him. He tried and failed three times to establish an independent existence: searching for gold in California in 1849; trying to run a sugar plantation in Louisiana in 1866; and seeking a position in business or government in Arizona in 1876. His only period of sustained success throughout his life was in the Union Army (even though he evidently owed his original appointment as colonel of his regiment to his father's political connections, he seems to have convinced himself that he had made it on his own). He often threatened to resign from the army, but it is evident from his letters, particularly those written near the end of the war and after, that he would have been happy to make a career of it.

While his letters reveal mixed feelings, or ambivalence, toward his father, he tended to divide his superior officers into good father figures, such as Sheridan and Rosecrans, and bad father figures, such as Buell and Foster, seeing little bad in the former and little good in the latter. Perhaps feeling like an underdog at home, in the army he identified with the enlisted man and consistently portrayed his troops in the best possible light. His loyalty to—and identification with—his troops led him to deny their weaknesses, not only in his official reports (most officers reported their men's behavior in flattering terms) but also to his family and, I believe, to himself. Thus, at Missionary Ridge, he described all of his men (except a few "skulkers") as heroes eager for the charge, although apparently he had to obtain Sheridan's help to get them out of the rifle pits and started up the ridge. Otherwise most of his observations appear to be accurate.

The difference in feeling tone between Colonel Sherman's loving letters to his mother and the rather peremptory quality of some of his letters to his wife rings the psychiatrist's bell. This difference, along with family discord evident in two or three of his letters at the end of the war, suggest that an earlier close attachment to his mother may have persisted into his marriage so strongly that it contributed to a conflict in loyalties.

From the beginning of his military career, however, Frank wanted to have his wife with him, or at least close at hand. For well over half his participation in the Tennessee campaign, she was away from their three children, either actually caring for her husband or standing by to care for him, should he need her. His letters suggest that he took her for granted; at one point, he left her to stay by herself in his quarters, while he enjoyed three weeks' home leave. She seems to have accepted her assigned role without complaint when they were together, although she comes across as much more vigorous and independent when she was not with him.

Colonel Sherman's letters and diaries thus provide an account of the Union campaign in Tennessee and Georgia, a soldier's response to Civil War politics in Chicago, and insight into a many-faceted personality.

ACKNOWLEDGMENTS

For this book, I am most indebted to my daughter, Carol Barkin, who first transcribed the letters and diaries and later rendered inestimable editorial assistance in putting them all together. Without her, the book would not have come into being.

I am deeply grateful to William Abbot, Robert Cross, Merrill Peterson, and Edward Ayres, professors in the Cochran Department of History at the University of Virginia, for their friendly and constructive help in steering me through the shoals of a discipline new to me. For their help at various stages of this endeavor, I also thank Robert T. Sherman, Jr.; Sherly Maier; Arthur Chitty; Archie Motley and the staff of the Research Library of the Chicago Historical Society; Carolyn Autry of the Indiana Historical Society; Beverly Millard of the Waukegan Historical Society; the staff of the Special Collections division of the Alderman Library, University of Virginia; and the editors and staff of the University of Tennessee Press.

Finally, I thank my wife, Julie, for her unfailing encouragement and support.

QUEST FOR A STAR

1

A Chicago Innkeeper and His Son: 1834–1862

At the start of the Civil War, Chicago was one of the fastest-growing cities in the United States. In a little over a quarter-century, it had grown from a tiny village of two hundred people to become a rowdy, energetic city of over one hundred thousand. Located at the base of Lake Michigan and on the Chicago River, Chicago was well situated for the transshipment of goods. As agriculture in the Middle West began to flourish, much of its production passed through Chicago en route from the Northern Plains to the East via the Great Lakes, or to the South via the Illinois and Michigan Canal and the Illinois and Mississippi rivers.

Chicago got its start in 1833 because of its waterways; in the 1850s, as rail transportation began to replace rivers and canals, the city became the major rail center linking the East and the South with the Middle West. Business was good, and Chicagoans wanted it to continue growing.

California recently had opened up, and Chicago was poised to become the take-off point for a proposed railway to the Pacific. To get Congress to finance this project, Chicagoans believed, the western territories would have to be admitted to statehood as expeditiously as possible. But controversy about the status of slavery in the new states could not be avoided, either in Chicago or in the rest of the country.

Many of Chicago's businessmen, much of whose trade was with the South, tended to distrust abolitionists and to favor compromise on the issue of slavery. They supported the Democratic senator from Illinois, Stephen A. Douglas (known as the "little Giant"), who had worked hard for the Compromise of 1850 and was the author of the Kansas-Nebraska Act of 1854, which allowed the inhabitants of those two territories to decide for themselves between slavery and free-soil. However, Chicago was a northern city, and many Chicagoans, including a substantial number of Democrats, felt strongly that slavery should be forbidden in any new state.

Even after the passage of the Kansas-Nebraska Act, vigorous debate over its implications continued to rage in Congress, in the territories, in Chicago, and throughout the North. In Chicago, it was the major issue on which the mayoralty election of 1856 was fought between two Democrats: Thomas Dyer, Douglas's candidate, who favored the Kansas-Nebraska Act, and Francis C. Sherman, who opposed any extension of slavery whatsoever.[1]

Although born in Danbury, Connecticut, Sherman was a pioneer Chicagoan. In April 1834, at the age of twenty-nine, he had ridden to Chicago from Buffalo, New York, on horseback with his eight-year-old son, Frank; his wife and their two younger children arrived by boat six weeks later. Chicago then had a population of only two hundred but was growing rapidly, and housing and transportation were in short supply. Responding to these shortages, the enterprising newcomer built a boarding house soon after he arrived. Once it was a going concern, he bought a wagon and a team of horses to meet incoming boats and to carry passengers between Chicago and Joliet, Peoria, and other Illinois towns. Sherman then turned his attention to the brickmaking business, in which he continued until 1850. In 1836–37 he used his own products to build the first four-story brick building in Chicago. This was the City Hotel, "the largest and most splendid hotel in Illinois,"[2] which he later renamed the Sherman House. Along with politics, managing the hotel was his major occupation until his death in 1870. He added two stories to the hotel in 1844; then, in 1861, just as the Civil War was beginning, he tore it down and built a new and even grander hotel.

Not long after arriving in Chicago, Sherman began his career in politics, and in 1835, as a pro-Jackson Democratic-Republican, he was elected town trustee. Two years later, he became an alderman, and in 1841 he rose to the post of mayor.[3] He was elected to the Illinois Legislature in 1843 and 1844, and in 1846 he was a delegate to the convention called to write a new state constitution. In 1856, in his bid to become mayor again, he lost by six hundred votes, after a bitterly fought campaign in which he was viewed as "the standard bearer of the Democracy against slavery extension."[4]

Sherman loved the rough and tumble of Chicago politics; despite frequent defeats, vilification by opponents, and his son's efforts to dissuade him, he kept on seeking office until he was sixty-two years old. He was a diamond in the rough; Upton and Colbert, who had nothing but praise for most of the distinguished Chicagoans they wrote about, observed that the mayor's opponents charged him with "a lack of polish and a deficiency of education." These qualities were offset, however, by his "strong practical sense and personal integrity."[5]

In 1857—Chicago's mayors served one-year terms until 1863—the upstart antislavery Republicans elected John Wentworth, a former Democrat, as mayor; Republicans would control City Hall, as well as most state offices, until 1862. The Democrats continued to be a strong minority in Chicago, although, when the war began, the city closed ranks to support the Union and the Republican administration enthusiastically. On the day of Lincoln's first call for troops, the *Chicago Tribune* proclaimed:

> Lenity and forbearance have only nursed the viper into life. Let expressed rebuke and contempt rest on every man weak enough to be anywhere else in this crisis than on the side of the country against treason—of Lincoln and Scott against Davis and Twiggs, of God against Baal. We say to the Tories and lickspittles in this community, a patient and reluctant, but at last an outraged and maddened people will no longer endure your hissing. You must keep your venom sealed, or go down! The gates of Janus are open, the storm is on us. Let the cry be, THE SWORD OF THE LORD AND OF GIDEON![6]

Chicago quickly recruited more than its share of the seventy-five thousand volunteers Lincoln called to enlist for a three-month term—enough time, it was thought, to put down the rebellion.[7] In the Civil War, volunteer regiments were recruited by the states and maintained their state identity throughout the war. Most of them were equipped with substantial financial and other help from local businesses and trade organizations. Political influence played no small part in the selection of senior officers; junior officers, up through the grade of captain, usually were elected by their companies. Political influence no doubt was the reason why, in November 1861, Francis T. Sherman, eldest son of the innkeeper and Democratic politician, was appointed lieutenant colonel of the 56th Illinois infantry regiment.

The young Sherman had been born in Newtown, Connecticut, on December 31, 1825, and had arrived in Chicago with his father on horseback when he was eight and a half years old. Later he wrote: "My earliest recollections of this period are of the Indians—the Potawatomies—who came in the fall of each year, until 1840, to receive their annuities from the government.[8] Astor had a fur station here and the Government had a one-company post, called Fort Dearborn. . . . My education was such as this frontier post afforded during the winter months."[9]

In spite of the limitations of his schooling, his penmanship, grammar, spelling, and vocabulary were excellent. As a teenager, young Frank helped his father in the brickyard, driving an ox-cart and hauling clay. At sixteen, presumably through his father's influence, he was appointed foreman of "Bucket Company Number One" in the volunteer fire department.[10]

At eighteen, Frank became a clerk in a wholesale grocery business, and a year later, in 1844, he moved on to become a post-office clerk, a position he held for the next four years. In 1848–49, he was secretary to the Board of Appraisers of Canal Lands but gave up that position for reasons of health. He appears to have suffered from bronchial asthma, which then was attributed to the swampy terrain around Chicago; although he continued to suffer periodically from asthma for most of his life, he seldom was incapacitated by it for more than two or three weeks at a time until his last years.

In the spring of 1849, when he was twenty-three, he joined the gold rush to California, in part to get rich, in part to get away from the asthma-inducing Chicago climate, and perhaps in yet another part to get away from the domination of his father. He crossed the plains in a hundred days by ox-cart; after a month on the road, he wrote his parents from what is now Kearney, Nebraska, that he was enjoying the trip and that his team had "passed every [wagon] train on the road with the exception of [army] mules."[11]

His enthusiasm, as well as his pace, diminished considerably as he climbed the western mountains and plodded across the desert, and he wrote to his parents from California, "I never would advise anybody to come to California to make a fortune." He was appalled to find "no moral restraint upon any one & men who at home were considered respectable, quiet, & orderly citizens here become great brawlers, gamblers, and drinkers."[12] He was not one to give up easily, however, and stuck it out for another year, at the end of which he returned by ship, none the richer. Back in Chicago, he went into the building materials business but did not prosper. Shortly before the war, he went to work in his father's hotel.

On October 4, 1851, he married Eleanor ("Ellen") Norton Vedder, when she was twenty-one. Her father, Philip, of Dutch descent, had been born in 1804 near Schenectady, New York, and had come to Deerfield Township, near Waukegan, Illinois, to buy a farm in 1844. He had married Margaret Haverly when she was but fourteen; she became an invalid after the birth of their fourth child in 1838 but lived until 1856.[13]

The Vedders and the Shermans apparently were not acquainted; the only available record concerning Frank and Ellen's courtship is a letter from Philip Vedder to Frank Sherman, dated March 23, 1851, in which the future father-in-law says, in the formal terms of the day, "You wished me to write you an answer in regard to my daughter. You are, as I might say, a perfect stranger to me; of you personly [sic] I know nothing, but if it is my daughter's wish to receive your visits I have no objection."[14] Ellen's older brother, Alman, had made the trip to California at about the same time as Frank Sherman and stayed for eight years. Although Sherman does not mention Alman Vedder in the available letters he wrote from California, the two may have become acquainted.

In the ten years after Frank and Ellen were married, they had five children, two girls and three boys. One boy died in infancy, in September 1860; another boy died at the age of five, in December 1861, a month after his father had accepted his first commission in the Union Army. Neither of the deceased children is mentioned in Sherman's letters.

The first of young Frank Sherman's three commissions was as lieutenant colonel of the 56th Illinois Volunteer Infantry Regiment. The new officer had had more preparation for military leadership than many officers in the Civil

War. He had spent three years as a second lieutenant in the Chicago Light Guard, a local military unit somewhat like the current National Guard. The Light Guard was described as "for years the crack corps of the Northwest . . . and to be a guardsman was to be envied by all less favored mortals."[15]

The Light Guard, however, did not prepare Frank for the peculiar nature of the regiment he joined on November 4, 1861. This regiment, called the "Mechanics' Fusiliers" because it was sponsored by the Mechanics' Union Association,[16] had a short life. In the summer of 1861, most of its volunteers had been recruited by an unconventional colonel named John W. Wilson, who, contrary to the rules, recruited not from a single state but from several midwestern states.[17] At least part of the regiment spent the month of October building barracks at Camp Douglas,[18] where Lieutenant Colonel Sherman reported for duty on November 4. While he left no record of his experience as second-in-command of the Mechanics' Fusiliers, it evidently was a turbulent time for the young officer. By the time Frank arrived, Colonel Wilson was out of town and had managed to make himself so unpopular with his men that he was advised to stay away for his own protection.[19] Mutiny apparently was in the air; although there is one mention of a regimental mutiny,[20] no details are given, and no report of a mutiny appears in Chicago newspapers of that time.

Apparently Colonel Wilson listened to his advisors and did not return to the regiment. In his absence, Lieutenant Colonel Sherman presumably was in command for the next three months of training prior to active service. Finally, on February 5, 1862, the regiment was mustered into active service. Then, on the same day, it was mustered out of service. Its roster on that day included Sherman, Maj. Matthew P. Wood, and ten captains, but the line for colonel is blank.[21] While the army evidently wanted no part of Colonel Wilson, it appears to have felt obligated to acknowledge the services of the rest of the regiment by making it official for a single day. The Mechanics' Fusiliers then disappeared from sight completely; three weeks later, another 56th Illinois Volunteer Infantry Regiment was mustered in at Shawneetown and served honorably throughout the war.[22]

Colonel Sherman's military career had gotten off to an inauspicious start; no doubt he was embarrassed to have been associated with such a fiasco. He never mentioned the 56th Illinois or the Mechanics' Fusiliers in his letters and often omitted it when recounting his military experience; there is no mention at all of it in his autobiographical sketch.[23] However, the unfortunate circumstances and abrupt end of his first command did not appear to affect the younger Sherman's future as an officer. He had another commission within a month, this time as a major with the 12th Illinois Volunteer Cavalry Regiment. He joined this regiment on March 8, 1862, about a month after it was formed, and spent the next three months in Springfield, Illinois, in training and in guarding Confederate prisoners at Camp Butler.

Camp Butler, in Springfield, Illinois, was a twelve-acre stockade with a twelve-foot plank fence around it, holding about twenty-three hundred prisoners.[24] Guard duty, while not glamorous, apparently was not too irksome early in the war. At that time, prisoners on both sides were treated well, and relations between prisoners and guards tended to be friendly, although they worsened as the war dragged on, as Colonel Sherman could testify. At Camp Butler, a Confederate prisoner, a soldier named Jordan (probably Pvt. J. D. Jordan), from Murfreesboro, Tennessee, became so friendly with the Shermans that he arranged for Mrs. Sherman to stay with his parents when she visited her husband a year later, after the Battle of Stones River.[25]

On June 25, 1862, the 12th Illinois Cavalry Regiment was relieved of guard duty, mounted, and sent to Martinsburg, Virginia. There it joined reinforcements for Gen. Nathaniel Banks's Army of the Shenandoah Valley, which, in April and May 1862, had been outsmarted and outmaneuvered by the Confederates under Gen. Thomas J. "Stonewall" Jackson.[26] In planning his campaign, Jackson had been given valuable information about Union troop movements by Belle Boyd, an eighteen-year-old woman with strong southern sympathies who was originally from Martinsburg. When, in early June, the strengthened Union forces forced Jackson to withdraw from Front Royal, Boyd was arrested there by Union troops. Although she was released because of inadequate evidence, she was kept under surveillance for the next two months. On July 28, she attempted to pass more information through two men in Confederate uniforms who claimed to be exchanged prisoners about to return to their units. Actually they were Union spies. A warrant was issued for Boyd's arrest,[27] and Major Sherman was sent to Front Royal with a detachment of the 12th Cavalry to take her into custody. In her memoirs, Belle Boyd described her arrest by three men:

> Major McEnnis [Provost Marshal Major Arthur Maginnis], whose face wore an expression of excitement and nervousness; a tall, fine-looking man, introduced to me by the name and title of Major Sherman, of the 12th Illinois Cavalry; [and] one of Secretary Stanton's minions [a Mr. Cridge, from the Secret Service]. . . . Major McEnnis turned to me and said,
> "Miss Boyd, Major Sherman has come to arrest you."
> "Impossible! For what?" I cried.
> Major Sherman here interposed, and speaking in a very kind manner, assured me that, although the duty he had to perform was painful to his feelings, he was, nevertheless, forced to execute the orders of the Secretary of War.[28]

By the time they arrived at Martinsburg, Belle Boyd felt unwell, and, again according to her account, "Major Sherman, compassionating my forlorn condition, very kindly stayed behind the cavalcade and prevailed upon his wife to accompany me to the camp."[29]

Ellen Sherman stayed with the young prisoner until Belle's mother arrived in the afternoon, whereupon the three ladies were permitted to go to a Martinsburg hotel to await transportation under guard by train to Washington for Belle's trial.

Mrs. Sherman was in Martinsburg to be with her husband; this was the first of several occasions during the war when she left her children with relatives or friends and went wherever her husband was located.

Mrs. Sherman is not mentioned in her husband's official report to his commanding officer concerning the duty which included the Belle Boyd incident. Since this was his first contact with the enemy—even though the enemy was an unarmed eighteen-year-old girl—Colonel Sherman may be excused for writing a longwinded report, which included a bit of unsolicited advice to his superiors. The report, in somewhat abridged form, follows.

Camp Wool, Martinsburg, Va. Aug 1st, 1862

To Col. Arno Voss, Cmdr. Post

Marched from Winchester at 2 P.M. 29th, arrived at Front Royal at 9 P.M. same day, observed nothing unusual on the route. Negroes were questioned by me as to the whereabouts of rebel forces and "Bush whackers." They reported several bands of these marauders and robbers in the neighborhood who employed themselves during the day as farmers, and at night prowled around the country destroying property and picking up stragglers. I did not deem it proper to weaken my command by sending out squads to discover the truth of these reports, as the orders I had were positive and for a specific object.

I reported myself and command . . . at Front Royal on the morning of the 30th. . . . At 9 o'c A.M. I arrested by order of the Government Agt. with us, Miss Belle Boyd and commenced our return march to this place. I was joined at 1 P.M. by 100 mounted men from Winchester, . . . increasing my command to 200 effective men rank and file. Believing that I had a larger force than was necessary to escort the prisoner, I sent out a detachment of men. . . . to scout over the country. . . .

Arrived at Camp Wool at 1 P.M. 31st [July 1862], and delivered my charge into your custody. I take pleasure in bearing testimony to the soldierly qualities of the officers under me, the discipline of the men, and the alacrity and cheerfulness with which they obeyed all orders delivered to them, and thank them for uniform and soldierly conduct, this being for the majority their first march where great danger [from bushwhackers] was to be apprehended. I take this occasion to respectfully suggest that parties of mounted men be frequently sent out for three or four days' march as being conducive to discipline and preparing officers and men for the peculiar service required of them, making them familiar with the country and enuring them to danger and fatigue.[30]

Major Sherman did not remain with the 12th Cavalry long enough to find out if his advice was followed. In late July 1862, the Chicago Board of Trade (which was to sponsor three Illinois Volunteer Infantry regiments, the 72nd,

Col. Francis Trowbridge Sherman. Courtesy of Library of Congress.

88th, and 113th) decided to launch its second regiment, the 88th, and offered its command and a colonelcy to Major Sherman. He immediately accepted the offer and resigned from the 12th Cavalry.

Colonel Sherman's new regiment had been in camp in Chicago for over a month by the time he returned to Chicago and assumed command. He was commissioned on August 15, 1862;[31] took command on August 27, 1862; and left the next day, with 926 officers and men, to join the Army of the Ohio.

The offer of a regimental command to Colonel Sherman well may have resulted in part from his father's improving political fortunes. The initial high enthusiasm for the war and for the Republican administration in Washington gradually had waned in Chicago, as it became evident that the Union forces would not overrun the Confederates in a few weeks and that business with the South was going to be cut off for some time to come. As the war dragged on, Democrats became loud in their criticism of administrative inefficiencies in Lincoln's government, and their criticism influenced an increasing number of Chicago voters.

While most Democrats freely criticized the *administration* of the war, some now began to question *participation* in the war. Many Democrats had serious reservations about the abolition of slavery, and some could even see advantages to a separate, slave-holding Confederacy, which would supply cotton for northern mills. These "Peace Democrats," or "Copperheads,"[32] who saw little to be gained by continuing the war, created a serious schism in the Democratic party, particularly in the Midwest. Colonel Sherman considered them traitors; his father, once a "standard-bearer of the Democracy against the extension of slavery," gradually became more tolerant of the Peace Democrats. The father's conciliatory approach made him acceptable to both factions of the party, and he was nominated for mayor again in 1862. His party appealed to the moderates by claiming that the Republican candidate, Charles N. Holden, was for both abolition and temperance. Sherman won, by a vote of 7,437 to 6,254,[33] taking office three months before his son again went off to war, this time for almost three years.

2

THE 88TH ILLINOIS GOES TO WAR:
AUTUMN, 1862

The Army of the Ohio, which Colonel Sherman and his regiment were ordered to join in August 1862, was at that time under the command of Gen. Don Carlos Buell, who in November 1861 had replaced the psychologically troubled Gen. William Tecumseh Sherman.[1] Buell was a rigid, conservative West Point graduate, a competent administrator but a cautious fighter. Like McClellan and Halleck, he tended to emphasize problems rather than opportunities.[2]

The ultimate goal of the Army of the Ohio, soon to be renamed the Army of the Cumberland, was to cut the Confederacy in two by moving eastward through Tennessee and Georgia. An important objective en route was to rescue the loyal people of East Tennessee from Rebel occupation.[3] So, in July 1862, two months before Colonel Sherman arrived from Chicago, Lincoln, through Halleck, ordered Buell to clear East Tennessee of Confederates by the end of the year.

Buell considered this order totally impractical. The time allotted was insufficient, his troops were too inexperienced, his supply lines were inadequate, and he faced a formidable enemy force. In his view, Chattanooga had to be captured before an East Tennessee campaign could succeed, and Chattanooga could not be captured until Nashville was in northern hands and could be used as a base for communications and supply routes via the Tennessee Valley.[4] Despite his reservations, however, Buell had no choice but to follow orders, although for the most part he moved more deliberately, carefully, and slowly than Lincoln had intended.

Before he could get started on the road to Nashville and Chattanooga, Buell faced a more immediate threat: the Confederate invasion of Kentucky.[5] In response to Buell's urgent request for more men to meet this threat, several new and untried regiments were sent to join the Army of the Ohio. Among these regiments was Colonel Sherman's 88th Illinois Volunteers, which left Chicago on August 28, 1862, to join Buell's Army.

The regiment's first destination was Cincinnati, where it was presumably needed to help fight off Confederate troops under Gen. Kirby Smith. The regiment went by rail; Private Francis complained that the troops were "crowded into open, shallow cars, used otherwise for transporting coal or other heavy merchandise" and were "nearly blinded by the black, sulphurous cinders and smoke that came upon us from the engine."[6]

When the men of the 88th arrived in Cincinnati, they found panicky citizens desperately putting up breastworks to defend the city against Kirby Smith's anticipated raid. Unbeknownst to the Union command, however, Smith had decided to abandon his push to the Ohio River, and it soon became evident that Cincinnati was not in danger. The 88th was then sent to Louisville, aboard an Ohio River steamer, which twice ran aground, finally requiring the regiment to proceed on foot. But there was no more action in Louisville than there had been in Cincinnati; Bragg and his Confederates had been slow in marching toward Louisville, and when Buell got there first, Bragg turned back to Tennessee.

The 88th Illinois went into camp near Louisville in September 1862, where it was assigned to Col. Nicholas Greusel's 37th brigade and became part of Gen. Philip H. Sheridan's 11th Division in Gen. Charles C. Gilbert's 3rd Corps. Thus began Sherman's association with Sheridan, which was to continue throughout the war and beyond it.

When the 88th went into camp, Colonel Sherman anticipated that it would undergo a period of training for combat before being sent into the field. But Buell was under a great deal of pressure from Washington to engage Bragg; in fact, Buell, because of his dilatory pace, would have been replaced by Gen. George H. Thomas, had Thomas not recommended that Buell be retained.[7] Buell therefore was eager to catch up with Bragg before his opponent could get back to his supply base. Furthermore, Buell, in common with many other West Pointers, had little patience with the volunteer soldiers and officers who made up the majority of his troops and seems to have believed that they would not benefit much from training.[8] Thus, with little training, inadequate supplies, and antiquated firearms[9] the army was soon on the road.

They were on the road, but where they were going was not at all clear. Most of September was taken up with "marching and countermarching, orders and rescinded orders, misunderstandings and recriminations."[10] Rumors that proved unfounded, about the location of Kirby Smith's troops, sent Colonel Sherman and his regiment on futile marches first to Frankfurt, Kentucky, and then toward Danville as far as Bloomfield.[11] The next destination was Perryville, where Sherman's recruits first came under fire.

The season had been unusually dry, and, as they approached Perryville, the thirsty troops were looking for water. On October 7, almost by accident, Col. Daniel

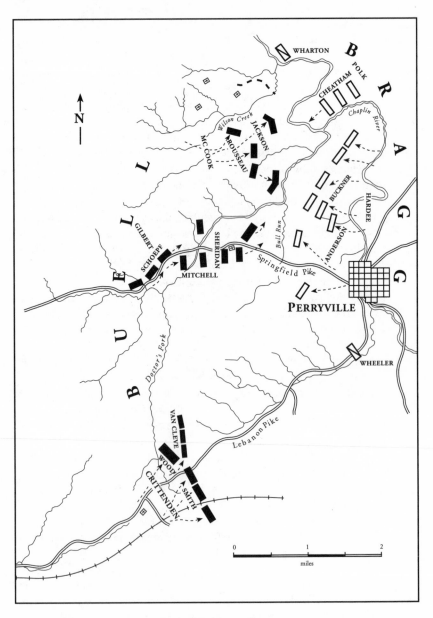

Battle of Perryville.

McCook's brigade, which included the 88th Illinois, encountered a Confederate force also looking for water. The consequent engagement was brief but sharp; the Union troops secured the stream bed and repelled a Confederate counterattack.[12]

The main battle was fought the next day under confusing circumstances; as Horn writes, "Seldom in the annals of warfare have the commanders of two contending armies been so completely befuddled as to the location and plans of the other."[13] At the start, the Confederate right drove McCook's green troops back two miles and forced the left of Gilbert's center to give way, although Sheridan, on Gilbert's right, was able to drive the Confederates opposing his brigade back into the town. While all this was going on, Crittenden, on the Union right, was waiting for orders, unaware that McCook and Gilbert were engaged with the enemy. The orders never came, because Buell, too, did not know that the fighting had started. Apparently a peculiar combination of wind and terrain called an "acoustic shadow" blew away the sounds of battle, and the Union commander remained in ignorance of the day's events until it was too dark to mount a counterattack. Although the outnumbered Confederates won the battle, they were too short of men and supplies to exploit their victory, and so that night they continued their retreat back to Tennessee.

Sheridan's brigade was about the only unit of the Union forces that distinguished itself at Perryville, and Colonel Sherman interpreted the engagement as a victory. The 88th Regiment had picked up what combat training it could get while on the march. Fortunately, Sherman had had experience training "green" troops while he was with the 12th Illinois Cavalry, and he told his father in his first letter home how proud he was of his men and how pleased he was with his own role in the battle. He was not so pleased with Buell's failure to pursue what he perceived as defeated Confederates. At the time of writing, Frank presumably was unaware of the troubles that had beset the rest of the Union forces. The letter, written three days after the Battle of Perryville, started out by describing the paucity of supplies:

Crab Orchard, Ky., Oct. 11, 1862

Dear Father:

The army left Louisville October 1st, and up to this time has marched or fought every day with the rebels. We have not had any tents with us and scarcely anything to eat. I make my coffee in a tin cup and cook my piece of bacon on the end of a stick, and this with a hard cracker constitutes our meals. The army, as you see, is marching light.

We are pressing the rebels close, and there is a continual skirmish going on with our advance and their rear guard. At the battle of Perryville on the eighth we ought to have taken the whole rebel force, if we had had a man to command this great army who has not got so much science.

I flatter myself, Father, that my regiment took a very prominent part in the Perryville battle. We were under fire for an hour where the bullets sounded like a hive of bees swarming, and the men behaved like old soldiers. The 88th engaged a brigade of rebels at what is called close quarters (say fifty yards) and made them beat a hasty retreat. In advancing to meet them I had four men killed and fifteen wounded. I think this is doing very well, considering everything. I saved many men by making them lay down when the rebels fired.

I do not suppose that we will be able to catch Bragg until he gets into Cumberland Gap where he is headed for now. We had a complete victory at Perryville and mighty hard fighting. My brigade commander [Col. Nicholas Greusel] mentioned me in his report in the most flattering manner.

Love to all, Your son, Frank

In his next letter, dated October 16, Colonel Sherman included a copy of part of his official report on the participation of the 88th Illinois Infantry in the Battle of Perryville. The report reads:

On getting into position the order was given for the regiment to open fire on the enemy, who were advancing on the charge to take our battery [which was] placed on the hill immediately in the rear. At the command, "Fire!" the whole line was in a blaze, and volley after volley was sent into the advancing ranks of the rebels, who by that time were within fifty yards of our lines. So continuous and sharp was our fire that their further advance was checked and they slowly retired until we were left in possession of the field, the rebels leaving 380 of their dead on the ground by actual account. During the engagement the officers and men behaved with the utmost coolness and bravery, not a man flinching or leaving his post, although under sharp fire from the enemy during the whole time.[14] The officers cheered on the men and exposed themselves freely to keep the men in place and our lines unbroken.[15]

Colonel Sherman's criticism of his superior officers at Perryville was explicit in his next letter:

near Bowling Green, Ky, Oct. 16th, 1862

Dear Father:

The battle of the 8th was a complete victory for the Union arms over the rebels, and had it been followed up then as I and many other officers superior to me think, it could have been as complete as was the victory at [Fort] Donelson, but instead of that the whole of the next day was occupied by shifting brigades and divisions from one point to another, and finally ended by occupying the camp that the rebels evacuated twelve hours before, leaving all of their dead unburied. In this camp we lay until the 11th, giving Bragg all the opportunity that he desired to get away. We had two divisions on the 8th that were not engaged at all. We might have closed in upon them and with a sharp fight on the morning of the 9th have captured some ten or fifteen thousand prisoners and destroyed the rebel army in Kentucky.[16] Such an opportunity we will never get again. I went over the field the next day and saw where whole [Confederate] regiments had thrown down their arms and fled.

We arrived at this place [between Crab Orchard and Bowling Green] last night and find that Bragg, with the main body of his army, was three days ahead of us, and Kirby Smith thirty-six hours, all pushing for Cumberland Gap, where we will have to go through such scenes as occurred at Corinth, Mississippi.[17] You will get more of the details from the papers at home than I can give you, as we do not know what we have to do until it is done, and then know only so much of the operations as we take an active part [in].

Gen. [Charles C.] Gilbert, who commands the Third Army Corps (in which I am), is not liked at all, and I have seen him take to the rear with his bodyguard at the discharge of two or three pieces of artillery. Gen. Buell no one likes or has confidence in, and like a pig's tail is always behind.

Today we have not moved. We left Louisville without a tent, nor has the army had any except generals commanding brigades, divisions, and corps. Half the time I have had nothing but hard bread with now and then bacon and coffee made in a common tin cup. I care not for this. I never was in better health, and the regiment generally is healthy.

Kiss the children for me. Love, your son, Frank

Like his views of General Buell, Colonel Sherman's criticism of General Gilbert appears to have had some justification. Gilbert's leadership style has been characterized as a "perfect illustration of the complete inability of a certain type of regular officer to understand or to lead volunteer troops."[18]

But while Gilbert stayed on, his superior was on the way out. His ineptitude at Perryville and his failure to pursue Bragg aggressively made it inevitable that Buell, already under criticism for the slow pace of his campaign, would be replaced in command of the Army of the Cumberland. Although General Thomas had been offered General Buell's job a month earlier, he had turned it down; now it was offered to Gen. William S. Rosecrans. Rosecrans was an excellent strategist, one of the best in the Union army, careful and imaginative in his planning and resourceful in the execution of his plans. He was popular with most of his officers and men; he participated in the fighting, at least until the latter part of Chickamauga, and he inspired confidence in his troops. Even after the defeat at Chickamauga, Colonel Sherman thought that the sun rose and set with General Rosecrans.[19]

Rosecrans took command on November 1. He was worried about the lack of supplies, the long sick list, and the shortage of cavalry, so, although he was under great pressure from Washington to get going, he moved very slowly during the next few weeks. On November 18, Colonel Sherman wrote about his sick list and about commanding, for the first time, a force of brigade strength:

near Nashville, Nov. 18th, 1862

Dear Father:

We are very pleasantly situated here opposite Nashville, about one mile from the city and the same distance from water. The health of the regiment has been very bad since we came here, but is mending rapidly. I have lost three men died here since we arrived on the seventh of November and have over two hundred men sick and in hospitals scattered from Cincinnati to this place. The regiment is no discredit, I am proud to say, to Illinois and the Board of Trade. The colors are at Mitchellville, thirty miles from here, and have to be brought through by express, the express wagon being one of my own regimental wagons. I have just received orders to go on a foraging expedition, having three regiments of infantry and two sections of artillery under my command.

I am going to send for Ellen to join me at this place, as the prospects are good for our regiment remaining here some little time. She can live here as cheap or cheaper than she can in Chicago.

My love to all at home, Your son, Frank

According to Private Francis, the foraging expedition found farms "untouched by war. The farmers had let their stock out, but the soldiers retrieved hogs, sheep, horses, and cows, and took stores of grain and corn."[20]

Near Mill Creek, Colonel Sherman appropriated a "milch cow," presumably to secure milk for his and his fellow officers' coffee. Private Francis, temporarily Colonel Sherman's orderly, reported that the colonel "was in a continual state of anxiety over that cow until it was safely haltered to a tree at the rear of regimental headquarters."[21] The cow may have been safely haltered, but most of the milk was pilfered by the men, who watered the colonel's milk and never were found out.[22]

Colonel Sherman did find out, however, about some illicit foraging late one night after he had retired, and it made him very angry. Private Francis recalled how, when the foragers were brought to his tent, he came out to confront the culprits, dressed in his red flannel underwear and looking "very much the Indian chief. . . . How he did give it to the unhappy prisoners! Cowards, thieves, scoundrels, prefixed by a selection of the most florid adjectives, were the mildest of his terms of reproach and denunciation." After the profane harangue, the colonel directed the guard to take the foragers to Colonel Greusel, which made them happy, "for they knew that Colonel Greisel (*sic*) had a much different disposition."[23]

With respect to foraging, General Sheridan wrote in his memoirs, "The feeding of our army from the base at Louisville was attended with a great many difficulties, as the enemy's cavalry was constantly breaking the railroad and intercepting our communications . . . So to make good our deficiencies . . . I employed a brigade about once a week in the duty of collecting and bringing in forage . . . In nearly every one of these expeditions the enemy was encountered."[24]

Colonel Sherman commanded three regiments on this expedition. Although it was a temporary command, he perceived it as evidence of his superiors' confidence in his ability, and he began to think that he soon might have his own brigade and then might be promoted to brigadier general. As the war dragged on through two and a half more years, he became more and more preoccupied with obtaining that elusive promotion. As his frustrations mounted, he often thought of resigning, but always he returned to his quest for a brigadier's star. He was encouraged in this quest by General Sheridan, who consistently advocated his promotion. Although Sheridan could give Sherman temporary command of a brigade and could recommend his promotion, the actual promotion required approval from Washington. And, while Sherman had plenty of political support, it all came from the wrong party.[25]

As the end of 1862 approached, the Army of the Cumberland perhaps was better fed than it had been in September, but it remained almost 150 miles from Chattanooga, the first of the two objectives that President Lincoln optimistically had set for the army to accomplish before the year was out. Since winter mud and cold were far from ideal fighting conditions, most troops went into winter quarters and postponed active warfare until spring. Colonel Sherman apparently believed that this would be the case for Rosecrans's army; unaware that he soon would be fighting in a major battle, he set about improving his domestic arrangements and bringing Ellen down to Tennessee.

The colonel seems not to have been too concerned about his wife's comfort as a Yankee in hostile territory, about possible wartime risks to her life, or about the needs of their three children. When she was sent for, she dutifully packed up, left the children with the mayor's family, and took the train to Nashville. No more bacon on a stick and coffee in a tin cup for Colonel Sherman.

3

BATTLE OF STONES RIVER:
WINTER, 1862–1863

The winter inactivity did not last as long as Colonel Sherman had anticipated. Rosecrans had been assigned to replace Buell because Buell was too slow in chasing the rebels out of Chattanooga and East Tennessee. Thus, while Rosecrans was reluctant to move until he was ready, once he was prepared to go, he moved quickly. What may have determined his decision to engage the enemy at Stones River was the information that Bragg had sent Brig. Gen. John Hunt Morgan's cavalry to Kentucky and Brig. Gen. Nathan B. Forrest's to Corinth. Even without Morgan and Forrest, the Confederates had twice as many cavalry as the Union had; nevertheless, the rebels' cavalry advantage was less than it had been before or was likely to be again.[1] Furthermore, Rosecrans was receiving signals from an impatient President Lincoln that, if he could not get things moving, he might well suffer a fate similar to General Buell's.

So, although Colonel Sherman spent Christmas of 1862 with his wife in Nashville, he left the next day with the 44,000-man Army of the Cumberland to find and confront Bragg. It took four days to catch up with the Confederates, as the southern cavalry harassed the supply trains and slowed the Union army's pace. On December 29, the Army of the Cumberland finally faced the main body of Confederates at Stones River, near Murfreesboro, thirty miles south of Nashville. On the next day, both armies reconnoitered and set their lines for the coming engagement.

Colonel Sherman and the 88th Illinois, about to face their first major battle, had been fortunate in being assigned to Sheridan's division. On the evening of December 30, General Sheridan and Gen. Joshua W. Sill, Colonel Sherman's brigade commander, warned their corps commander, Gen. Alexander McCook, that the Confederates were likely to focus their attack on their corps.[2] McCook,

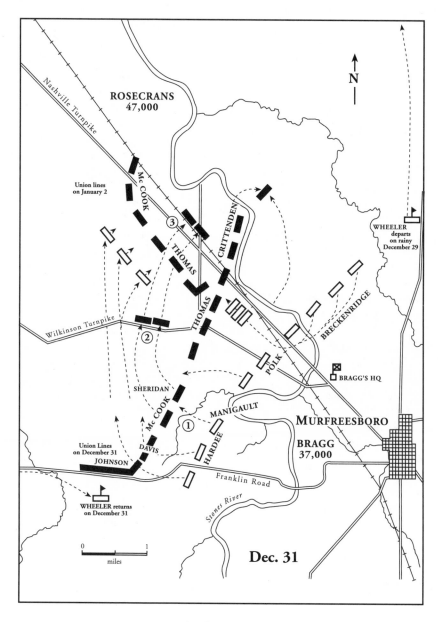

Battle of Stones River.
Legend: 1. Johnson and Davis break. 2. Sheridan holds his line.
3. Sheridan's "orderly retreat."

however, disagreed; Rosecrans planned to attack the Confederate right, and both Rosecrans and McCook thought that the Confederates would have their hands full and could not launch the attack that Sheridan and Sill predicted. By the time McCook reconsidered, it was late, and he did not press his brigade commanders to prepare to meet an attack. Thus, early in the morning on New Year's Eve (Colonel Sherman's thirty-seventh birthday), when the Confederates struck McCook's corps, Sheridan and Sill (and Sherman) were ready, but the other two divisions on the Union right—those under Gen. Richard W. Johnson and Gen. Jefferson C. Davis[3]—were taken by surprise and rolled back.[4] Three times the Confederates charged, and each time Sheridan's lines bent but did not break. Eventually, as their ammunition ran low, the Union troops were able to conduct a skillful "fighting withdrawal." As Sheridan observed, "By afternoon the Union army was drawn up in an arrowhead formation, right and left wings standing almost back to back; and there, finally, as the cold day waned, they made their stand and held on grimly, beating off the last of the rebel attacks."[5]

By his brilliant leadership that day, the youthful Sheridan strengthened his reputation as one of the top Union generals. His division's "performance ranked among the very best in this, or any other, American war."[6] Sheridan's losses, however, were heavy. Stones River was no Perryville, where Colonel Sherman's green regiment had reported only four men killed and fifteen injured. In the four hours of fierce fighting at Stones River, Sheridan's division lost 40 percent of its men killed, injured, or missing; all three brigade commanders were killed, including General Sill, in command of the brigade which included the 88th Infantry. According to Colonel Sherman's diary, after the battle his regiment "mustered 270 men out of 420 [who] went into action." In proportion to the size of the forces engaged, the first day of Stones River was one of the bloodiest days of battle in the war.

Bragg believed on the evening of December 31 that he had won a substantial victory, and he felt sure that Rosecrans would fall back during the night, but the Union army held its ground. The fighting diminished in intensity on January 1; after an ill-advised Confederate advance was repulsed with heavy losses on January 2, it was Bragg, not Rosecrans, who retreated.

Colonel Sherman wrote to his father and to his sister about Stones River. The first part of the letter to his father and the last part of that to his sister are missing, but, between extant parts of the two, an account of most of the fighting can be found. Frank graphically described the fighting on December 31 to his sister, reaffirming his pride in his regiment:

> Camp on Stone River, Jan'y 12 '63
> Near Murfreesboro, 3 ms, So.
>
> Dear Sister:
> I received the family letter written on Christmas day containing the wishes of you all for me and Ellen, which, thank God, I am able to send

back to you all at the present time the same wishes for your present and future happiness, and a reunion at no great lapse of time of us all at our home in Chicago. I received two letters for Ellen from our daughter Ella, and it gives me pleasure to note the improvement she is making; tell her to keep on. Altho Pa and Ma are a long way off our dear children are not forgotten.

William writes me that he has sent me $100 by mail. I have not as yet received it; when I do I will acknowledge receipt of the same. Ellen is in Nashville stopping with a Dr [Peter A.] Westervelt and is tolerably comfortably situated. She will come to Murfreesboro in a few days and will stop at the house of a Mr Jordan whose son was a prisoner of war at Camp Butler when the 12th Cav'y was there. He remembered her and me and invited her to go to his father's house when she went [to Nashville].

Father says he is going to Washington and if I will get a recommend from Gen'l Rosecrans he will try and get me a "Star" in place of my eagle. I confess I would be glad to mount the "Star" but I have considerable delicacy in asking Gen'l Rosecrans to do me so great a favor. Tell him to try without the recommend and I will try to get it from some of the commanding generals over me. If [Adj.] Gen'l [Allen C.] Fuller had dated my commission on the eighth of August 1862 I would now be in command of a brigade.[7] Have father try and have a new commission made out at that date.

In a letter written some days since I gave some account of the battle, I think up to Tuesday night of the 30th, and the part taken by my Rgt. up to that time. During Tuesday night the regiment lay in a cotton field (in the mud) in line of battle with our skirmishers acting as pickets about 50 yards in advance of the battalion and 150 yds. from the rebel pickets. This was the second night we had to lay out without fires [during] a heavy frost and with the men wet through. Nothing occurred during the night except an occasional shot from the pickets as some one of them exposed himself to view. At daylight I had every man in the Reg't in his place and awaiting the coming fight which came so near to being disastrous to our Army. With daylight came the sharp crack of the Enfield rifles as our skirmishers exposed themselves to the enemy. Both sides were busy trying to pick off any unfortunate soldier who had not sufficient cover to protect him. I will attempt to here give a diagram of my position and that of the rebels as they advanced to the attack at sunrise on Wednesday morning, the 31st of December, 1862. I do not know if you can make out anything by my diagram.[8]

I discovered the Rebels moving forward in columns of battalions, one [column] directly at the 88th Ill. and the other at the 36th Ill. On they came with steady front and firm tread with colors flying as if on the parade ground, their officers leading in advance of the column and cheering on their men. As they advanced my skirmishers delivered their fire and rallied upon the battalion in fine style and lay down in their places (the whole battalion at this time laying on their faces). Some five or six of them were killed or wounded at this time.

For a few moments everything was still as death as that dark host moved forward to our front. Never shall I forget those few anxious moments that intervened before the terrible work of death commenced. The men of the 88th I am happy to say were under complete control and though there was many an anxious eye turned towards me I saw nothing but determination and a fixed purpose then and there to make a record on the enemy that will not soon be forgotten, and that they had faith in me to bring them through the contest in which they were about to engage with thrice their numbers. The benefits of discipline and obedience to orders was visible here; not a man offered to discharge his musket but patiently waited for the order which they anxiously waited to hear. I am proud of my reg't and proud of the part they took in that day's fight, and I think the Board of Trade of Chicago are proud to acknowledge us.

All this time the rebel horde was advancing, their lines extending beyond my right and left flank. They were now within one hundred yards of us, when they took the double quick and with a yell they came to the charge bayonet and came on for twenty five yards further. I let them come; when within seventy five yards of us I gave the command to the 88th to fire and aim low. At that command every man raised to his knee and a long line of bright barrels for one instant gleamed in the early sunlight as they were leveled on the advancing foe, and the next moment they vomited forth their contents on the gallant men who were rushing on to their destruction. Like the grass before the scythe of the mower[,] the ranks of the enemy went down as that volley went crashing and tearing through their ranks. It brought them to a dead halt for a moment, and then on again they came. That halt was fatal to them; it gave my men time to reload. Again another crashing volley tore through their decimated ranks. Still stubborn these brave but infatuated [*sic*] men lay down and attempted to return the fire but the advantage was ours; we being on the highest ground, their balls whistled harmlessly by.

'Twas now that I ordered the battalion to rise and give them h———l. At the word every man sprung to his feet and we poured in such a fire upon them that they were forced to leave the ground on the double quick and retire into the timber beyond. [several pages missing]

This was our first fight in which the enemy were handsomely repulsed. (Please send me any newspaper account of the battle or mention of the 88th as we are all anxious to see the reports sent back home.)

The regiment met with a severe loss in the death of Dr George Coatsworth, our surgeon, who died of pneumonia contracted in the discharge of his duty amongst the wounded. He was a splendid man, a good officer, and one of the best surgeons in the Army. We cannot replace him.

Write me often. Remember that I cannot sit down at any time and write; we are here today and away tomorrow. Our rgt. is 3 miles south of Murfreesboro on the Shelbyville pike, and as usual our Div. is on the front, our pickets and the rebel pickets posted in sight of one another. I will write again in a few days if we are not moved. During the battle I lost 5 pounds of flesh but am now in good health. My love to you all and my respects to all enquiring friends.

Good-bye

Your brother, Frank

Tell mother I was made happy by the few lines she wrote and to write more. God bless her; to her I owe all that I am.

Colonel Sherman continued his narrative of the Battle of Stones River in the existing portion of the January 4 letter to his father, beginning his account a few hours after the repulse of the Confederates on December 31, described in his letter to his sister. In the intervening period, the 88th had been unsuccessful in its attempt to dislodge the Confederates from their position in the woods and, almost out of ammunition, had withdrawn. Colonel Sherman's letter to his father relates what occurred after the withdrawal.

We finally found protection behind the railroad track. Here we were able to fill up our empty cartridge boxes after having been under fire for 5 1/2 hours and fought over two miles of as hard contested ground as any that has been fought over during this war, and one mile of it [with bayonet and] without ammunition. Nobly and manfully did the officers and men of my regiment go through this terrible fiery ordeal, and we now rank with any of the old regiments in the service, having received the kind of praise we got from our commanding general.

With a supply of ammunition in our cartridge belts we were once more ready to face the so far victorious enemy. Our Division had now fallen back on the Center of the Army under command of Gen. [George H.] Thomas. Here the enemy were checked and stopped, after a severe fight of two hours' duration, in which many noble spirits went back to the Giver of all Good.

Again our division was ordered into the fight by our brave commander Gen. Sheridan, who seemed to bear a charmed life as he was everywhere present in the thickest of the battle. One more charge and the rebels fell back with fearful slaughter on both sides. We drove them back over half a mile of the ground that they had pushed us over. The battle for the day was over and the remnant of our gallant division was permitted to rest for the night, after having fought for eleven hours over 2½ miles of ground.

The loss to our division out of 5500 effective fighting men was 1755 killed, wounded, or missing. The loss that the 88th sustained was 150 men out of 420 who went into action. Enough of the missing have returned to reduce our loss on that memorable day to 116—the missing are supposed to be prisoners. I had one first lieutenant killed [Thomas F. W. Gullich], 1 captain [George W. Smith] and 1 lieutenant [actually two: Homer C. McDonald and Dean R. Chester] wounded. Major [George W.] Chandler was wounded slightly. Our Division Commander Gen. Sheridan was told by Gen. Rosecrans that our division saved his Army. This is a great compliment to him, and to the officers and men under him.

Jan. 1, 1863, opened the new year and in the morning quite a sharp fight took place. From then until the Rebels began their evacuation our Division was not in any general engagement, although we were ready at any moment.

They [the rebels] were awfully whipped the next night [January 2]. I say night, because the fight did not begin until four o'clock and lasted until dark. They were driven back at the point of the bayonet for over a mile, and many were killed. On Saturday [January 3] they commenced evacuating Murfreesboro, and on Monday following, our brigade and division was moved to where we are now [close to Stones River]. How long we shall remain here I do not know. Ellen is still in Nashville.

The Rebel Cavalry captured my Headquarters wagon and destroyed all of my private property, my blankets, papers [perhaps including his 1862 diary], everything. For two days we lived on corn and the rest of the time on half rations.

You may have published if you think proper so much of this letter as may be of interest to the sponsors of the regiment [the Chicago Board of Trade], although it gives but a faint outline of what we went through from the 26th of December, 1862, to the 4th of January, 1863, during all of which we were either skirmishing or fighting.

Regimental colonels were appointed by governors of the respective states; in Colonel Sherman's case, although his father had arranged it, the actual appointment had been made by Gov. Richard Yates of Illinois. Colonel Sherman wrote a somewhat more formal account to the governor on January 13 from Stones River and kept a copy in his papers:

I have the honor to report to you the part taken by my regiment in the recent battle of Stones River, near Murfreesboro, Tenn.:

On the morning of the 30th day of December at 7 o'clock the brigade to which my regiment is attached, being then under the command of Brig. Genl. Sill, marched on the pike towards the town of Murfreesboro. About 9 A.M. I was ordered to the right of the pike where skirmishing was going on with the enemy. I immediately formed in line of battle on the left of the 36th Ills. in front of [Capt. Charles] Houghtaling's and [Capt. Henry] Hescock's batteries and threw out my two flank companies as skirmishers with Companies F and G as supports. My skirmishers advanced to the rear of Harding's house and orchard and from behind a rail fence skirmished moderately with the enemy until about 3 o'clock P.M. when an advance was ordered.

Changing front to the left I took position with the regiment in a cotton field on a ridge just in the rear of a strip of bottom lands beyond which the enemy was posted in the timber, with my skirmishers a short distance in advance. During the remainder of the day skirmishing was brisk, in which I lost one man killed and a number wounded.

Night having set in I received orders for the regiment to remain on the field—the skirmishers to act as pickets. The night was cold and windy; the men were allowed but little fire by which to warm themselves and make a cup of coffee. They got but little sleep and at daybreak the following (31st) morning were in line of battle when skirmishing was renewed. About 7 o'clock the enemy made an advance across the "bottom"—one brigade charging directly upon my regiment. I ordered the men to hold their fire until the enemy should be within short musket range. This was a trying moment for them but they quietly lay upon the ground until the enemy in full view had advanced to within seventy-five yards when the order was given for them to rise up and fire which was obeyed with a coolness and bravery worthy of veteran soldiers. At this the enemy halted and as our men reloaded and fired into their ranks, rapidly they turned their backs to us, leaving many brave men dead and dying. This repulse was complete but a charge on troops to our right was more successful and we were obliged to retire, which was done in good order[9] but with great loss of men. In this retreat Lieut. Thos. F. W. Gullich was shot in the head and killed instantly. In his death his company and his country have lost a faithful officer and a gallant soldier.

The enemy having broken our right we retired across the Wilkinson Pike and made a stand in the cedars but after a severe engagement for about twenty minutes we were ordered to fall back. We fell back to the railroad when firing ceased the whole length of the lines.

The enemy's cavalry had been making attacks on our trains on the Murfreesboro Pike and about noon we were ordered out to support our cavalry in resisting the attacks. We had no engagement and at night went into camp on a hill just beyond Overhaus [sp?] Creek about two miles from the battlefield. Early the next morning (January 1st) we marched again to the battlefield and took position on the right where we remained until the close of the battle.

Colonel Sherman, generous as usual in his praise of his subordinates, ended his letter to Governor Yates about the battle with commendations for his company commanders, "all of whom remained steadily at their posts, urging their men to stand firm under a galling fire from the enemy." Lt .Col. Alexander S. Chadbourne and Adjutant Alexander S. Ballard were both sick, leaving Colonel Sherman with only one field assistant, Major Chandler, about whom he wrote to Governor Yates, "I take special pleasure in mentioning Maj. [George W.] Chandler, whose conduct throughout the conflict was characterized by calmness and the most determined bravery. His services were invaluable to the regiment as his gallant example infused itself into the spirits of the men, making them cool and steady when obliged to retire in the face of the enemy. Although wounded and having his horse shot from under him, he remained steadily at his post until the close of the battle."

At the end of the letter to Governor Yates, Colonel Sherman commented on the regimental surgeon: "Major Geo. Coatsworth was not with us on the field but at the hospitals in the execution of his duties as Surgeon of the regiment. He was untiring in his efforts for the alleviation of suffering, laboring almost continually for 48 hours and exposing himself greatly. His associate surgeons gave him all praise and acceded to his superior abilities. The labors and exposure he endured were too much for him and after an illness of one week he died on the 9th inst. He died gloriously—at his post of duty."

In his letters about Stones River, as in other battle reports, Colonel Sherman described the outcome in somewhat more positive terms than history confirms. Although Stones River was hardly as decisive a victory as Colonel Sherman believed it was (Rosecrans's army suffered three thousand more casualties than Bragg's), the Union forces did win the ground. In a period that included Second Manassas, Antietam, and especially the disaster at Fredericksburg, Stones River reassured Lincoln and the North that its troops could hold their own, at least in Tennessee. Lincoln's gratitude to Rosecrans for the Stones River victory may have been one reason why the cautious general remained as commander of the Army of the Cumberland as long as he did.

Sheridan had lost all of his brigade commanders at Stones River, and Colonel Sherman apparently was now being considered for the command of a brigade. It would be a temporary command, without a promotion to brigadier general, which would require War Department action. To command the brigade, Colonel Sherman needed to establish seniority over Col. Charles H. Larrabee, the commander of the 24th Wisconsin regiment (in Sheridan's division), whose commission was dated five days before Sherman's. Although Sherman tried to have the date of his own commission advanced by a week, Colonel Larrabee's seniority held. Shortly thereafter, however, he took over as brigade commander in Larrabee's absence.

Meanwhile, Rosecrans, with sparse supplies and in no hurry to risk another Stones River, settled his army for the winter in Murfreesboro and began planning his spring advance on Chattanooga. On January 30, 1863, Colonel Sherman started home with his wife on leave; when he rejoined his troops in February, she remained in Chicago. Upon his return, he wrote to his father about his new assignment as brigade commander and the conditions at camp.

Murfreesboro, Tenn., Feby. 18, 1862

Dear Father

I have not much to write you. It is very rainy and muddy and Rosecrans' army cannot move for the present on account of the state of the roads. And we have the pleasure of being up to our necks [in mud] with no prospect of the weather or roads getting better. When I got back from leave I found myself in command of my brigade, Col. Greusel having resigned during my absence. I am to all intents and purposes a brigadier with a rank of colonel and have the paraphernalia about me when I am on duty that belong to the high and exalted station of a star. Almost all the regimental commanders are pleased at the change, so they say, and I take their words for it. Changes in the army are rapid and I who started out as junior colonel of our brigade am now its senior with but one exception, Col. Larrabee of the 24th Wisconsin who is at home recruiting his health and his regiment.

We are going through the usual routine of camp life which is not very exciting. Guard, picket, and forage duty fills up the time, and is very disagreeable on account of the inclemency of the weather. It is not cold, but like April with us at home, but with more rain. All the birds of May are here, such as meadowlarks, robins, and the others that inhabit our climate during the spring and early summer.

Many resignations are being offered and accepted. Some deserting is taking place, and many, very many, are sick. This army has not been paid yet, for some reason unexplained, although the paymasters are at Murfreesboro and have been there for more than a week.[10]

Colonel Sherman did not command his brigade for long. He wrote his father a bitter letter about the loss of his command on April 21, 1863, the same day that his father was reelected mayor. Since his father had just waged a political campaign emphasizing the alleged inefficiency of the administration's war effort, he was hardly the right person to press his son's interests at the War Department. The colonel persisted, however, in insisting then and later that his father intercede for him to obtain his promotion:

Murfreesboro, Tennessee, April 21, 1863

Dear Father:

I have been relieved from the command of the brigade and am now with my regiment. This was brought about by Col. Larrabee, who is my senior in rank by five days. He went to Gen. Sheridan, who would not listen to him and kept me in command. Larrabee then went to wire-pulling and succeeded in getting himself assigned to the command of this brigade unbeknownst to Gen. Sheridan or to Gen. McCook, contrary to all military usages. Well, be it so.

By the provisions of Sections 19 and 20 of the Act for the "Enrolling and Calling out of the Forces of the U.S." (Conscription Act), I am liable to be mustered out of the Service for not having five hundred men or more [in my regiment].[11] I do not wish to get out in that way. I believe that I have fairly earned promotion. This I can get by a little exertion from my friends at home. If they will write to Generals Rosecrans, McCook, and Sheridan I think they can get such answers to their inquiries about me that will induce the President to give me the appointment that I desire. You can talk with Mr. Tuttle[12] and give him this idea, and if the Board of Trade [which had sponsored the 88th Illinois regiment] are desirous of having anything done for me in that way, they with their influence can easily bring it about in a short time. If nothing can be done I shall probably come home, as the prospect is anything but encouraging for me to go into another battle, and lose more men in fighting for my country with that law staring me in the face. No matter whether I do well or not I must be mustered out. That is a very just law, is it not?

Colonel Sherman did not resign his commission, then or later, despite many threats to do so, but his resentment over the loss of his brigade command continued to rankle.

4

CHICAGO POLITICS:
SPRING, 1863

In 1862, Mayor Sherman had been nominated for Congress on a non-partisan ticket. The platform on which he ran pledged a vigorous prosecution of the war, but was highly critical of the Republican administration for inefficiency in the conduct of the war. It opposed the extension of slavery and slavery itself, but at the same time it viewed emancipation as radical and unconstitutional. While the platform opposed secession, many of the Chicago "Peace" Democrats, who supported Sherman, would have welcomed a peace that recognized the Confederacy. Colonel Sherman, as his letters make clear, vigorously opposed any peace short of complete surrender and the total dissolution of the Confederacy, and he objected strongly to his father's softened stand on the war.[1]

In the bitter campaign for Congress, the Republicans freely accused the Democrats of traitorous sympathy with the Confederacy. Much of the campaigning was carried on in the partisan press, led by the Republican *Chicago Daily Tribune* and the Democratic *Daily Chicago Times*.[2] On October 15, 1862, the *Tribune* called Mayor Sherman "a tail to [the most notorious Copperhead, Clement] Vallandigham's kite." On election day, November 8, 1862, its editorial trumpeted, "Every disloyal man in Chicago will vote for Frank Sherman for Congress today. Not a vote will be cast for [Isaac N.] Arnold [the Republican incumbent and candidate] except by men whose loyalty and patriotism have never been impeached."

The mayor lost his bid for a seat in Congress; although he won the city by 150 votes, he lost in the outlying districts. His margin in the city, however, encouraged him to plan to seek reelection as mayor in the spring of 1863. His son opposed his father's plan, since he believed, perhaps not as strongly as the *Tribune,* that the Democratic party in Chicago wanted to end the war, even if that meant strengthening states' rights and continuing slavery in the South.

The Hon. Francis Cornwall Sherman.
Used by permission of the Chicago Historical Society.

Colonel Sherman's unhappiness with his father's political associates, particularly those who were talking of making peace with the Confederacy, is evident in the last three paragraphs of his letter[3] of February 18, 1863:

> There is considerable talk amongst officers and soldiers about the present political differences that are agitating our state. So far as I have heard there is but one opinion amongst us, and that is that our people are determined to sacrifice us to their partisan ideas, leaving us to take

care of us as best we may. And our idea is that we have some rights left and are entitled to consideration. We cannot vote and do not want to,[4] but we shall insist that the North, and especially Illinois, shall stop giving aid and comfort to traitors in arms by dissension and the talk of peace conventions.

Carrying forth to the southern traitors and bolstering up their waning fortunes [encourages them to believe] that no more men can or will be raised to crush out the so-called Southern Confederacy. It appears to me that the extremists in both parties are mad, and the patriots, if any there be left, apathetic. They must awake from their lethargy or our country is lost. It is not now to punish traitor and suppress rebellion only that we are fighting for, but to save the country and the government from anarchy worse than that which paralyzed Mexico through the past quarter of a century.

Why will not the people of the north see this and arouse in their might and save us and them from utter ruin? When it will be too late they will see that they have been led by a will-of-the-wisp to their destruction. There will be a meeting of officers and soldiers from Illinois in a short time on the course being pursued in our state by extremists in political affairs. I would prefer not to have this meeting if Illinois will only come to her senses. If not the soldiers must try to help her to them. *They will be heard from.*

Soon thereafter, Colonel Sherman indeed was heard from, in an impassioned and somewhat longwinded letter to Frederick Tuttle.[5] The letter was written from Stones River on February 18, 1863, and turned over to the *Chicago Daily Tribune* by Tuttle, apparently according to Colonel Sherman's wish. Five days later it was published. After a preliminary paragraph describing his current command, the colonel continued:

The rebels are becoming more confident every day of success in dividing our beloved country from the fact of the political differences in the North, and especially the states of Illinois and Indiana.

What can our people be thinking of when they go so far with their partisan feeling as to lose sight of the fact that our country is now passing through the darkest hours of our history? With armed rebellion in our front, and insidious foes and traitors in our rear, she needs that all true patriots should step forth, at whatever cost or sacrifice, and crush out traitors at home who are trying to poison the minds of the weak and fearful, whose minds are worked upon by their hellish cunning and damnable sentiments of party, and who wish to serve the country through dishonorable overtures to rebels in arms, and make us, as a people, a byword for treachery for all time to come.

The soldiers here, when they look back to their homes and firesides that they have left for love of country, feel that, in the recent political struggles for power and party, they have been ignored by all parties, and left here to contend against disease, death, and an ever vigilant foe alone, whilst the fanatics of the North are giving aid and comfort to rebellion, and revive their broken fortunes by their (the North's) infernal dissensions.

Let the disunionists of the North take heed. We do not propose quietly to allow them to trample on our rights, and help dig our own graves. What we expect and look for is that men will not long be allowed to utter traitors' sentiments at our homes; that there is true patriotism enough left to save the country, and rub out traitors of all degree at home, who act in the guise of loyalty, to whatever party they may belong.

The soldiers here recognize in the President one who is constitutionally authorized to administer the laws and direct the operations of the army and the navy. As Commander-in-chief he has the undoubted right to issue orders and proclamations, whenever the exigencies of the service require it to suppress armed rebellion against the Government that he, as the Chief Magistrate, has sworn to protect.

We the soldiers of the United States, called forth to save the country, dropped our political differences and took the oath that we would obey the orders of the President of the United States and we intend to do it, and every officer and soldier that I have talked with in regard to our duty agrees with me, i.e., that we will sustain to the death our Commander-in-chief, the President of the United States in all measures and orders that he may issue for the thrashing of the rebellion in the Southern States, and we call on the North to lay aside their bitter feelings, engendered by strife for power, and unite, and come up with a steady front on the war question, and demonstrate that it is the determination of the North, at all hazards, to furnish men and means to prosecute this war to a finality; that traitors shall be punished; and, my word for it, this war will not last one year longer. Those of us who are left can then lay down our arms and return to our homes, and we shall again have a happy and prosperous country respected and feared by all the nations of the earth.

Pursue the mad policy of partisan politics, and we are lost; unhesitatingly yielding to the demands made upon us by the Government to root out their great wrong that is threatening one of the fairest portions of man's inheritance, and all will be well. But rest assured of one thing: the soldiers are loyal and will support the government, and they would as soon war on traitors in Illinois as in Tennessee. The soldiers must not be ignored, nor must it be forgotten that we yet have rights, and a voice at home, and an interest in our country.

Yours respectfully,
Francis T. Sherman,
Colonel commanding 88th Illinois Volunteers

We can only guess how the mayor responded to his son's excursion into politics and his not-so-veiled criticism of his father, at that time busily campaigning for reelection as mayor. Two weeks later, Colonel Sherman defended his position in a letter to his parents:

Franklin, Tenn., March 8th, 1863

Dear Father and Mother:

It seems that my letter to Mr. Tuttle has made a great stir in the Chicago world. Well, let it. There is no such thing as peace so long as one armed rebel pollutes the soil of our country. As to having turned myself over to the abolitionists, that is not so. I only wrote my honest sentiments about this unhappy war and its consequences.

I went into this war from motives of patriotism[;] and as a Democrat, a loyal citizen, I want to see our government reinstated and placed where she belongs. I want to be proud of the name 'American citizen.' When I cannot serve my country without being able to call into question the authority of its legal head or to complain if he happens to step beyond the limits of the law, I shall resign and return to my home, nor be mean enough to partake of the honors or emoluments she may bestow. This I call honorable and what she expects of me. Enough of this.[6]

A week later, after he had received another letter from his father, he included this somewhat more conciliatory comment:[7]

My letter to Mr. Tuttle seems to have made considerable excitement amongst the good people of Chicago. Father, there is nothing written or implied in it but what you or any other good loyal citizen and Democrat can subscribe to. There is mention of neither party and only those who would accept peace with dishonor from rebs in arms will put on the shoe. I know you are true and loyal, and I care not for all the little slurs and innuendos as to my motives, so long as you do not mistake or misconstrue me. You may tell the editor of the [Chicago] *Times* if you see fit that he need not spare me for connections sake, with his dirty fling about my going out with my regiment under protest of its officers, and that I despise his praise or condemnation. He will be hung yet for a traitor if he keeps on.[8]

Colonel Sherman may not have intended his letter to Frederick Tuttle to be a personal attack on his father, but the opposition *Chicago Daily Tribune* chose to view it as such. Its election day editorial diatribe against Mayor Sherman said: "His own son, who is in the field, wrote home an indignant rebuke of his father's apostasy, which was published in the loyal papers of this city."[9]

On April 3, Colonel Sherman expressed his feelings again in a long and impassioned letter to his father:

April 3, 1863

Dear Father:

I see that politics runs high with you yet. I hope you are not so wedded to any party that you will allow it to carry you beyond patriotism and the love of country. Excuse me for writing thus, but it does seem to me, Father, that there is neither democracy nor patriotism in the acknowledged organ of the so-called Democratic party, the *Times*. I do not believe that you endorse the sayings and doings of this filthy sheet, which is heaping dust upon the self-sacrificing soldier who has left his home and all that he holds dear for love of country to face the perils of the field and the camp.

Suppose you differ with the present administration as to many of its measures and blunders in the conduct of this war, as to the enforcement of the laws and bringing back a portion of the refractory subjects who have been misled by the sophisms urged upon them by designing men who wished for nothing more than their personal aggrandizement and to gratify an inordinate ambition to rule or ruin, what then? Must a great principle be perverted by demagogues; must we be bound by chains of steel to the chariot of party, and forget that we have a country without which we as the people who have for the last eighty years been working out the great problem 'Is man capable of self-government' must come to naught, anarchy, chaos?

The question now is shall this principle become active and diffuse happiness for all to come and those who shall come after us, or shall it be buried in the ruins of demagogism and party strife through the weakness of those who are controlled by the trammels and narrow views of selfish politicians obscuring the minds of the people as to the great results and benefactions which are to be transmitted to future generations, and build up a nation the like of which will never have been before formed on earth by the hands of man.

Cast aside, I implore you, Father, all considerations of party until this infamous war is closed and peace once more sits enthroned in our once-happy land. Cast not a straw in the way of the wheels of state which are now creaking under the heavy burden put upon them, and by your position and influence show the world that you can rise superior to party when the stake played for is our country. God bless her, my country, the United States of America, first or last, right or wrong, still my country. Its legal representatives and constituted authorities shall receive my whole and undivided support with all the capacity and power that an all-wise God has endowed me with for the purpose of crushing this rebellion and once more reuniting this unhappy country and people, one and indivisible.

Great responsibility rests upon the men of influence and substance at home, and it becomes them to take the side of patriotism and of this country in this her hour of trial. Be warned! No terms must be offered to treason but absolute submission to the offended laws. It must, it cannot be otherwise; the laws must be avenged or we become a second Mexico— all that we hold dear gone, vanished, without morals, law, or stability— the laughing stock of the world, knocked about like a battledore and shuttlecock at the caprice of every adventurer who may for the time gain the ascendancy by means of any advantageous circumstances which he may be smart enough to seize upon. Father, there should be one party at the present time and its platform should be death to traitors wherever found, and the last man and cent that can be raised or found to prosecute this war, to maintain the birthright that we inherited from the glorious fathers of the revolution.

I know you are true and patriotic, a firm supporter of our country and desire nothing more than the triumph of the Union cause. You want peace; so do I, but not dishonorable peace. That can never be. I claim to be as good a Democrat as ever I was. That does not interfere with my support of the government under which I was born and whose protecting arm has ever been ready to shield me, one of her sons, from wrong. Shall I shrink now that she needs me? Shall I forget the many blessings she has show-ered upon me and mine? No, never! Then rally around the old flag, see it not trailed in the dust and all will be well. Amen.

These thoughts have been suggested to me by your letter and the ac-counts of party strife now going on at home for power, the loaves and fishes, and the impediment thrown in the way to stop the return of ab-sentees and deserters who have received the bounty of their country and sworn to protect her, by those who call themselves 'Democrats.' You and I, Father, belong to no such party as that. The true democracy should rise en masse and trample out such scoundrels.

I am well and so is Ellen. We both join in sending love to you all. I have no news to write you but what you have heard. We are laying in camp here doing the usual routine of duty with an occasional skirmish. Again, love to all, and believe me as ever your loving son, Frank.

Colonel Sherman may have been "as good a Democrat as ever I was," but his political sentiments seemed more Republican than Democratic. He did not remain a Democrat to spare his father's feelings; changing parties doubtless would have had less impact on his father's feelings than his public criticism. Perhaps he felt that he could have more influence on his father's politics if he remained a Democrat. More likely, he may have thought that he would lose the support of his father's political associates in his quest for promotion if he deserted their party. (Later, however, he sought help from the powerful Chicago Republican "Long John" Wentworth and from two Republican governors.) Whatever the reason, he remained a Democrat all his life, and after the war he was elected to the state legislature as a Democrat.

Colonel Sherman's recommendation to "cast aside all considerations of party" did not deter his father from continuing to campaign in what was called the most bitterly fought campaign the city had yet seen. Two days before the election, the *Chicago Daily Tribune* warned its readers: "By voting for Sherman for mayor you cripple the administration, paralyze the government, and compromise with traitors."[10]

On the next day, the *Tribune* continued its attack: "Every man who is opposed to the fire-in-the-rear on our soldiers in the field will vote for [Thomas B.] Bryan and the Union ticket. Every Copperhead will vote for Sherman. A man is known by the company he keeps. . . . We don't say that every man who votes for Sherman is disloyal, but we do say that all the disloyal voters in this city will vote for him, and that they control his party."[11]

On election day, the *Tribune* made its final pre-election pitch: "[The Copperhead snake] today seeks to cast a censure on the flag and an Odium on the Union cause by the election of a man who has never had one word of sympathy for the cause of his country. He is the puppet of men whose sole work is treason, whose only sympathies are with the armed enemies of the Government."[12]

Nevertheless, the colonel's father won reelection as mayor of Chicago, this time for a term of two years rather than one. The *Tribune*'s editorial deplored his victory: "For two years more the concealed secessionists in our midst have a tool in the person of the chief executive officer of the city who will do their bidding. Chicago, until another trial of strength, is ranked among the disloyal cities of the land. A bad day's work has been done; the city has been dishonored."[13]

It took a while for Colonel Sherman to bring himself to congratulate his father after his victory. His next letter, written about May 1, is somewhat restrained:

Dear Father:
    I have not heard from home very often of late and suppose the reason is because you have been very busy in the political world. I saw that you have been re-elected mayor by a hundred and eighteen votes. That is what I call a close rub [actually it was 157 votes—still a "close rub"]. I am very glad that you have succeeded in whipping them.
    I wish I could rejoice over the election of the whole ticket, but I cannot. Such men as O. G. Rose,[14] who never had a principle, being elected to a responsible position in the city government is a disgrace to all with whom he may come in contact, and more so to the Democratic party. Well, that is no business of mine. All I have to say, Father, is that that man will bear watching. I hope your administration of the city government will give the lie to all of your calumniators. I know it will.

On May 7, 1863, just over two weeks after the election, Colonel Sherman formally communicated his felicitations, but then could not refrain from lecturing his father.

Murfreesboro, Tenn., May 7th 1863

Dear Father:

Allow me to congratulate you upon the victory you have achieved over your personal and political adversaries. The 'government as it was, and the Constitution as it is' is a good platform,[15] but that platform can never be carried out again in this country. The day is past and [it] is beyond the control of human power to restore this government 'as it was' before the rebellion. The north will surely suppress the present revolt notwithstanding its gigantic proportions. And in doing so the blot of slavery on our free institutions will be wiped out, and the stain upon the 'Declaration of the Rights of Man' will be no longer the mark of Cain upon our nation and country.

This war must never cease until the fire brand of slavery is utterly quenched. There is no use of blinding ourselves. Events which none but God control are taking place, which will inevitably work out the problem under which this country is laboring, and its throes and agony at the present time makes the civilized world look on in wonder and amazement at our powers of endurance.

I am as good a Democrat as ever,[16] and there is in the word no significance which tends to treason or disloyalty to our beloved country. There may be those who cloak themselves under its broad mantle to hide their foulness and bring discredit upon the party that has always been first in loyalty.

Even Douglas the patriot and statesman has been called traitor by those who now quote [his speeches when he is] dead [but] who spat forth venom on him [when he was] living. He was the first of Democrats and he was the first to pledge himself and the party he represented to the President of the United States (A. Lincoln) to maintain the laws of the country against treason in arms to its destruction and annihilation. That is my democracy until the last rebel north or south has paid the penalty of his treason.[17]

In his frequent lectures to his father about his political associates, Colonel Sherman never directly accused him of being a Copperhead, although he may have suspected that his father was more of a Copperhead than he acknowledged. While Mayor Sherman generally was perceived as a moderate and a compromiser,[18] in one report he was alleged, probably falsely, to have been a member of the Order of American Knights, a secret society of southern sympathizers headed by Vallandigham.[19] If Colonel Sherman believed that his father was more than a fellow traveler of the Copperheads but felt that he could not confront his father directly, in view of the latter's denial, it would account, at least in part, for the frequency and intensity of his diatribes concerning his father's politics.

5

A Quiet Spring in Camp, 1863

While his father was campaigning in Chicago, Colonel Sherman, in winter quarters in Murfreesboro, was becoming increasingly lonely for his Ellen. On March 3, 1863, he sent her a rather peremptory letter with the terse heading, "Wife":

> What I want you to do is to pack and come here to *me* at once. Lieutenant [Frank M.] Bouton has written for his wife, and you both had better come together. At any rate I want you to come. See father and tell him to pay the children's school bill out of the money left with him by me. So come, lassie. Telegraph me from Louisville so that I may know when to look for you. If I am not at the depot in Murfreesboro when you arrive you had better go to Jordan's[1] and send word to camp. Our division is going out on a scout for five or six days, and I may be away with it when you arrive.

In his March 8 letter to his father from Franklin, Tennessee, he described without much enthusiasm four days of maneuvers ("on a scout"). The mud he had complained about at the end of January was still with him and would get worse:

> Our division left Murfreesboro on the morning of the fourth of this month in light marching order without tents, one wagon to a regiment, to be gone four days. We arrived at Versailles the same day, the next Eagleville, the next Triune, the next we camped seven miles from here [Franklin]. Arrived here today at two o'clock and have bivouacked. Tomorrow we march again.
>
> Our destination I do not know.[2] It has rained incessantly since we left and is raining now. Such roads as we have passed over are terrible to think of, much less to travel over. Men wet through, and up to their knees in mud,

artillery stuck, transportation trains stuck, mules down, horses down, men down, and such swearing down south here that would put to shame 'our army in Flanders.'[3] Still, dear parents, this is all for the old flag and borne by all with cheerfulness for we are after rebs and traitors in arms.

One of our brigades—not our division—was led into an ambuscade and twenty-two hundred captured at Spring Hill.[4] We expected to have caught them, but they have given us the slip. I think we shall have a battle soon, not one like Murfreesboro [Stones River] but a good one nevertheless. If we are anyways near matched we shall whip them certain. It is going to be my fortune to be in all the battles, as we have a fighting general [Sheridan], one on whom Gen. Rosecrans places great reliance. I may have been in a fight long before this reaches you. It looks very much like it. If you hear of a battle near Franklin or Columbia before you hear from me again be sure that the 88th will be there, and I shall be with them.

The original "destination" in this maneuver that Colonel Sherman did not know was Spring Hill. The division had been ordered to join Col. John Coburn's force and attack Confederate Gen. Earl Van Dorn's cavalry. The operation was a Union fiasco, as Van Dorn surprised and captured Coburn's troops before Sheridan arrived and retreated back to safety across the Duck River. As the next letter suggests, Colonel Sherman seems not to have realized that Sheridan's troops were supposed to be fighting alongside Coburn's.[5]

The "five or six days" Colonel Sherman expected to be away from the camp near Murfreesboro stretched to eleven. Once he returned, the colonel wrote his father:

Stone River, March 15th, 1863

Dear Father:

I am nearly tired out and so are the men and very much pleased to get back here where it seems like home to us. We had terrible weather and roads. It rained seven days out of the eleven without tents or other covering other than such as we could make out of rails to protect us at night while we slept wet to the skin. During this time we marched fifteen to twenty miles a day and skirmished with Van Dorn's forces, driving them before us to Columbia and trying the men's endurance to their utmost capacity. They submitted cheerfully and were eager to redeem Col. Coburn's disaster at Spring Hill (which, by the way, was one of the most stupid and disgraceful affairs that has happened to our arms in a long time).

When Gen. Rosecrans found out what had happened [at Spring Hill] he ordered our division over to Franklin to drive back the rebs which we did some twenty miles across the Duck River at Columbia. Our force being too small to go further or remain, we returned here having marched 120 miles going and coming through storm and cold.

Col. Coburn's brigade was captured by Van Dorn's forces, which were composed entirely of cavalry, about twelve thousand strong. We lost by this fourteen hundred prisoners and about a hundred and twenty killed and wounded. If Coburn had shown a little more grit he could have brought his brigade out, or at least held his ground until reinforcements were sent to him. We marched over the spot of their disgraceful affair. He could not get out, it is true, unless he fought well, but it was not done. The rebels may well glory over this affair; it was a brilliant exploit for them.

Van Dorn kept his forces out of our reach after we arrived on the scene of action. Everything favored his getting away; the rains had swelled the small streams and creeks into mighty rivers that went plunging and roaring through and over their banks, and the rebs destroyed their bridges behind them. We came up to their rear guard at Rutherford's Creek and exchanged compliments with them. That was all the fight that we had.

On our return the men came in with very sore feet and were generally leg weary, making a march the last day twenty-two miles across the country through mud a portion of the way. On the whole the trip has done us good. The signs are that this army will move before many days; then look out for a battle. If the rebs stand they will be whipped, and I expect they will be for showing us a fight at Shelbyville, and then at Tullahoma.[6]

Colonel Sherman, outspokenly critical as usual, appears to have been too rough on Coburn. It is true that, in the "ambuscade" at Thompson's Station near Spring Hill, Van Dorn's Confederate cavalry captured Colonel Coburn and 1,221 of his men. Confederate reports, however, stated that Coburn's outnumbered men made a "stubborn stand," "maintained their position with genuine courage," and were a "fine body of men, as shown by their stout fighting."[7] Furthermore, if Sheridan had not slowed his pace by looking for forage, he might have joined up with Coburn in time to forestall the debacle.

Two weeks later, 750 of those who had escaped from Van Dorn at Thompson's Station were captured at Brentwood by Gen. Nathan Bedford Forrest, Van Dorn's second-in-command. Losses like these, plus Rosecrans's inactivity, increased the pressure for Rosecrans's removal. Colonel Sherman, always a fan of General Rosecrans, thought that the period of inactivity, much of it due to the weather, was about over. But, instead of moving, the army remained in camp for another two and a half months. On March 25, Colonel Sherman wrote an uncharacteristically brief letter to his father:

The rebels made a dash at our picket lines on Saturday last when we had a sharp skirmish and drove them back. On Monday we had a grand review of our division[8] by Gen. Rosecrans who gave us the high compliment of being the best equipped and having the most soldierly appearance of any that he had reviewed. Our division is considered the best in this army, and there is a host of good soldiers here. Gen. Sheridan has been promoted and confirmed a major-general.

After this storm is over and the roads get dried up again, we shall be ready for the spring campaign. Then look out. There is to be some tall fighting. Ellen is here and has got a sidesaddle and a horse on which she perambulates to her satisfaction.

Love, your son, Frank

General Sheridan's promotion was a cause for great celebration, as Colonel Sherman related in his diary:

Thursday, April 16, 1863

The officers of the 3rd Division, 20th Army Corps, presented Gen. Sheridan with a $1000 sword, belt, and sash, a pair of revolvers, an elegant wine case & saddle with all the trappings, costing in all about $2000.

Those lavish gifts indicate the high esteem with which Sheridan was held by those who fought with him.[9] He was noted not only for his skill as a soldier,

Gen. Philip H. Sheridan. Courtesy of Library of Congress.

but also for the concern he consistently demonstrated for the well-being of his men, a concern which did not keep him from being a firm, and on occasion a harsh, disciplinarian. He had a hot temper but usually got over it quickly, although he was known to hold a grudge.

General Rosecrans's recommendation got General Sheridan his first star, and Colonel Sherman may well have hoped that Sheridan would do the same for him. Sherman found much in common with his youthful superior—Sheridan was five years younger—and they became close friends.

In his restrained initial congratulatory letter of May 1 to his father upon his reelection as mayor, Colonel Sherman wrote:

> There is not any news of importance here to relate. We are in camp with now and then an excursion against the Rebs. Last week our forces went to McMin[n]ville, captured a railroad train and some few prisoners, burnt thirty thousand pounds of bacon, destroyed two wagon trains, burnt a lot of cotton, one factory, and two grist mills, driving the butternuts before them like dust before the wind. Altogether the most successful raid that we have made this spring.
>
> I do not think we shall move forward very soon, and there will not be a great battle in these parts for the present. The work on the fortifications is being pushed with great energy and soon the combined army of Davisites could not drive us out of this place. We have three months' provisions on hand, and our desire is that Bragg or Johnston should try to retake Murfreesboro. Rosecrans' army is in the best possible condition and improving every day.

A week later, however, Colonel Sherman had begun to anticipate more fighting. In his second letter to his father congratulating him on his win at the polls, he expressed concern about his own mortality:

> I have not much news to write you from this department. All sorts of camp rumors are afloat as to what Rosecrans is going to do or what the rebels [will do]. We are kept continually at work at something or other, and I do not get much time to write.
>
> There is something in the wind and before long there will be stirring events tak[ing] place which will materially affect our cause. A great battle has yet to be fought here, and when again the hosts of rebellion are met by the gallant soldiers of the Union under Gen Rosecrans we shall be triumphant and victory perch upon our banners though thousands fall in the crash and clash of arms of the opposing forces. I will write you a few lines whenever it is certain that we shall march out to meet the foe.
>
> If I fall in the terrible struggle which is near at hand I leave to you my wife and children as a legacy. It has been my support in the day of battle

heretofore [that] if I should fall, there were those who would watch over and protect them from want in this world. To God and you, my Father and Mother, I leave all that I hold dearest in this world in the full faith and trust of a loving son, should I by the casualties of the field lay down my life for the preservation of our loved country and its trampled laws.

Do not think that I am despondent or have an idea that I shall not get through the next great battle alive. Ellen is here and well, and has a good place to go to whenever we have to march, at Murfreesboro at Mr. Ned Jordan's, a good Union man of Tennessee who has kindly offered her a home when she needs one. Let me know what you think my chances of promotion are and what has been done in that direction. It requires pressing.

Love to all, Your son, Frank

The next letter is dated May 24, following the gloomy news of the Union defeat at Chancellorsville:

We feel here that the Army of the Potomac is played out and that Gen. [Joseph] Hooker has received a most terrible whipping at the hands of the rebels. Fighting Joe has received a most signal rebuke, and his testimony against [Gen. George B.] McClellan is a record against himself for want of generalship.[10] As you say it is bad for the army and for the country to be changing commanding generals so often in any way or for any cause except that of absolute incompetency. If the policy is kept up by the administration of promoting only those who are out-and-out Republicans and ignoring those who are Democrats and making politics the test of merit the country will lose the services of hundreds of able and patriotic Democrats who hold commissions. If this rebellion is to be crushed there must be no political preferences, and men fighting to preserve this government from the hands of traitors must be recognized for their merits and nothing else.

There is not much news here to relate. We are jogging along at about the same pace as for the last three months. The speck that at one time loomed up into a battle has passed around us for the present. We are under orders to march at a moment's notice and have been for the last two weeks. Ellen still stays with me in camp but has sent her baggage into town [Murfreesboro].

Tell Mother that I appreciate her suggestion about the farm and would be glad to have my family all together once more but I am afraid that I should not be able to make both ends meet with my ideas of economy, especially as long as this war lasts. After it's over and I should live through, a farm may have great attractions for me and I could be induced to retire to its quiet and rural employments. I wish this war was over, but, Mother,

if we have a war with England I must have a hand in the mess; when that
is over I will agree to lay down the sword and follow the plow.

Love to all, your son, Frank

Colonel Sherman's threats to resign from the army because of politics were
apparently taken seriously enough by his mother to lead her to suggest an al-
ternative. The Shermans owned a small farm south of Chicago, and Colonel
Sherman's mother thought—better, hoped—that a farmer's life could appeal
to her son. His response did not radiate enthusiasm.[11]

The next letter, dated May 30, is addressed to Colonel Sherman's mother; it
includes the first (and mildest) of many complaints about the lack of mail.
Colonel Sherman was feeling a little sorry for himself.

Stones River, Tenn., May 30th, 1863

Dear Mother:

Of late I have not received letters very regularly and I sometimes think
I am forgotten in the great whirl of prosperity that is flooding the north,
in Chicago in particular. Thank God that this terrible devastating war is
being waged far from your home and fireside. No description that I can
give or write can picture to your minds the desolation that now rests upon
this land of Tennessee, with its thousands of homes deserted and left to
the ruthless ravages of civil war. Pray all that God in His goodness and
mercy may keep back the waves of this terrible scourge from our beautiful and prosperous homes.

Never mind the promotion. I can wait, if only the people of the north
can wake up to the responsibilities which are upon them and put a stop
to the flow of blood that is draining the life and energies of this once great
and happy country. Politics! Mother, that word is sending thousands of
the brave and noble of this land to untimely graves. What will democracy or republicanism amount to without a country? *Democrat.* Because
I am one and bare my bosom to the foe and risk all that I hold dear on
earth (my family), any merit that I may have must not be recognized. So
be it. My country calls, and I have answered her demands.

Love from your loving son, Frank

P. S. I was on picket when Vallandigham was passed through the lines
to his friends the rebels. May he have free speech to his heart's content
with them.[12]

Through the spring of 1863, Rosecrans avoided a direct assault on Bragg's
forces. Bragg had blocked and fortified the main road to Chattanooga at both
Shelbyville and Tullahoma, and Rosecrans sought to force Bragg out into the
open by flanking movements and by a threat to the Confederate rear. Colonel
Sherman, along with the War Department, was more impatient; he kept hop-

ing that they would fight a battle. He was not a particularly blood-thirsty soldier, but, like most of Rosecrans's troops, he felt strongly that the sooner they fought, the better for the Union cause. Meanwhile, he was not ready to take up the plow; what he saw of rain and mud in the farm land of Tennessee was no encouragement to do so.

In early June, he wrote after a skirmish at Franklin:

Outpost duty near Salem, Tenn.

Dear Father:

For three days everything has been loaded in the wagons ready to start. The men in addition to their tents, guns, ammunition, and blankets have seven days' rations to carry, three days in the haversack and four days in a knapsack. This looks like work. The Army of the Cumberland has shook itself. We should by now have been in Shelbyville if it had not been for the rebs, who demonstrated along our entire front on the 4th with their cavalry. They also attacked Franklin the same day, and it sounded around us once more like war. Heavy rains have delayed our visit to Mr. Bragg and his followers. One thing is certain, we were going out in fighting trim, and there would have been bloody work had the two armies come together.

I have no doubt that the rebel army in front of us is larger than ours.[13] I also doubt the policy that moves us forward, but old Rosey [Rosecrans] knows best and we all have faith in whatever he undertakes. The whole army has become tired of inaction and camp life, and are anxious once more to cross blades with the chivalry of the south.

If we meet them anywhere near on equal terms they will be the worst whipped lot of traitors that ever came in contact with the sturdy mudsills of the North since Jeff Davis laid the cornerstone of the bogus confederacy. It has become evident to us that the men of the northwest must crush this hydra of the south; the Grand Army of the Potomac, the pet of the Union, with its boasts of what it is going to do, is played out. Let it rest in garrison around our national capital and keep the wolf from its door until the army of the west can wipe out treason in the southwest and swing around to the great stronghold of treason in the east. It will take us this year to complete the contract here if we are allowed to do so without molestation from the [indecipherable word] of the east and we receive the support from our people that our cause demands. Fill up our thinned ranks with conscripts or volunteers; place them side by side with the veterans who have been tested in many a skirmish, battle, and march, and we will soon make soldiers of them.

Hooker occupies Fredericksburg after Lee abandons the place. Glorious achievement, and the reb army gone where echo answers. Look to the west; Grant has Vicksburg in his coils; Rosecrans the wily is waiting to pounce upon Bragg, and success has perched upon his banner wherever he leads.

Tomorrow we march, and two hours after we are in motion we shall have the sharp rattle of musketry and the heavy boom of artillery to keep step to. The advance will be contested over every foot of ground, but like an avalanche we shall gather forces by our momentum and hurl back the obstacles in our way to their supports at Shelbyville, and then a battle. Who of us shall come out of this struggle with life and limbs God only knows.

Love to all, your son, Frank

There was neither rattle nor boom, however, and the disappointed colonel wrote to his mother the next day, concerned about the prolonged inactivity and how warlike he had become:

in camp near Murfreesboro, June 7th 1863

Dear Mother:

Once more back in our old camp, as you will see by the heading after having everything packed and loaded for four days ready to march. Something has turned up, and old Rosey has allowed the Army of the Cumberland to lay down again after having fairly shook it up. Do not think we are in a torpid state, far from it. Vigilance and discipline are not relaxed. On the 4th [of June] the enemy made his appearance along our whole front, which produced a series of skirmishes and at one time sounded very much like a fight. For three months we have not heard the roar of cannon and musketry, and as the echoes of the fray were borne to us on the southern breeze I verily believe that the men rejoiced in the prospect of once more meeting the rebel foe in open conflict. You ought to see them; their eyes sparkled with the light of battle; they leapt for very joy that the long truce had at last come to an end. See what training does for human nature. A few short months ago their cheeks would have paled, and they would have gathered in knots and with hushed voices talked over the chances of a fight.

Mother, war is a horrible trade. With what eagerness do we thirst for the blood of our enemy and tear down the fabric made in God's own image. I confess that there is something terribly intoxicating in battle when our sympathy for the mangled and torn of its destructive work is passed by us without a thought or feeling for the poor wretches writhing in mortal agony beneath our feet. War is horrible but it is in this case waged for a good and holy cause. We shall win, and if I do not live to enjoy the benefits of our government as a single unit, my children will. The fathers of the Revolution died that we might reap the harvest that they prepared for us. Father, would we not be degenerate sons of such noble sires, men who pledged their lives and sacred honor to the principle of self-government in man, if we let the flame be quenched just as its light began to break on the millions of the downtrodden of earth? No. Never. We have not forgotten what our fathers of the Revolution passed through that we might be a great, a free, and happy people.

How long we shall remain in camp I do not know. We are watching Grant; when Vicksburg falls we shall have plenty to do. Blackberries are getting ripe here, and there are acres of them. Cherries are ripe; apples and peaches will soon be ripe enough to eat. New potatoes here, but not in large quantities. There are no farms or gardens going on around us, and fresh vegetables would be a luxury. I have seen lettuce but once this spring.

I think that the rebs intend to attack us here or try to flank us and take Nashville. Well, to tell you the whole truth, I think there is something in the wind, and you will probably know of it as quickly as I do. Ellen and I were at a dinner party given by the staff mess of the commanding general last week. Gen. Rosey was there and also Gens. Sheridan and [later President James A.] Garfield.

Love to all, your son, Frank

❻

TULLAHOMA CAMPAIGN:
SUMMER, 1863

There was indeed "something in the wind." Finally, on June 23, the order to march was given; at five o'clock the next morning, the army of sixty thousand men was on its way. Colonel Sherman had time for only a brief note:

June 23rd, 1863

Dear Father:

I have but a short time to write you as we have very unexpectedly received marching orders. This time we shall make a go of it I am certain. Our destination is as far into Dixie as we can penetrate. What opposition we shall meet with I am unable to tell, but presume that the rebels will contest every inch of the ground. We shall have to skirmish and fight our way through to Shelbyville, where Bragg's headquarters is. Whether he will give us battle here is doubtful. At all events we are ready to try [indecipherable word] with him for the crops which are now harvested.

I am well and so is Ellen. I do not know but what she will go home after a little if there is no general engagement within a week to see the children and to look after them.

Love, your son, Frank

During the previous weeks, Rosecrans had developed a masterful plan for a swift campaign to drive Bragg south and out of Chattanooga. Rosecrans's plan, consisting of feints to the left and center and drives around Bragg's right, was brilliantly conceived and executed, and it resulted in the "least bloody major [Union] victory of the war."[1]

Whether these plans would have resulted in a major battle if the weather had

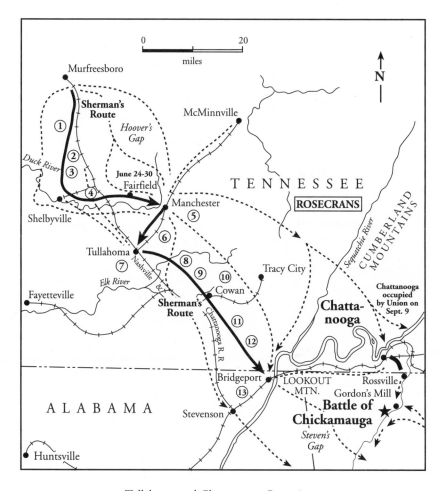

Tullahoma and Chattanooga Campaign.
Legend: 1. 6/24; 2. 6/25; 3. 6/26; 4. 6/27; 5. 6/28; 6. 6/29; 7. 6/30;
8. 7/1; 9. 7/2; 10. 7/3–29; 11. 7/30; 12. 7/31 13. 8/1–9/7.

been at all normal never will be known. The weather was not at all normal; instead it rained, and rained, and rained. As Colonel Sherman reported:

Manchester, Tenn. June 28th, 1863

Dear Father:

It commenced raining the day we marched and has rained almost incessantly ever since. What was first hailed as a blessing in laying the dust has proved to be almost intolerable. The dust was allayed and became muddy, from that to mud, from mud to slosh, slosh to an almost impassable quagmire, and still it rains. I never saw anything like it: artillery, wagons, mules, and men were engulfed in the plastic clay. Oaths, curses, and obscene adjectives ruled the hour, whilst the unrelenting clouds discharged their reservoirs upon us for thirty consecutive hours without interruption. Still, on we struggled without murmur from the soldiers, shouts of laughter going up as some luckless wight made a misstep and was submerged in the yellow liquid. When the sun finally did come out, as if to add to our misery, it scorched and parboiled us in our wet and mudstained garments.

Our division had the advance on the Shelbyville pike the first day [June 24], and after marching nine miles we came out on the enemy in position in Guy's Gap. The musket was soon at work. Then followed the boom of artillery, echoed by heaven's artillery, whilst nature wept over the evil deeds of man. After skirmishing some two hours with them Gen. [Gordon] Granger's command came up from Triune, and we turned over the Gap and the rebs to him and struck across the country for Liberty Gap.

At this point [Gen. Richard W.] Johnson and [Gen. Jefferson C.] Davis with their divisions of our corps were sharply engaged. On we went [to support them] the mud increasing at every step, but before we reached them the fight was over. Again we moved on and bivouacked for the night. At 3:00 the next morning we were up again, got such breakfast as we could, and moved on. This day [June 26] it took us sixteen hours to make three miles.

The next day we got through to the Manchester Pike at the entrance of Hoover's Gap, which Gen. [George H.] Thomas' corps had taken from the rebels the day before. We [then] took the road to Fairfield [where] we found the rebs taking supper, and had it not been that we had to cross the Garrison Fork of Duck River we should have gobbled them all. As it was they left their supper and tentage after an hour's fighting. The whole number of skirmishers that charged on our side did not exceed a hundred men. Our loss to the division in this affair was three men wounded.

Again we moved on and bivouacked six miles from here [Manchester]. This morning [June 28] we arrived at eleven, tired out, having had nothing to eat for twenty-four hours except a biscuit. Shelbyville is ours and we are south of Duck River, and Bragg and his army are traveling at full speed for some place. He has been completely outgeneraled, and I am confident that he will not risk battle this side of the Tennessee River. In my opinion it is a footrace; if we get there first he will be [indecipherable word]. I will keep you posted of our movements.

Love to you all. I am well. Your son, Frank

In the next letter, written on the first day of the Battle of Gettysburg, Colonel Sherman reported Sheridan's division still struggling through the mud in pursuit of Bragg.

Cowan, Tenn. July 1st, 1863

Dear Father:

We are here waiting for the elements to subside so that we may be able to move on. We have had but little fighting to do, because we have in Gen. Sheridan a man and an officer, one who knows his business. He has out-maneuvered them whenever they made an attempt to stand. At Fairfield on the 27th he could have made a great fight, but instead of bringing up the artillery and shelling the woods, he sent out a line of skirmishers that soon became engaged. After working about for an hour the skirmish line was ordered to charge, and with a yell they went in and put to flight two regiments of infantry and chased them for a mile or more. The Rebs left everything they had behind. The whole number of skirmishers on our side did not exceed a hundred men; our loss was three men wounded.

Monday the 29th we left for Tulahoma [sic] in the rain, which was pouring in torrents on the Lynchburg Road. After six miles we went into camp in the heaviest timber ever I saw. We were now within six or seven miles of Tulahoma, where it was supposed Bragg would give us battle. Gen. Rosecrans began massing his troops in thickets of timber, for the purpose of advancing to the attack. There were no positions for artillery, nor could the cavalry do anything; all rested on the musket and the bayonet. The infantry was cautioned to hold their fire until they were in short range, and then fire, following it up with the bayonet. It would have been a bushwhacking fight, and we could not see them until they were within a hundred yards of us.

That fight did not come off, and the next day [June 30] our division marched into the stronghold of Tulahoma with colors flying and drums beating [Bragg had evacuated Tullahoma and headed for Chattanooga]. No rest was given us and on we went in pursuit of the fleeing army. We pursued them to this place [Cowan] and halted [on July 3]—for the last fifteen miles driving their rear guard before us. We have forded rivers waist deep in the chase, but all to no purpose—they would not fight, even though we were 24 hours' march ahead of the main army and six hours ahead of the cavalry.

We have taken two or three hundred prisoners who state that Bragg's army is very much demoralized, and that the Tennessee troops will never cross the Tennessee River. We have only the story of the deserters and prisoners to vouch for the truth of these statements. The Appalachian Mountains are between the two armies now, and Bragg has escaped from our clutches. He can thank God and his rain for the safety of his hosts.

It looks now as if we were to remain in camp here for some time. One thing is certain; all that part of this state from which the Rebs expected to draw large supplies is lost to them. Shelbyville and Tulahoma with all their works erected with great labor and cost were wrested from them with scarcely a blow struck to save them. The immense fields of wheat and corn from which we drove their men who were detailed to gather the harvest will go into the ground or into Uncle Sam's granaries. The country through which we marched was one vast wheat and corn field— the Confederacy has received a blow from which it will never recover, and the victory [so] gained is almost equal to the destruction of their army. Had it not been for the rain we should have not only outflanked him, but got into his rear and cut him off from his line of retreat and forced him to the west on to the Tennessee River, where without supplies his whole army would have been easily bagged by us, and the War over, as far as this Department is concerned. All honor to Gen. Rosecrans, the greatest of American generals. Honor to his brave and noble army who so bravely seconded him under almost unsurmountable difficulties. But the best of plans fail where the elements interfere to frustrate them.

What our next movement will be I am unable even to surmise. Old Rosey, as we love to call him, is as close as a sepulchre, and his plans only unfold to us when they are being executed. One thing I am sure of, he will not be idle. This town of Cowan is a place of three or four houses and a railroad station situated in a valley that bends into the hills toward the north, and with a hill forming an ox-bow around it. The soil is rich and the fields are planted with corn, rye, and wheat. Blackberries and whortleberries are ripe and in great quantities. I am well and expect to hear from you before long. Love to you all.

Your son, Frank

This was the last letter for almost a month, so far as we know. The army apparently was not engaged in fighting, and Colonel Sherman did not have much to write about. There was one incident near Cowan that would have been worth describing, but we know of it only from General Sheridan, who in his memoirs called it "A Foolish Adventure":

Having heard during the night [of July 5] that the enemy had halted on the mountain near the University—an educational establishment on the summit [the University of the South at Sewanee]—I directed [Col. Louis D.] Watkins to make a reconnaissance and find out the value of the information. He learned that

{52}

Wharton's brigade of [Confederate] cavalry was halted at the University to cover a moderately large force of the enemy's infantry which had not yet got down the mountain on the other side, so I pushed Watkins out again on the 5th [of July], supporting him by a brigade of infantry,[2] which I accompanied myself. We were too late, however, for when we arrived at the top of the mountain Wharton had disappeared, and though Watkins pursued to Bridgeport, he was able to do nothing more, and on his return reported that the last of the enemy had crossed the Tennessee River and burned the bridge.

Nothing further could now be done, so I instructed Watkins to rejoin the division at Cowan, and being greatly fatigued by the hard campaigning of the previous ten days, I concluded to go back to my camp in a more comfortable way than on the back of my tired horse. In his retreat the enemy had not disturbed the railway track at all, and as we had captured a hand-car at Cowan, I thought I would have it brought up to the station near the University to carry us down the mountain to my camp, and, desiring company, I persuasively invited Colonel Frank T. Sherman to ride with me.

I sent for the car by a courier, and for a long time patiently awaited its arrival, in fact, until all the troops had passed us, but still it did not come. Thinking it somewhat risky to remain at the station without protection, Sherman and I sent our horses to Cowan by our orderlies, and set out on foot to meet the car, trudging along down the track in momentary expectation of falling in with our private conveyance.

We had not gone very far before night overtook us, and we then began to realize the dangers surrounding us, for there we were alone and helpless, tramping on in the darkness over an unknown railroad track in the enemy's country, liable on the one hand to go tumbling through some bridge or trestle, and on the other, to possible capture or death at the hands of the guerrillas then infesting these mountains . . .

At every turn we eagerly hoped to meet the hand-car, but it never came, and we jolted on from tie to tie for eleven weary miles, reaching Cowan after midnight, exhausted and sore in every muscle from frequent falls on the rough unballasted road-bed. Inquiry developed that the car had been well-manned and started to us as ordered, and nobody could account for its non-arrival. Further investigation next day showed that when it reached the junction at the foot of the mountain the improvised crew followed the main line (instead of the branch) across the range down the Crow Creek Valley, where the party was captured.

I had reason to remember for many a day this foolish adventure, for my sore bones and bruised muscles caused me physical suffering until I left the Army of the Cumberland the next spring, but I had still more reason to feel for my captured men, and on this account I have never ceased to regret that I so thoughtlessly undertook to rejoin my troops by rail, instead of sticking to my faithful horse.[3]

Colonel Sherman does not refer to this episode in his letters or diary. Perhaps this omission stemmed from his loyalty to General Sheridan; he may not have wanted to communicate anything to his father that did not reflect well upon Sheridan.

When the army moved from Murfreesboro, it left Ellen there. Shortly thereafter, she wrote to the senior Shermans—the only letter we have that gives an idea of her mixed feelings about being in Tennessee:

Murfreesboro, Tenn. June 25th, 1863

In accordance with Frank's wish I write you. The Army of the Cumberland moved yesterday. They had been out but a short time before skirmishing commenced and was kept up all day with some cannonading which we could distinctly hear. It commenced raining about six in the morning and rained all day and night without any cessation. I had a note from Frank this morning which said they had advanced about ten miles and skirmished most of the way. He said that he was soaked with the rain and covered with mud, but quite well.

I hear this evening that there are quite a number of wounded being brought in, but none from Sheridan's division. We heard no cannonading today until quite late this afternoon and concluded that the army did not move [earlier] on account of the mud and rain.

The town of Murfreesboro looks deserted and God forsaken. All the Union people wear very long faces, for they expect the rebs will come in and rob them and destroy what little they have left. Nearly every one has left who could get away, and it is thought by many that [railroad] cars will not run after tomorrow. Frank is a little anxious about my staying here for he thinks, as many others do, that this town will be shelled, but I am willing to run some chances for the sake of being in reach of him in case he is sick or wounded.

I am very anxious to be home with the children, but am quite undecided at times to know whether it is my duty to stay or go. I know I cannot do Frank any good by staying in Murfreesboro, but if he should be sick or wounded, I never should forgive myself if I went home.

It wants but a few days of Ella's [her daughter's] vacation, and it does seem to me sometimes that I cannot stay another day, that I ought to be there. I know duty says stay and duty says go. If I do go home it will be impossible for me to get back, however much I would be needed here, and so I think I shall have to leave my children to the care of our friends a little longer until we see the result of this move. Then if all is well I shall go home at once. In the meantime if you will look after Ella I will be very grateful.

I am almost ashamed to send this horrid scrawl, but I am so harassed in my mind that I can neither read nor write. I think and think but cannot put my thoughts on paper. My love to Martha, Will, and George, and a good share for you both. Kiss the children for me when you see them, and God bless them.

Love, Ellen

Mrs. Sherman's presence with the 88th Illinois was a morale booster not only for her husband, but also for the rest of the regiment. Stella Coatsworth, whose husband was the 88th's medical officer until he died of pneumonia after the Battle of Stones River, quoted from his journal: "On the appearance of Mrs. Colonel F. T. Sherman in camp (for she frequently visited the camp of her husband's regiment or brigade during the war), the soldiers drill better, they obey more promptly, are more courteous, neat, and affable. As she passes through the camp all hats are raised and the hearts of thousands turn toward home and its sweet associations. She seems like a ministering angel among the weary wounded boys; and she has performed a work among them unexcelled in the space of time by any lady in the army."[4]

Ellen Sherman finally left Murfreesboro and went back to Chicago and her children, but she did not stay home long. She had returned to Murfreesboro by the time Colonel Sherman wrote to his sister "and all at home," from Cowan, Tennessee, on July 26. In this letter, he is sarcastic in his resentment of the fair-weather friends who criticized him for his published letter of February 18 to Frederick Tuttle, and bitter about Colonel Larrabee, who, he believed, had pulled strings in order to replace him as brigade commander. Colonel Sherman wrote that he was studying hard, apparently both for promotion and to defend his rights against Colonel Larrabee:

Cowan, Tenn., July 26th, 1863

Dear Sister and all at home:

Yours of the 19th has been received together with all the letters written me up to this time with one exception. That is Father's letter sent by Col. Chadbourne who was unfortunate enough to lose his valise. We have some hope of finding it again. I have received all the books that I sent home for; they will prove of great value to me. All the leisure time that I have is devoted to study and the posting of myself in the duties of my position and [that of] a higher grade. The books as you discovered all treat of war and martial law. Every officer should know something of the profession which he has adopted so that he may at least have some knowledge of the fundamental principles which govern the prosecution of war.

I am pleased to hear that I have numerous friends at home. To those *true* friends who wish me well—and have done so when the dark clouds of jealousies and bitter invective were heaped upon me—I return their kind wishes with grateful feelings and an open heart. To those additional *warm* friends who came forward to me with their remembrances I return in kind. You all know with what affection I contemplate their voluntary offerings which have been brought out in the sunlight of success that made the reputation of a regiment which, I flatter myself, the City of Chicago and the State of Illinois are proud of.

Sister, I do not require that class of friends to encourage me to do my duty to my country. I find no consolation in the sacrifices of home and the family broken up and its members scattered and left to the care (in some measure) of strangers. The satisfaction is in having done my duty. You may think me egotistical but I can't help it. I have no faith in friends who are made from success. Those who stood by me nor wavered under the sore trial which I have passed through and came out of with some degree of credit can command me for I feel under true and great obligation. I have tried to do right and I shall continue to try.

I have many trials here yet—not in my regiment for that I believe is loyal to me—but from other sources. I am in the way of Colonel Larrabee and I am satisfied that he is in an underhanded way trying to injure me. His own reputation as an officer is very poor and he has never forgiven me for not giving up the command of the brigade to him. By wirepulling he got Gen'l Lytle assigned to the brigade and me relieved after he found out that the command would not be given to him. He is very disagreeable and keeps us all in hot water, more or less, besides which he is drunk half of his time (and, I am sorry to say, our Brigadier is not entirely free from this vice). One thing is certain: no drunken officer can ever command me or my men in battle.

So you may set it down that I am not in high favor at Brigade Headquarters. Well, I ask no favors from them and they know it. They also understand that I am not to be run over with impunity, and am about as well posted in my duties and rights as they are. In fact I have made them back down two or three times and they do not like it. I can paddle my own canoe and will come out all right yet. I have sailed in rougher waters and come into port safe.

I have no news to write and therefore my own personal matters fill up the sheet. I cannot truckle and play the courtier; it is not in my nature. It looks as if we were going into permanent camp and probably shall remain for a month or more. Where Bragg's army is and [what it is] doing is not fully developed. Ellen is at Murfreesboro and will shortly join me. The rebel citizens and soldiers are tired of the war and ask for peace. The beginning of the end has come.

Love to all; kiss the children; tell Ella that Pa will write her a letter.

Your brother, Frank

By the first part of August, the Army of the Cumberland was closing in on Chattanooga. Although Rosecrans had outmaneuvered Bragg, he still had plenty of troubles, particularly with supply. His lines were long and getting longer. Roads, poor at best, were almost impassable due to the rains. The Confederates had destroyed railroad lines and bridges in their retreat, and Rosecrans remained dangerously short on cavalry. Furthermore, the Confederate Army had been substantially reinforced, while Rosecrans had been unable to get any reinforcements from the Union high command. Nevertheless, he continued to move toward Chattanooga, which required crossing the Tennessee River, whose bridges had been destroyed or damaged by the Confederates.

Rosecrans planned to cross the river below Chattanooga, while leading Bragg to believe that he was going to cross above the city. In anticipation of the crossing, Sheridan's division was sent in early August to repair the bridge at Bridgeport, just below the Alabama line. From there, Colonel Sherman wrote again to his sister, on August 4. By this time, Ellen was back in the field, and her husband was responding to a rumor which turned out to be unfounded:

Bridgeport, Tenn., [Ala.] Aug 4th, 1863

Dear Sister:

Yours of the 25th reached me on the march from Cowan to this place. I rec'd the books sent to me in the care of Mr. [Thomas] Maple and those that Col. Chadbourne took charge of for me. His lost baggage consisted of a valise in which there were some letters which he had in charge for us. The Colonel has learned of its whereabouts and will get it before many days.

So far as the reports which have reached you in regard to my feelings of a father being called forth again? I do not know but it may be so but Ellen and I have as yet failed to discover any symptoms that would lead us to suppose there is any truth in the reports which have reached you. Ellen would probably know if anyone if she was about to force the feelings of a father upon me once more. That report is bosh.

Since my last letter to you we have changed camp and position, as you discover by the caption to this. We are now on the extreme front. Bridgeport, you would suppose, would indicate the name of a town, but there is no town here; it is at this point where the Memphis and Charleston R.R. crosses the Tennessee River. There is not even a station house here. The river is divided by an island about six miles long, the main channel of the river being on the south side. The river on the side next to us is about 500 yds. wide and is crossed by a bridge of nine spans of 150 feet each. The island at this point is about 500 yds across. The main channel of the river is crossed by a bridge of five spans and a draw for the passage of steamboats. These bridges are the finest in the Confederacy, and the rebels in their haste to get away from the Yanks burnt six out of the nine spans on our side of the river.

Never was there an army so outgeneraled as that of Bragg's by Rosecrans. The last part of their flight was a complete rout, nor did they stop or look back until the waters of the Tennessee floated between the two armies. Bridges were burnt that did not take us an hour to repair. The roads were filled full of trees and every method resorted to to stop our pursuit but that of fighting. This great victory has not been heralded over the country by the boom of cannon and the slaughter of thousands, but nevertheless the advantages gained are of so substantial a character that I believe the rebels feel it more than the loss of Vicksburg.

The country from which they have been ejected by Rosecrans and his army is planted to corn and wheat, which they hoped would be gathered for their commissariat. I saw one field of corn on my march that contained not less than 2000 acres, as fine a crop as ever grew under the sun. There is forage enough in the country to supply our whole army for a year.

We are encamped upon a hill that overlooks the river and is about 250 yds. from it. The position we occupy is a commanding one and overlooks both bridges and the island. Very considerable earthworks with long lines of rifle pits have been thrown up here by the rebels, the timber having been cut off for ½ a mile all around to get range for artillery and repulse any attack that might be made upon them and for the protection of the R.R. bridges. The position is so strong that 500 men might hold it against 20,000 men for an indefinite period.

The rebs are in plain sight on the opposite bank and sometimes a very interesting conversation is carried on between the pickets back and forth. By common consent there is no firing, and only sharp words and repartee indulged in on both sides. Our men are in bathing every day within easy range of their sharpshooters, and some have swum ⅔ds. of the way across and talked with them. Our men have not yet succeeded in making an exchange of papers with them nor will they bathe in the river on this side.

The weather is extremely hot and we do not attempt to move about except in the morning and evening. There are six regiments and a battery of six guns stationed here, all from Illinois, under the command of Col. Luther B. Bradley, myself being second in command. The total number of troops is about 2300 men and we feel ourselves equal to five times that number by virtue of our position. What our next movement will be I am unable to surmise. I hardly think a new campaign will be commenced so long as the extreme hot weather lasts.

I have been in command of the brigade for a few days whilst Gen. [William H.] Lytle was commanding the division. He will resume his command tonight and I will become once more a plain colonel. I have no news to write as we are so far away from all direct communication with the outside world and even our own army. I would like to be home with you for a month or more if I could get leave but I can hardly hope to get away at all.

Ellen is in Murfreesboro and well when I last heard from her except for her spinal affliction.[5] She will hardly join me here and you may expect her home to see after the children. Tell Ella to write me all about herself and how she gets along and send my love with kisses to Lulu. Kiss Ida and Edwin for Uncle Frank and tell them that he thinks of them often. My letters must be considered addressed to you all.

My love to you all, and may we all be speedily reunited is the wish and prayer of:

The son and brother, Frank

By the time of Colonel Sherman's next letter, the resourceful Ellen had managed to find her way to Bridgeport and was again escorting Confederate ladies:

Bridgeport, Tenn. [Ala.] August 12, 1863

Dear Father:

Ellen is here. She joined me last week. She is in tolerable health. She is now on the extreme front, and on Sunday morning last she crossed the river with a flag of truce that was taking the mother of General [James] Patton Anderson (a Reb) through our lines to her son who is in command of the Rebel forces on the opposite side of the river. She was very much pleased with her trip across the Tennessee into the land of Dixie. There she met some Reb officers who were sent to receive Mrs. Anderson. The chivalry were very polite and pleasant, and after half an hour spent in chat, the party broke up and each went their way.

The pickets are in plain sight of each other and are continually calling to each other. The other night came the cry across the water, "Hello, Yank, where is Rosey?"

Yank: Upon the hill back here. What do you want to know for?

Secesh: Why Bragg has sworn to kill him.

Yank: How's he going to do it?

Secesh: By running him to death chasing him.

This is all the amusement the boys have on either side, as strict orders are given not to fire on each other. The weather is hot and oppressive during the day. The nights are generally cool. Every morning a fog settles down on the valley where we are and does not leave until eight or nine, which I fear is going to make it unhealthy for me. I have suffered from a cold and asthma ever since we came here, the first of my old complaint since I went into service.

The prospects are that we shall not long remain here, as we have received orders to reduce our baggage to the smallest possible limit and have the surplus ready to be sent to the rear. The enlisted men send their knapsacks and carry with them an extra shirt and pair of shoes with one blanket. We are evidently on the eve of a campaign into the mountains and I think our mission is to take possession of east Tennessee and relieve its loyal citizens from the heavy burden of treason and oppression. God grant that such may be the case, for those people have remained true and loyal to the government and the flag under all of their trials. The Rebs, in my opinion, will fight at Chattanooga, as it is a natural fortress. It is idle for me to speculate on what is going to be done, and I am content to let time and the march develop the plans of Gen. Rosecrans.

When we leave here Ellen will probably go home for a time and look after the children and their wants. The letters that I get are few and far between from home. Give our love to Mother, Martha, Will, and all at home. Kiss the babies for us, and, believe me, we are your affectionate children,

Frank and Ellen

A note from Col. Sherman's diary, dated Aug. 15, reads:

This morning at midnight the bridge over the main channel of the Tennessee River was discovered to be on fire. The destruction of the bridge by the rebels, they hoped, would stop our march into Alabama, and at a quarter before one o'clock the bridge fell into the river.

Four days later Colonel Sherman wrote to his mother:

Bridgeport, Tenn, [Ala.] Aug 19th, 1863

Dear Mother:

Again we have orders to be ready for the march, in consequence of which our baggage and tentage are to be sent to the rear to be stored during the campaign. Where we are going and at what point we are to strike is in the dark. Rosey has moved his headquarters to Stevenson, and I hear that our corps is concentrating at that point. We are within thirty miles of Chattanooga, where Bragg has his headquarters. Our pontoon train is coming up and with it we shall cross the Tennessee somewhere. One thing is sure, we cannot go far before we run into the rebels. They are in plain sight at work on the opposite bank of the river. Last week they burned the bridge over the main channel. When we discovered it was on fire we opened on them with shell. What damage we did I do not know; they did not answer.

Every day deserters come in who have swum the river. The last that came in are Mississippi troops. They all tell the same story, that thousands would desert if they could get away and were sure that we would treat them kindly. They report that orders have been read on dress parade that the Yankees hang every Confederate soldier that falls into their hands.

Their cause, I am satisfied, is becoming desperate. Let our people support the draft and shove forward the men to us speedily and this rebellion will be short-lived. We are waiting for drafted men; when they come we will soon make soldiers of them, and they shall have the best chance there is to smell powder and show their patriotism.

Ellen is here with me and has been here for the last ten days. When we march she will go directly home and stay there until the children are fitted out for the winter and the army has come to some permanent camp, when she will rejoin me. My opinion is that after the conscripts have come forward and have been in soldier life and duties, we shall not give the rebels much rest. I have been in the enjoyment of asthma for the last month, and were it not that we are to move, I would try to get a leave to go home. When I shall be able to see you all again depends on God and the rebels.

Tell Father to make as much interest for the 88th as he can amongst the drafted men, so that I can have my regiment filled up. Have him speak to the leading members of the Board of Trade; if they wish to help their regiment, that is the way to do it. The conscripts, as I understand, choose the regiment they prefer to serve in. I shall keep you all posted as far as I can of my future movements and what we have done to the rebellion.

Love to all, your brother Frank

Colonel Sherman's leave came sooner than he had anticipated, and it may have saved his life.

7

DEFEAT AND REORGANIZATION: AUTUMN, 1863

Through August, the colonel's asthma got no better and in fact became so severe at the beginning of September that he no longer could march with his command. He returned to Bridgeport and was granted twenty days' leave, which he spent in Chicago. He was still there when, after Rosecrans had taken Chattanooga and was chasing the rebels into Georgia, the two armies met at Chickamauga Creek and the Union army was soundly defeated.[1]

The Battle of Chickamauga was fought on September 19 and 20; Colonel Sherman returned on the 27th. En route back to his brigade, he wrote to his father:

> Nashville, Tenn. Sept 24th 1863
>
> Dear Father:
>
> I arrived here this morning at one o'clock. We had a slight scare on the S and N Railroad yesterday which detained the train for seven hours. The cause was an attempt by a party of guerillas to burn the railroad bridge at Nolan. They left and the fire was put out by some women and a Negro man. The damage was not so great, and the train was able to cross over. There are all sorts of rumors here as to how badly Rosecrans has been whipped and his army cut up.
>
> The battle [of Chickamauga] is not yet over, although there seems to be no doubt that our army is in such position as to resist successfully any attempt by Bragg to dislodge us until reinforcements are brought up. I fear the loss of officers and men on our side [at Chickamauga] is much heavier than reported. My [McCook's] corps has been very roughly handled and lost heavily in Saturday's fight. Gen. [William H.] Lytle, commanding my bri-

gade, killed; Lt. Col. [Duncan J.] Hall of the 89th killed, together with four captains of the same regiment. Of the fate of our division and my regiment I can hear and learn nothing.[2] I cannot get any further for a day or two than this place, as all cars are being used to bring up the wounded from the front. I shall go on the first opportunity I get.

I do not believe Bragg can drive Rosey from his present position. Our army is in a critical position, but I believe that Rosecrans is equal to the emergency. Burnside has not formed a junction with him yet.

Love to all, Your son, Frank

He added a postscript: "I have just seen Captain [Elijah H.] Crowell of the 21st Michigan of our brigade who was wounded on Sunday. He says the brigade mustered five hundred men out of the fourteen hundred they had when they went into the fight. The loss is terrible and sickening."

Two days later, back with his men, Colonel Sherman wrote:

Chattanooga, Sept. 29, 1863

Dear Father:

I arrived here on Sunday feeling better than when I left home. My asthma has not troubled me since my return, and I have comparatively quiet nights' rest. My strength is returning, and I breathe with ease except when I exercise hard. This is encouraging as everything here wears a sad aspect and requires all of our animal spirits to keep up a show of cheerfulness. The men and officers have not yet recovered from the fatigue and wearing of their late marches, to say nothing of the terrible ordeal of the battle. None but a soldier knows how much flesh and blood can endure in times of great physical trials. The battle is over and the march ended for the present. Anxiety and danger give place to security, and our men are fast recovering and resuming their cheerfulness.

The recent battles here have partially taken the conceit out of the Army of the Cumberland, and they admit they are not invincible against vastly superior numbers.[3] The feeling of invincibility was all that saved Rosecrans from utter defeat.

Everything looked blue for a while, but from that the men have recovered, and every day shows the works rising under their hands. Our lines and the enemy's are about 300 yards apart and have remained so for the past week, with now and then a skirmish. We are in a strong position and are making it still stronger. One thing is certain, if Bragg [abandons] Chattanooga, it will cost the Confederacy so dear that they will be ready to lay down their arms in this part of their dominions.

My regiment, the 88th, has from all accounts behaved splendidly during this campaign and battle. It has gained great praise for its steadiness and the magnificent manner in which they went into the fight. I am proud of them, for they have given evidence in more than one fight of their devotion to their flag and country. Our loss is five officers and eighty-three enlisted men wounded [a considerable reduction from Captain Crowell's earlier panicky estimate].

I am again in command of the brigade [succeeding Gen. Lytle, killed at Chickamauga]. Will write again soon. They keep us very busy making reports and superintending the erection of works. No reinforcements yet. Rebs are throwing up works in plain sight.

My love to you all. I had to leave everything behind me at Nashville to get here.

Write, your son, Frank

Colonel Sherman discussed the military situation in broader terms in his next letter:

Send me some postage stamps; those that I have are all stuck together. Chattanooga, Oct. 6th, 1863

Dear Sister:

I have not as yet heard from home since I left. The presumption is that you have written. It takes a long time for a letter to reach us here on ac-count of the difficulties of transportation across the mountains. Heavy reinforcements I understand have arrived and are arriving at Bridgeport and Stevenson [Alabama]; some say four corps, two from Grant com'ded by [Gen. William T.] Sherman and [Gen. James B.] McPherson and two from the Potomac commanded by [Gen. Oliver O.] Howard and [Gen. Henry W.] Slocum. We shall again be able to have breathing room if this is the case. The 20th and 21st Army Corps commanded by Gen'ls. [Alexander M.] McCook and [Thomas L.] Crittenden, it is reported here, have been consolidated under the title of the 4th Army Corps to be com-manded by General Gordon Granger. This is, I think, a good move.

There will be in my opinion a general reorganization of the entire army. Regiments will be consolidated with one another, new brigades and di-visions formed and the excess of officers mustered out of the service. This is all right and I am for it, as our present commands are mere skeletons. Many reg'ts do not number more than 180 to 240 effective men for duty whilst scores of others do not number 100 men. The Army of the Cum-berland has over 150 regiments and cannot muster over 30,000 fighting men or about 40 maximum regiments. So you see, instead of having an immense army we in truth have but a small one. But small as it is, it yet has to learn what defeat is.[4]

I enclose orders sent to the Army of the Cumberland by Gen'l. Rosecrans. It is truth itself and brief as it is shows the true state of the campaign. The rebel cavalry made a raid on our rear last week and burned upwards of 500 gov't. wagons (including 114 ammunition wagons) loaded with commissary and quartermasters' stores. The rebs shot over a thousand mules in the harness and left them. This is war. In consequence of this raid our men are on half rations and have to go ragged and cold.[5]

The weather is very cold here, especially at night. The two armies are still facing one another; we are shut up in our lines and the rebels in theirs all around us (except for the river). They have Lookout Mountain which overlooks all of our works. They have been busy planting batteries that command us all over the sides of the mountain, and yesterday at one o'clock they commenced to play upon our works and the town. For four hours nothing could be heard but the explosions of artillery and the screams and bursting of shells as they came flying over and into our lines. My brigade was and is on the extreme outer line doing picket duty. We had many narrow escapes but no one was hurt. One shell stuck in the earth about two rods from me; another burst over my head without any damage to me. We have dug pits into which we lay down when the rebs have cold iron to bestow upon us; I confess it is not the most comfortable feeling in the world to lay and dodge those iron messengers, particularly when we are unable to return as good as they send. I have only heard of two casualties during the whole cannonade and they want confirmation.

The shelling commenced again during the night and continued at intervals. There has been no firing this morning but they may open at any moment. This state of things cannot last long; when our reinforcements arrive Bragg will be compelled to raise the siege and retire from his present position unless he has an immense force. I have no doubt the great battle of the war will be fought on the soil of Georgia. God grant that the victory will be ours and we can again have a happy and united country. We want a Waterloo and here is the place to have it.

My health has improved since I left home and arrived here—no touch of the asthma which is a great blessing. Otherwise my health is not as good as I wish. Could I have two or three weeks' quiet I should be all right; now I have to be on the *qui vive* night and day. Expectation is continually on the stretch as we know not what an hour may bring forth. All this is very trying to the nerves and consequently to the health of us all.

The prisoners taken from Longstreet's Corps say they never had such fighting on the Potomac as they met with here, and that when they had got our lines broken, instead of running from the field as the Potomac men do, we fought them as we fell back and punished them so that it was impossible to follow up their advantage before we were reformed in line again to receive them.

My love to you all at home; kiss the children and write me often. My love to my darling wife, Ellen.

Your bro., Frank

Colonel Sherman's brigade command again was short-lived, and he was replaced by Gen. James B. Steedman, whom he called "General Steadman."[6] Disappointed and angry, Colonel Sherman wrote to his father on October 12 about politics in the army:

General Steadman is from Ohio; he is an old member of Congress[7] and has had a command in this Department in the Reserve Corps (i.e., after we took and fortified the towns and were ordered still farther on into the enemy's country, the Reserve Corps came up and garrisoned the places we left). He is from Ohio; so is Rosecrans and Garfield, his chief of staff, and consequently Ohio has all the best positions for her officers in this reorganization. Again I am ordered back to my regiment with less show than ever to rise from my present position unless influence is brought to bear on the appointing power in Washington.

I had a long talk yesterday with Gen. Sheridan about the way things are working out here. He told me all that he could do was to save his whole division intact and keep it under his command, with such additions as old Rosey might think it proper to make, and that he was not consulted as to who was to command brigades under him (in the reorganized division). The old division has not received the compliment of even one brigade commander from those who have followed its fortunes and led its brigades in every battle and skirmish from Louisville to Chickamauga.

The reason given is that there are no divisions of old enough date in the old Third Corps, and therefore the reserves and other corps have been searched to find those who rank us by date, and they have been found— Ohio has them. Illinois has more regiments in the division than any other state, but Illinois has no officer whose commission dates far enough back to entitle him to a brigade. Ohio and the regular officers run this army, and there is not much chance for volunteer officers of other states getting any advancement.

Gen. Sheridan is from Ohio and a regular, but I believe he is not actuated entirely for his state or for regulars. He has frequently complimented me as an officer, and yesterday told me he would rather I would have command of one of his brigades than any man in the army, and backed up his assertion by offering to help me to promotion.

He told me if I desired he would recommend me to be appointed a brigadier, and that he would get the endorsement of Generals Gordon Granger and Rosecrans, together with that of [Charles A.] Dana, Assistant Secretary of War, who is here at the present time. I accepted his offer, and he told me he would go to work at once, and forward the papers on to Washington.

He also asked if I could bring any influence in my favor from home. I then told him of the proposed action of the War Committee. He had no doubt if that was done but what the two recommendations would get me appointed at once. Now, Father, a little exertion at home from my friends will make everything easy.

Mr. Tuttle told me he was going to Washington, that he would see [Secretary of War] Stanton, and urge my claims. Get Mr. Tuttle to do this and all will be right. Try and get a letter from the governor in my favor. Pile up the testimony, and my star will exceed George's.[8] I leave all with you. Mr. Tuttle, I know, will do all he can. Show him this, but do not let any portion of it get into the newspapers.

I have no news to write; the two armies hold the same positions. Give my love to mother and all, and when I write next will try and give some news and not fill up the paper with my affairs.

Your son, Frank

However, in his next letter, five days later, he was still preoccupied with his promotion, although he seemed less confident:

Chattanooga, Oct. 17th, 1863

Dear Father:

Lt. Col. [Alexander S.] Chadbourne [who commanded the 88th Illinois in Colonel Sherman's absence] has resigned and will be the bearer of this. His reason for leaving the service is the fact that the regiment is very poor in numbers and does not require three field officers to command it. His reasons I consider valid, and I advised him to resign. No blame ought or can be brought against him for this step. He has done his duty faithfully and earnestly and would, I have no doubt, enter the service again if his country needed him; Gen. Rosecrans considered his reasons valid and gave him an honorable discharge.

There are a great many resignations being offered and accepted. To tell the truth I have seriously thought of doing so myself and for no other reason than that there is no disposition shown to fill up our decimated ranks. I will wait a little while yet. Gen. Sheridan has been as good as his word; he has recommended me for promotion and shown me the papers. All that it wants is the recommend that has been promised at home by the governor and the War Committee and all will be right as far as the appointment is concerned. All that it wants thereafter is someone in the Senate who will interest himself to have me confirmed.

The situation here remains the same. There are rumors that the Rebels are receiving large reinforcements, that Jeff Davis is visiting his army in front of us and making great promises of what he intends to do,[9] that Bragg is relieved and either Longstreet or Joe Johnston is to be his successor, and that on Monday next the Rebel host will assault us in our works and try to annihilate Rosecrans and his army. All this comes from a Rebel officer who came out on the neutral ground between our lines and exchanged [news]papers with one of our officers. There is one thing certain; they are very busy doing something which means mischief. We are not idle on our side and every day adds to the strength of our position. They will be met with a warm greeting if they attempt to visit us.

Love to all at home, Your son, Frank

Colonel Sherman's next letter continued the familiar themes of weather, supplies, and promotion:

Chattanooga, Oct. 17, 1863

Dear Father:

It has been raining heavily for the last sixty hours, and everything is full of water. The river is rising rapidly, and the roads are almost impassable. It looks as if we would have to go hungry before the Rebs are got out of our immediate front. Rations have to be hauled twelve miles over the mountains to feed the army. Hundreds of horses and mules are dying for want of forage and exposure. Every ear of corn is guarded with jealous care so that none shall be wasted.

I am now in full command of the new brigade, Gen. Steadman having gone home on twenty days' furlough. Gen. Hooker and his command are at Bridgeport, at least four days' march from us as the roads now are. What he is going to do I have no means of knowing.

The news of the defeat of Vallandigham [in the Ohio gubernatorial election] reached us yesterday and three times three was given over the glorious news. The candidate from Canada, I reckon, will find some secure retreat and retire into private life, despised as a miserable traitor deserves.[10]

Love to all at home. Kiss the babies for me,

Your son, Frank

Two days later, Colonel Sherman wrote again, complaining that his brigade had been moved from the extreme right of the army to a position closer to the center:

Chattanooga, Oct. 19, 1863

Dear Father:

Today I received orders to move my brigade, which has been located on the army's extreme right, to a new position closer to the center. It makes a complete break-up throughout the entire army. The ground we now occupy is not nearly as good as that we left. We are on low, level ground which is hard to drain and make the troops comfortable, as they were in their old camp. All the little chimneys and fireplaces have to be rebuilt, and all the lumber which the men had found to make sheds has to be pulled down, moved about a mile, and fixed up again.

I wish you were here two or three days just to see what necessity does for the soldier, and how he makes himself a shelter from the weather. There is not a hog sty in all Illinois that is not roomier and warmer than that which the enlisted man of the Army of the Cumberland has. And still he never grumbles or growls, but takes his lot as a matter of course, be he wet or be he cold, be he warm or be he dry, or has he half enough to eat or has he plenty. If you saw what I see every day you might wonder how they can be kept in the service of their country.[11]

I am at present quartered in a one story cottage house with green blinds and no furniture, about two hundred yards to the rear of my brigade and am now prepared to live like a prince, provided the rebels do not shell me out of it, which they could do if they open up on our works. We are in a much more exposed place than we were before. My command is in the trenches which cover one of the principal roads leading to this place, and up which the rebs will have to march part of their forces to attack us. We have good rifle pits for the men to get into, and bastions for artillery. They will find it a slaughter pen if they attempt to cross the open ground in front of us, which they will have to do for half a mile before they reach us.

General Sheridan showed me yesterday the recommend that he had written to the President on my behalf, with the endorsement of Generals Granger and Rosecrans, asking that I be appointed brigadier general. It is now on the way. It seems to me that there will be no difficulty now if things are pressed a little at home. If the appointment can be made and sent to me in the next thirty days I can retain my present command, which I desire, for I have one of the finest brigades in the army, made up of old and tried troops with whom I am acquainted, and they with me, and I have the egotism to think would be glad to have me retained in command.

There have been rumors of a battle on the Potomac and that our armies have met with a reverse. Everything has [been] kept very still here about it. I know not what to believe or what to think so I will wait.

I have received but two letters from home since I left, and I have written more than a dozen back to you. I wish some of you would write every day.

My love to Ellen and the children. Your son, Frank

In the Civil War (and in every subsequent war), mail call was a high point of the day during the long waiting periods between fighting. Colonel Sherman's unhappiness about the lack of mail from home is revealed in this poignant—albeit somewhat histrionic—letter:

Chattanooga, Oct. 25th, 1863

Dear Mother:

I have written very many letters home since I left you. I have sent them by mail and I have not missed an opportunity when it offered of sending you by private hands letters keeping you all posted in regard to the conditions and position of things here. I have told you of the different changes which have taken place since the battle of Chickamauga in the Department and in the Army of the Cumberland. Most of the letters must have reached you long ere this, and enough time has elapsed for answers to be made in return. To this date, I have received the enormous number of four from home, including those written by Ellen. Do not think that I wish to impress upon your minds that I have been neglected or forgotten. I know that that is not so. A dear mother watches and prays for her boy without ceasing that the storm when it breaks will pass him harmlessly by. That boy is not unmindful of her solicitude for his well-being and safety, that he may travel over the dangerous path which lies before him. In the faith of Him who works out the wonders of the world I put my trust. I feel, Mother, that if your prayers could be answered my safety from physical harm would be assured, and I can enter the conflict with the protecting armor of a mother's love and a mother's petitions that will ward off the deadly bullet and the screaming shell and bring me back home free from harm.

Now, dear mother, write me. You cannot know how much I prize the few letters that you have written me. I know that it requires an effort on your part, and I know that your silence is not that of indifference. I also know you feel that it is difficult for you to write out your thoughts. But surely you can write your son, who reverences and honors you as having led him up to life's journey to manhood to guide him on to noble acts, worthy of your love and unceasing care. That love and that care has been the bright halo which has directed my wavering steps and brought me back to the paths of virtue and honor whenever I have strayed from the right. Mother, your love shall not be lost, nor your sacrifices in vain. And Father, the stern, the kind, the true, him do I honor, love, and respect. In him I have had the example of what a good and pure life, coupled with perseverance, energy, industry, and honesty can wrench from the cold and grasping world.

God bless you both, and may you long be spared to your children as the models on which their lives are molded. Many heartaches I have caused you both. I trust that I may have enough of life spared me to extract those things and gladden your hearts to the end of life's journey.

I have no news to write, nor am I in a mood to touch on other matters. Write me all. Love to you all, kiss the children, and now good night.

Your son, Frank

On October 28, still in Chattanooga, the colonel wrote to his father:

Yours of the 17th inst. has just come to hand. I have thought it somewhat strange the paucity of letters that have reached me. I have written numerous letters home to you all; some of them must have miscarried. I have sent by private hands letters whenever I found anyone going home on leave or resignation. It is very dull as far as news from the outer world is concerned and we are at present completely cut off, so that when a letter from home makes its advent it is hailed with emotions of joy and pleasure.

I regret to learn that mother's health is bad and trust that a few days at the most will again see her at her usual health. If wishes could bring it about, her sickness would be of short duration. I hope to hear in the next letter I get from home that she has entirely recovered.

As to the elections they have terminated as I expected. I did not believe the people of the great states of Ohio and Pennsylvania would be swayed by the radical school of Vallandigham and ignore the brave and patriotic men in the field confronting the enemies of their country and spilling their blood like water to maintain its integrity against rebels in arms. "Hurrah" say I for the patriots who at the pass have come forth nobly in defense and put down the subtletrys [*sic*] of treason under the guise of Democracy. Our party is redeemed from that disgrace, and will be once more looked upon as the true *War* party which cannot be led astray by any logic or sophistry by such men as Val and Merrick[12] and others of his ilk. Father, I feel that our country is saved, and now let our President fill up our decimated ranks by volunteering and drafting and this war will soon be over. I am tired of it but not so tired as to leave before the work is done.

Tell Mother I cannot come home yet; I have put my shoulder to the wheel and so long as my country needs my services she must have them. When she can do without me I am ready to go home, and I do not care how quick the turn may come around.

The situation here has not materially changed. The Rebels are still in our front and on our flanks. Hooker is trying to move up the river and regain possession of Lookout Mountain. There was considerable cannonading today from that direction. The Rebs opened a battery today from the very pinnacle of Lookout, twenty-four hundred feet above low water mark of the Tennessee River. We have a pontoon bridge laid across the river below the mountain which leads into Lookout Valley, and we expect our forces to cross and occupy it. To retake this position from the enemy is no easy task, but if we take it we believe a division could hold it against the whole Confederate army. The importance to us is vital, and so long as Bragg holds it our position is scarcely tenable on account of the difficulties getting supplies.

The mountain covers the approach to this place by river and the Chattanooga–Nashville Railroad. We hold the position of Bridgeport, which is twenty-seven miles by rail and about forty miles by river. We have steamers here that could, if we succeed in opening up the river, move back and forth between here and Bridgeport and bring up all the rations and clothing needed by the army. The railroad would soon be in working order and would enable us to accumulate the necessities which would put this place permanently under the armies of the Union.

At present we have to draw our rations by mule team nearly sixty miles over a rough mountain road, which becomes almost impassable after a short rain, and when the wet season comes on it will be impossible to feed the army by this precarious method. The present ration issued officers and men alike is a half pound of hard bread, a quarter ration of sugar, a quarter ration of coffee, and a full ration of salted fresh beef—only about a third [of the] ration allowed by law. It is piteous to see the men half fed and half clothed, with keen appetites and no way to satisfy the cravings of the stomach. Officers are no better fed.

It is a proud sight, under such circumstances, to see the pluck and courage of the American soldier. No thought of leaving this place does he allow. No griping or grumbling is heard from them, and when asked how they get along the inevitable reply is it is rough living on a third ration, but they would stand a still further reduction before they would give up the place. With this spirit animating them I think the rebels will find it a hard road to travel before they get us out of the stronghold of the south.

I wrote you some time since that Genl Sheridan had written a letter to the President recommending me for promotion and that Generals Granger & Rosecrans had put endorsements that were very flattering to me. With what the War Committee will or have done in that way, I think there will be no doubt on the appointment being made.

My love to you all at home: Mother, [sister] Martha, [brother] George, [brother-in-law] William, and the babies. My love to Ellen. My health is good. Now, write often, some of you, and let me know what is going on.

Good night, your son, Frank

Bragg's strategy of starving out the Union troops appeared to be working, and, except for a raid on October 28, there was little fighting in the next few weeks. In the only entry in more than a month, Colonel Sherman's diary records:

Wednesday, October 28, 1863

Night attack made by Longstreet forces on 11th & 12th A.C. in Lookout Valley. Rebels repulsed with loss. Our loss about 400.

There is no further communication from him until a letter dated November 9 from Chattanooga:

Dear Father:

I have an opportunity of sending you a letter by Mr. Titsworth[13] who

is here on a short visit to the Army. I yesterday wrote William in answer
to one I received from him. I have not any news to write; one day is so
nearly like the other that it is becoming very monotonous and tiresome,
for we have to stay closely to our posts and be ready for any emergency
that may arise. Whilst I am writing the enemy is banging away from his
battery upon Lookout Mountain. This has become an everyday occur-
rence and does not disturb my camp as they cannot reach us. Picket,
guard, and fatigue duty follows one after the other in regular routine. Our
rations have been increased from ½ to ⅔ and we hope soon to have full
rations to issue. The Paymasters have arrived and the Army will be paid
off. I am happy to say that my pay has been stopped on account of some
informalities in the ordinance returns sent forward by the regiment
through the company officers. It is very annoying as I am out of money
but will manage in some way to get along until the restriction shall be
lifted. There is four months' pay due me now and I expect that I shall
have to wait four months longer before I shall receive any pay, as that is
as often as the P.M. gets around to us here. I may have to draw on you
for money to carry me through.

The weather is clear, bright, and cold for this latitude. The leaves have
nearly all disappeared from the trees and everything betokens the approach
of winter, and the sunny South has a cheerless aspect. We are all preparing to send recruiting parties to Illinois to give the patriots there an opportunity to make good their boasts and to take a hand in the field with
us. This aid we need more than money, and this fall and winter is the time
to get men and make soldiers of them so that we may be ready for the
spring campaign to strike vigorous and giant blows which will bring peace
once more to the homes of our land. Now, Father, as you wish to see the
accomplishment of this end so devoutly looked for by we who have so
many times bared our breasts to the foeman's bullet: take every means in
your power to have the sturdy and brave sons of the North come to our
assistance. Throw away all party feelings and strife; bury the hatchet of
political warfare and all unite for the single purpose of restoring our government and country to her former proud position, and one flag. After
this is done, we will go back to our political principles once more. But
show the world that we as a people can forget our differences in regard
to the administration of the government when it is assailed by treason in
arms who desire to overthrow the temple and destroy the foundation of
our liberties.

We get rumors of numerous skirmishes and small fights from East
Tennessee. I have no doubt in my mind that the rebels are making a strong
movement in that direction with the hope of defeating Burnside and
driving him out of that country entirely.[14] By so doing they would make
our position untenable and we should have to evacuate this place. Large

bodies of rebel troops have gone that way, Longstreet's Corps amongst the rest. This we get from deserters; also that other troops take the place of those who are sent away. All the men captured at Vicksburg have been exchanged and are here in front of us. The concentration of troops by both sides here shows the vital importance in which our position is held. And if we are as active as our enemies and oppose force by force that they cannot defeat or dislodge, their cause will rapidly sink and rebellion will receive a blow from which it will be hard for them to recover. We have or shall have an active friend in their midst if we fail in the great undertaking. That friend is discontent, and he is busy now sowing the seeds of discord in their midst. If the 300,000 men are forthcoming promptly and our decimated ranks filled up, the rank and file of the rebel host will despair and their eyes will open to the hopelessness of their cause. Follow this up with a successful battle and, my word for it, peace will soon again dawn upon our war-stricken land. But if we are forced to leave our present position for want of men to hold it and lose the territory we have gained in the last year's campaign, God only knows when the end will come. It is for the people of the North to say, and with them lies the salvation of this country. It is within our grasp now; shall it be allowed to be wrenched from us? I trust not. Then let Illinois, as she has always done, put her shoulders to the wheel, nor wait for her sister states.

Gen'l Grant is here but I have not yet seen him.

My love to you all at home. I hope Mother and Martha are both well ere this time. There is no prospect of a battle here at present that I can see, so have no fear or uneasiness on my account. I do not hear from you very often—from that fact I suppose that you are all well and busy. Again love to you all; kiss the babies for me. And believe me I am truly and affectionately

your son, Frank

As the troops sat in Chattanooga, Rosecrans's star was rapidly setting. He had received little credit for the brilliant Tullahoma campaign, which was much less dramatic—and cost far fewer casualties—than the more spectacular Gettysburg or Vicksburg. Already criticized for his inactivity during the preceding months, he was blamed for the Union defeat at Chickamauga; in marked contrast, General Thomas, who had held his ground, was credited with saving the army. And now Rosecrans had led his army into a situation in which it was short of supplies and faced the possibility of having to retreat from the Chattanooga area.[15]

After the victories at Gettysburg and Vicksburg, the Union could afford to turn more of its attention to the Army of the Cumberland, and Union reinforcements from the east under Hooker and from the west under W. T. Sherman moved toward Chattanooga. Rosecrans held on until October 16, 1863, when Gen. Ulysses S. Grant became overall commander of the newly formed District of the Mississippi, which included all of the territory between the Appala-

Gen. William A. Rosecrans. Courtesy of Library of Congress.

chians and the Mississippi River. With Grant's arrival, the atmosphere changed from caution to action, and plans for a major battle were drawn up. Grant's first move was to replace Rosecrans with Gen. George H. Thomas.

Colonel Sherman was not at all happy with the change in command. On November 15, he wrote his father an impassioned defense of his general:

Dear Father:
    As to the reason why General Rosey was relieved from the command of this Department, I am as much in the dark as are you. I can surmise:

first, General R. was getting too popular with his army and the masses of the north. Two, he has been too successful in handling this difficult Department to suit old Brains [General Henry W. Halleck] and, therefore, he and the Secretary of War determined upon his removal whenever there was a shadow that they could use against him. Chickamauga furnished the excuse. Three, old Rosey had a mind of his own and did not always move his army against his judgment and good sense at the orders of those who were a thousand miles away and could not comprehend the difficulties to be overcome. Four, he had met with uniform success in all his movements and campaigns and wrested more territory from the enemy than any other general in our armies, inflicting such stunning blows upon rebellion as almost to have crushed it, and this, too, without having had a single man sent to him by way of reinforcement. Five, because Rosecrans with forty-five thousand men could not defeat and wholly annihilate eighty thousand veteran Rebel troops[16] and end the rebellion, and was forced to retire back to this place by overwhelming numbers—and when here [he was able to] hold Chattanooga, the key to east Tennessee, the depot where most of the rations, the coal and the nitre were drawn from to supply the army of the rebellion.

These are the only reasons that I can give for this, in my opinion, most unfortunate removal of a general who was uniformly successful in every campaign. I have no doubt that Gen. Rosecrans made a mistake in trying to do more than he had laid out. False information led him to believe that Bragg's army was in full retreat, and by a rapid pursuit it could be dispersed and rebellion crushed in this region by the occupation of Rome and Atlanta which, had he accomplished, would have cut the Confederacy in two. He failed and was forced back here, holding all that he started out to do in the first place.

Had this army only Bragg's army proper to contend with, all would have been accomplished, as we could whip them any day in the year. Well, reinforcements were sent when it was too late, with generals to command them whose commissions were older than that of Rosecrans and, of course, it would not do for a junior to command his senior. Draw your own inferences.

As to the idle tales and newspaper articles that are in circulation about drink and opium eating, they are not worth refuting. Of one thing I am certain, Rosey has not lost one jot or tittle of the confidence of the officers of his army because of his late movements in the field, nor has his removal abated that confidence. We shall see what we shall see and wait for the future. Time will test the wisdom of the President's act.

General Thomas, who succeeds Rosey, is universally respected and esteemed throughout this Department for his sterling qualities as a soldier and a great commander. Our men will fight under him with the greatest confidence wherever and whenever he will.

General Grant has his headquarters here. I have not seen him yet. Generals [Joseph] Hooker, W. T. Sherman, and [Oliver O.] Howard are here today; Gen. Sherman has arrived with two army corps. We are now a very respectable army, one that will trouble the rebs ere long or I lose my guess.

The situation has not changed. The enemy holds Lookout Mountain yet and sends their favor in the way of shells from its summit daily. They have not as yet done any damage; our men scarcely look up when they hear the boom of the guns. There are a great many deserters coming into our lines every night. They say that only a portion of their army is trusted to do picket duty for fear of the men coming over to us.

[Gen. James] Longstreet's forces have gone to east Tennessee with the intention of trying to cut off Burnside. We expect to hear of a battle being fought that way soon, and reinforcements have gone there from here. I think Burnside will be able to drive the Rebs back. The troops are now in excellent condition and spirits. They get three quarter rations. My love to you. Write often.

Your son, Frank

Four days later, Colonel Sherman wrote to his father, anticipating the coming battle and its possible consequences to himself:

Chattanooga, Nov 19, 1863

Dear Father:

On Saturday the 21st there is to be a general demonstration by our army against the enemy with a view of driving him out of Chattanooga Valley. It is more than likely that this movement will lead to a battle unless Bragg retires his army at once, which I do not think he will do unless compelled by us to fall back. In any case there will be severe fighting unless we can create a general panic in their army, which is problematical. At all events we are to move on the enemy. Hooker will try to take Lookout Mountain, and Sherman will cross the river onto Missionary Ridge by means of a pontoon bridge. Our generals think that the Rebs will give up the valley; if they stay to fight there will be a bloody time of it, and if we whip them, it will be a decisive battle which will cripple the Rebel Army so badly that, in my opinion, there will be nothing left for them to do but to throw down their arms. I pray to God that such may be the case.

I wish to write you about my wife and children. If anything should happen to me they will be left helpless, and to your care I leave them. Be kind to them for my sake, nor let them suffer from want. If anything can be gotten from the wreck of my business and property I want Ellen and the children to have it; I hope something may be saved for them.[17]

Love to all, your son, Frank

The planned demonstration did not come off on the 21st, as Colonel Sherman's diary related:

Friday, November 20

Recd orders to be ready to move in the morning against the enemy. Brigade all ready. 8 o.c. P.M. orders countermanded.

Saturday, November 21, 1863

Did Not Move.

Sunday 22

In Camp.

On Monday, the "demonstration" began:

Monday 23

At one oc P.M. 1st Brigade moved out in conjunction with Division. whole Army in 4 Corps moved. heavy Skirmishing on our left; Drove enemy back; Captured 300 prisoners. No fighting on our front. Bivouac for the night, rainy.

Tuesday, November 24, 1863

During night changed position to the left. Nothing important on our front. At 11 am heavy firing on the west of Lookout. At 2½ P.M. mountain taken by Whittaker's [Gen. Walter C. Whitaker} Brigd 14th Corps supported by troops under Hooker. Rainy. [W. T.] Sherman's forces crossed Tenn. on enemy's right in force.

Although Colonel Sherman did not then know it, the next day was to be the high point of his military career. In the plan for the "general demonstration," Thomas's divisions had been assigned a mere holding action; however, due to the vagaries of combat, they ended up making a frontal assault over almost impossible terrain, an assault which culminated in the decisive Union victory of Missionary Ridge. The Army of the Cumberland was to regain the reputation it had lost at Chickamauga, and Colonel Sherman was to play a significant part.

8

MISSIONARY RIDGE:
NOVEMBER 1863

In the plan for the battle of Missionary Ridge, Colonel Sherman, again in command of one of Sheridan's brigades, was scheduled to play a very small role. Since the Confederate position along the five-hundred-foot heights of the ridge was considered impregnable to frontal assault, Grant planned to attack on the flanks, relying on reinforcements recently arrived on the scene. Hooker was to attack Bragg's left over Lookout Mountain, and W. T. Sherman was to attack the right over Tunnel Hill. Grant planned only to hold the center, assigning the holding task to Thomas's battered Army of the Cumberland, still smarting from its defeat at Chickamauga.

Skirmishing began and continued through November 24, while Thomas's troops in the valley watched Hooker's men take Lookout Mountain. But on November 25, both Hooker's and W. T. Sherman's troops bogged down. Believing that a threat to the center would lead Bragg to draw some of his troops away from the flanks and so ease the pressure on Hooker and W. T. Sherman, Grant ordered Thomas to carry the enemy lines of rifle pits at the foot of Missionary Ridge, but not to continue further.

Sheridan and Thomas's other division commanders could see, however, that if their men stopped after carrying out these orders, they would be exposed to devastating artillery fire from the heights of the ridge. Sheridan shared this concern with his brigade commanders, including Colonel Sherman, as he recalled in his memoirs: "[I had] already begun to doubt the feasibility of our remaining in the first line of rifle pits when we should have carried them. I discussed the order with [Gen. George D.] Wagner, [Col. Charles G.] Harker, and [Col. Frank] Sherman, and they were similarly impressed, so while anxiously awaiting the signal I sent Captain J[ames] S. Ransom to ascertain if we were to carry the first line or the ridge

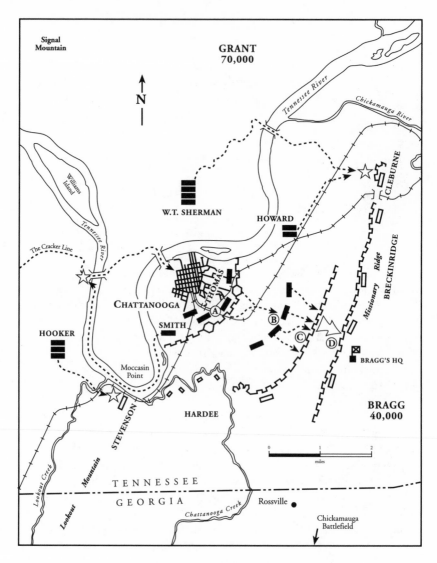

Battle of Missionary Ridge.
A to B shows movement of Thomas's troops, on Grant's orders. Exposed to Confederate fire, Thomas elected to charge, clearing the rifle pits at C and then clearing the Confederates off the ridge at D.

beyond. Shortly after Ransom started, the signal guns were fired, and I told my brigade commanders to go for the ridge."[1]

Go for it they did. Thomas's troops stormed up the heights, broke the Confederate lines, and drove the enemy troops all the way out of Tennessee. They almost captured General Bragg, and they cost him his command. By its unanticipated assault on Missionary Ridge, the Army of the Cumberland not only surprised General Grant and his staff, but also redeemed itself after the disaster at Chickamauga.

Missionary Ridge was one of the few successful frontal assaults on protected positions in the Civil War. Such assaults generally were unsuccessful, and Grant and Thomas, as well as Bragg, appear to have been convinced that it would be not only futile but disastrous for the Army of the Cumberland to undertake such an assault on the seemingly impregnable barrier of Missionary Ridge.[2] When Grant realized that an assault was under way, he sent a staff officer with orders to abort the attack, but by the time the officer caught up with the rear of Colonel Sherman's brigade, it was too late to stop the advance.[3] Wagner did get the order and fell back, and Harker followed suit, but the orders were modified, and both brigades resumed their charge.[4]

The Battle of Missionary Ridge was the high point not only of Colonel Sherman's military career, but of his entire life, and he wrote several accounts of it. Two of them are included in this book: first, his official report; and, second, his most complete account, part of a long letter to his brother. The official report was sent from Knoxville on January 22, 1864, to Lt. Thomas W. C. Moore, acting assistant adjutant general:

Sir: I have the honor to submit the following report of the part taken by the First Brigade at the battle of Mission [sic] Ridge on November 25, 1863.

On Monday, the 23d, my brigade was ordered to be in readiness to move to the front and beyond our lines of works at Chattanooga at 1 P.M. At the hour named the brigade marched, following the Third Brigade, and took position with my right resting on the Dalton Road. By command of General Sheridan, the Brigade was drawn up in two lines. The first was, by my order, placed under the command of Col. Silas Miller, Thirty-Sixth Infantry Illinois Volunteers. The second line was by me placed under command of Col. B[ernard] Laiboldt, Second Missouri Infantry Volunteers. During the afternoon the brigade lines were advanced 600 yards, and remained in position during the night, the men sleeping on their arms.

At 3 A.M. of the 24th, I received orders to move the brigade by the left, and take a position in reserve and rear of the Third Brigade, which was promptly done. At 4 A.M. orders were received to place three regiments of my brigade on the right of the Third Brigade, in prolongation of their first line, beyond hastily constructed rifle pits. [The 44th, 36th, and 73d

Illinois] were thus placed [with the 88th and 74th Illinois] in the rear as support.

This disposition of the brigade remained unchanged until 12 M. of the 25th, when the entire division line was moved forward some 300 yards. The other regiments of my brigade were moved to the right and rear of the line, where they were formed in the following order:

First line: 44th, 36th, and 73d Illinois, Col. [Wallace] Barrett commanding;

Second line: 88th Illinois and 24th Wisconsin, Col. Miller commanding;

Third line: 22d Indiana, Col. Michael Gooding commanding;

Fourth line: 2d and 15th Missouri, and 74th Illinois, Col. Laiboldt commanding.

With a heavy line of skirmishers on my front and flank, under command of Major [George D.] Sherman, 36th Illinois, whom I commend to the general commanding.

At 2:30 I received instructions from General Sheridan in person to hold the brigade in readiness to advance and assault the enemy's works at the base of Mission Ridge at a signal which would be given from Orchard Knob by the firing of six guns at intervals of two seconds.

At 3:00 P.M. the signal guns were fired, and the brigade moved forward, in conjunction with other troops of the division, in quick time, through the timber to the open plain beyond, which lay in front of the enemy's works.

The troops at this point, taking the double-quick step by order, swept across the open ground under a most terrific fire of artillery and musketry with unbroken ranks, and cleared the first line of the enemy's works at the point of the bayonet, taking many prisoners. After a brief halt for breath, the order to advance and carry the second line of works, behind which the enemy had rallied, was received by the troops with a cheer, and gallantly did they do their work as they dashed on through the storm of iron and lead hurled against them by our foes. In ten minutes' time the works were taken as before, the enemy, with broken ranks, retiring in confusion up the slope of the ridge to their third line, upon the crest. The troops, being much exhausted by their rapid advance and hard fighting, rested a few minutes behind the parapets of the rebel works of the second line, gathering their energies for the final advance to the third line, upon the crest of the ridge. From the second line the hill rises abruptly to an angle of nearly 40 degrees, and was covered by fallen timber and brush, which made the ascent very difficult and fatiguing. Again the order to advance was responded to with cheers, the colors, borne by their brave and gallant men taking the lead, each bearer wishing to be the first to place the banner of his regiment upon the crest of the rebel works. Slowly and surely we pressed up the hill, overcoming all obstacles, defying the enemy in his efforts to check our determined advance. Officers and men alike vied with each other in deeds of gallantry and bravery, cheering one another on to the goal for which we were contending. In this manner we gradually worked our way to the summit, over the rugged sides of the ridge, every foot being contested by the enemy. Rocks were thrown upon our men when the musket ceased to be of use, but to no purpose. When within 10 yards of the crest our men seemed to be thrown forward as if by some powerful engine, and the old flag was planted firmly and surely on the last line of works of the enemy, followed by the men taking one battery of artillery. The battle was won and Mission Ridge was taken, while the enemy fled in great disorder from before our victorious troops, who took whole companies of the rebels prisoners.

The brigade was reformed, the ranks being broken in the ascent of the ridge, and bivouacked for the night on the crest of Missionary Ridge. At 12 midnight we were, by order of the general commanding, marched on the road to Bird's Mill about 1½ miles in pursuit, and halted until 11 A.M. of the 26th, when we were moved to the Chickamauga Creek. At 4 P.M. orders were received to return to our old camp at Chattanooga, at which place we arrived at 6 P.M.

To Cols. Laiboldt, 2d Missouri, and Miller, of the 36th Illinois, I am indebted for their untiring exertions and [the] gallantry they displayed in encouraging and leading their respective commands to the assault, and by their example aiding in the successful termination of the battle.[5]

Colonel Sherman went on to commend his staff officers and the commanding officers of all but one of his regiments; the reasons why he left out the 22d Indiana and Colonel Gooding are unclear.[6]

Colonel Sherman wrote a more lyrical account of the battle to his brother-in-law (the first paragraphs of this letter concern the Knoxville campaign and can be found in chapter 9):

[Late January, 1864]

Dear Bill:

. . . In your letter you state that no correspondent has given in detail the part taken by brigades and regiments in the battle of Missionary Ridge of the 25th of Nov. which resulted in such a glorious and decisive victory for the Union Arms. Who is the man who will with his pen ever be able to picture the scene of conflict, to draw to life the many acts of heroism displayed that day? Whose the pen will be able to blazon forth to the world the undying valor displayed by the "boys in blue," and single out instances, individuals, or commands as they ascended that ridge? Would that I could seize upon the incidents of that fearfully grand drama and give you the shifting scenes of the play as it was enacted upon that bright and beautiful autumn afternoon, but that is beyond my poor skill. For the part which I took, I will briefly relate.

At two o'clock on the 25th I received instructions from General Sheridan in person, to prepare my brigade to make an assault on the first line of works at the base of the hill known as Mission Ridge. A signal would be given from Orchard Knob by the firing of six pieces of artillery at intervals of two seconds.

I immediately reformed my brigade into four lines of battle with a heavy skirmish line to the front under the immediate command of Major [George D.] Sherman of the 36th Illinois Inf'try. After my formations were completed the Regimental Commanders were instructed in the presence of their men what was expected of them and of their commands. Having formed our positions as assigned, we waited the signal which was to conduct many a brave and gallant man to a better world. In silence we then lay waiting that fearful summons which would lead us to victory or death. In front of us we could see a thin strip of timber and then a level open plain for near a half mile before we could reach the first line of rifle pits which we could see were alive with men in grey moving to their appointed posts in expectation of our attack.

The glintings of steel thrown off the burnished arms by that sun as it moved slowly towards the western horizon in a cloudless sky told that Death held his court there and seemed to wait in grim satisfaction for the banquet which man was preparing to glut his insatiable appetite with, and build upon the lifeless corpses that soon would strew that fair field and plunge a nation into mourning over its fallen brave.

As the anxious moments swept by, no levity was there and no careless joke. As you looked down that long line of bronzed faces you could see by the stern look of resolve and the compressed lip their firm purpose and unflinching resolve to do or die, and I was satisfied that victory ere long would throw its halo of glory around those veterans, whose stamina had been so often tried before and never found wanting. The thoughts of home, of Mothers, Fathers, Wives, Sisters, and Brothers in the far off land of the North may have passed through their minds as a panorama unfolding scenes of other days when happiness and peace abounded. Still with unblanched cheeks and clear eyes those sons and Brothers lay beneath the folds of that flag which had ever waved for the right.

Hark! Boom! Boom! thrice repeated broke upon the ears of that startled host. The hour had come, and as the cannon bellowed forth the charge, like some mettlesome courser with nostrils distended and eyes ablaze, eager for the chase, the Fourth Corps sprang from their recumbent position. In an instant all was life and motion, and ere the echoes of the cannonade had died out from the walls of Lookout, that noble band swept on. My brigade was on the extreme right of our division and corps, its flank covered by a cloud of skirmishers who would protect it, thus exposed, from an enfilade fire.

On we went through the belt of timber, nor slackened our pace. The open ground was gained and before us was our work. Long lines of blue stretched towards the left as far as the eye could reach, with the old banner proudly waving borne along in their midst, reflecting back in rainbow hues the rays of an autumn sun. A salvo of artillery and the sharp crack of small arms greeted our coming, and now more swiftly we moved forward to answer its greeting as the lines of blue redoubled their pace. On, on they went, banner and men. More furious beat the storm full on their breasts with no shield to screen them. One hundred yards and the work is ours, goes forth a shout from twelve thousand throats as they sped on to the shelter of the parapets. One hundred yards! It was the journey of a life, and many never gained its end. On swept the wave carrying the destiny of a nation on its combing billow as it rolled toward the breach, gathering volume ere it should break and overwhelm the barriers in its way. Relentless in its force, it rushed on throwing its spray (skirmishers) over the work engulfing all that came within its vortex.

The Rebels left their first line of works, throwing down their arms and retreating to the second line some four hundred feet farther up the slope of the Ridge. Hundreds yielded themselves as prisoners by falling flat in the rifle pits so as to be covered from their own fire. Thus far we had come without firing a shot and at double quick, taking the first work with the bayonet. The men were completely exhausted by their long run and exertions, and lay down behind the parapet to recover their breath. *We had now done all that we had orders to do.*

The Rebels in the meantime had rallied their men in the second line of works and had opened fire on us from them. All this time they were plying their batteries with vigor, and the air was literally thick with grape, canister, and bursting shell, whilst the pellets of lead from their musketry fire sounded like the swarming of bees as they went rushing by. To stay where we were was destruction, to go back the same, and it became evident to me that there was no choice for us but to advance and carry the Ridge with its works.

The men were elated with the success they had gained, and were eager for the order to advance. It was given and with a shout it was responded to. Up and over the first works went the men of the 1st Brigade, the Regimental Colors leading on to the second line of rifle pits, behind which the Enemy had rallied. It was a race of but ten minutes and they were ours. The 88th Illinois led the way; prisoners of every grade from Colonels down fell into our hands by the hundred, and were sent to the rear receiving the benefit of the fire of their own comrades.

A few minutes rest and again the old flag leading our brave boys pushed up the slope, which at this point rises abruptly to an angle of nearly forty degrees, broken by rocks and fallen timber which made the ascent very difficult. Still on [went] these heroes, Officers and men, determined to overcome every obstacle to gain the goal. Here the gallant [Col. Silas] Miller of the 36th [Illinois] rode out the storm animating his men by his daring. There could be seen the lithe and agile form of Richard Realf, Sgt. Major of the 88th, pricking up the skulkers with his Sergeant's sword. Yonder the veteran Leibold [Col. Bernard Laiboldt] of the 2nd. Mo., bearing a charmed life, moved through the hail of bullets leading on his gallant Germans; and far on towards the crest were the banners borne by the dauntless bearers in advance of the struggling line, waving defiance to the enemy and giving cheer to the boys below.

Slowly and surely advance the colors, slowly and surely follows the 1st Brigade in their trail. Nine Regimental Colors were there, all on a line and all making superhuman efforts to be first to unfold the stars and stripes upon the last of the works of the "impregnable" position of the rebels. There to the right goes the 88th unwavering and firm under a heavy cross and direct fire. Their gallant Commander [Lt. Col. George W.] Chandler[7] sees his men falling and, taking their position in at a glance, wheels a company to the right and pays his compliments to the foe who is annoying his flank.

At this point [Lt. Charles H.] Lane and [Lt. Henry L.] Brigham surrender their young lives, a fit sacrifice upon the altar of patriotism to the Moloch of treason. Peace to their ashes for they died as soldiers should, with their harness on and their faces to the foe. Here, whilst urging on his men, the cool and quiet [George W.] Smith, Capt. of Company "A," received his wound. As the wave was about to surge up and over the crest of the Ridge, [1st Lt. Dean R.] Chester, [1st Lt. Sylvester] Titsworth, and [2d Lt. Lewis B.] Cole, officers brave and true, were left behind. Colonel [Jason] Marsh, the venerable Commander of the 74th [Illinois], urged on his men to near the summit, and fell, pierced through the shoulder. [Colonel James F.] Jacques[s] of the 73rd [Illinois] was there, leading on his "fighting Regiment of Preachers."[8] All were there, Illinois, Indiana, Missouri, Wisconsin, and all struggling to plant the old flag where the cross bars had so long defiantly waved in our faces. All this time the tide rolled on up the scraggy sides of the hill; many wayfarers fell by the way, nevermore to rise again. Still, "On" was the cry. Hark! "Chickamauga" came drifting down the hillside to the ears of the panting heroes struggling up, by the voices of those who served under the Bars, in derisive tones. As if an electric shock had been felt, throughout the whole command that cry impelled them on with new force. Thus was the contest raging and every moment brought us nearer and nearer to the crest. Hoarse cries mingled with the rattle of musketry; eyes stared out of smoke and powder-begrimed faces were wild with the light of battle. The proud old flag had nearly reached the rebel lines; many of its brave and noble bearers had been struck down, but ere it could fall to the ground it was raised boldly aloft and moved on steadily.

As the Brigade gradually reached the summit, the steepness of the hillside forced the rebels to expose their persons to get anything like a correct line of fire on our men. Scarcely a man on their side lived to repeat the shot, as they were picked off as fast as they came into view, and when finally there intervened only ten or fifteen yards between our lines and the last line of works upon the crest, the enemy threw rock and stone over them on our men below. For some fifteen minutes our advance was checked, not through the efforts of the enemy, but from sheer exhaustion. This rest gave them time to recover their energies for the last and final throw which would give us the victory.

At last it came. With a mighty effort and with a shout that rose clear and loud above the infernal din, they precipitated themselves upon the last works. It came down with irresistible force, and swept all before it. There on the crest waved the war-worn banners, and in rapid succession and with scarcely an interval, the regimental banners of my brigade, nine in number, were planted. Over the rude barriers of logs rolled the tide of blue that had so bravely faced the storm and braved the torrents of iron and lead [which had] poured without intermission for an hour and a half upon their devoted heads.

The crest gained, on rushed our men after the fast-receding lines of Grey until, broken and dispirited, they disappeared behind the knobs and the thick woods beyond. The recall was sounded and "Halt" was the order, which was reluctantly obeyed. In breaking over the crest a battery of six guns was captured, two of which had the names of Lady Buckner and Lady Breckinridge painted upon the breech and were posted near the headquarters of General Bragg.

The rout was complete and one of the most substantial of the war. The 1st Brigade 2nd Division 4th Army Corps was the first to gain the crest and plant the flag of our Union upon the summit,[9] of all that grand army of heroes who had fought with such unflinching courage, its way to victory over obstacles natural and artificial, which was deemed impregnable by the sagacious and wily Bragg. Who shall attempt to portray the wild joy of the men when they realized the great achievement they had accomplished? The huzzas long and loud, the throwing up of hats, the shaking of hands, the embracing, and the tears which were shed, told of hearts full to overflowing. That scene is graved upon the tablets of my memory, never to be effaced.

For an hour all rank was waived and congratulations were exchanged by officers and men alike. General Sheridan riding up, the men seemed determined to carry him horse and all about upon their shoulders. He dismounted for a moment and spoke a few words which were drowned in shouts of joy going up about him. He was seized upon by the boys, for everyone wanted to shake our lion-hearted General by the hand. One large fellow forced his way through the crowd to where the General was standing, and slapping him on the shoulder with no light hand, sang out at the top of his voice, "Bully for you, General." All was taken by him in good humor for he knew that the men around him, were ready to do or die when he led.

I had the same experience, and when I got to where the 88th were, I thought for the moment that they would devour me for joy, as they had heard that I was wounded seriously, and when I stood amongst them unharmed, they could scarcely believe their own senses. Well and truly had they sustained their reputation that day for good fighters and adding new luster to the wreath woven by the men of Illinois in this war. Hers was the flag that first floated over Mission Ridge, borne by the gallant [Sgt. John] Cheevers. Illinois and Chicago need not blush to own the 88th for she deserves well of you all, and although we are debarred the privilege of filling up our thinned ranks by recruiting, we yet can strike telling blows against treason, and will do so when opportunity offers.

The sun sank to rest as we had fairly accomplished our work, and the men bivouacked where they had last seen the rebel foe. Our joy and exhilaration were somewhat dampened when we came back to look for those who were missing; 307 officers and men of the brigade were left by the way, three hundred and seven heroes whose names should be written in gold on the fairest leaf of history's page. God bless them, they had given earnest of their devotion and patriotic ardor for their country.

My brigade is composed of the following regiments: 88th Ill., 73rd Ill., 74th Ill., 44th Ill., 36th Ill., 22nd Ind., 24th Wis., 15th Mo., and 2nd Mo. Vols. Five of these regiments have nearly served out their time; four of them re-enlisted as veterans and are on their way home to be furloughed and to re-organize.

At 12 midnight I received orders to march in pursuit of the enemy; rations and ammunition were issued and in an hour we were on the road and following up the enemy to Chickamauga Creek, capturing prisoners and material of war which was abandoned by the rebels in their hasty flight.

That evening of the 26th [of November,] we were ordered back to Chattanooga which we reached at 6 P.M. We had hoped that we would be allowed to remain here and get such rest as we all required. Alas for hopes, no rest was there for the 4th Corps. Our brethren in arms far up in east Tennessee were shut in by the flower of Southern chivalry under the redoubtable Longstreet, and to save them from capture we were required to make a forced march of one hundred and forty miles and cross four rivers. Seven days of marching did the work, the rivers were spanned and the distance overcome, and Burnside was free.

In reading over what I have written you, I am not satisfied with the tale as told, but such as it is you have it, and when I look back to the scenes I have tried to depict, it seems more like a dream or a fable than a reality which will fill a page in history—one of the brightest in the annals of this damnable rebellion.

Give my love to all at home. Kiss the babies for me; also love to my wife when you see her. And believe me I am Brother Frank, still.

If any of this is published I do not wish my name to appear. I want every expression which would indicate the author altered. I do not care to have any of it published, it is written for you *all* at home. F.

Apparently not all of Sherman's men were "eager for the order to advance" from the first line of rifle pits. Although Colonel Sherman's mention of Realf's "pricking up the skulkers with his sergeant's sword" is his only suggestion of any lack of enthusiasm for the charge up the ridge, a less subjective account gives a different version: "Colonel Sherman, perhaps because of the nearer, more accurate fire to his front, had a more difficult time motivating his men than did [the other brigade commanders, Gen. George D.] Wagner or [Col. Charles G.] Harker. An alarming number of men from his first line either dropped behind or refused to leave the first line of rifle pits, so Sherman sent his aide-de-camp [presumably Sergeant Realf] back down the slope to urge the laggards forward."[10] Eventually, with some opportune assistance from Sheridan, who cursed and swung his saber at timid troops, Sherman managed to get his men on their way up the slope, although, "while cowering in the rifle pits, Sherman's regiments had become hopelessly tangled, probably more so than any other brigade in the corps." But, "once they started, Sherman's men had no trouble rolling over [Confederate Brig. Gen. Otho F.] Strahl's weak intermediate entrenchments."[11] Colonel Sherman faced a particularly difficult challenge in his area, because, at that point, the slope of the ridge was steepest and the second line of rifle pits was closest. Colonel Sherman, as usual, underplayed any deficiencies he found in the troops he led.

Sheridan made the only effective follow-up after the victory at Missionary Ridge. General Grant later gave his blessing to Sheridan's decision to follow up, saying, "To Sheridan's prompt movement, the Army of the Cumberland and the nation are indebted for the bulk of the capture of prisoners, artillery, and small-arms that day. Except for his prompt pursuit, so much in this way would not have been accomplished."[12] Sheridan had tried hard to persuade General [Gordon] Granger to provide support for this follow-up operation, even to the extent of simulating an engagement with the enemy, but he could not get help and eventually halted his pursuit for fear of being cut off from the main Union forces. Sheridan complained, "I was much disappointed that my pursuit had not been supported, for I felt that great results were in store for us should the enemy be vigorously followed."[13]

9

"A Series of Blunders":
Winter, 1863–1864

For Colonel Sherman, the excitement of the victory at Missionary Ridge soon would be followed by frustration in the course of a cold, hungry, and seemingly fruitless trip to East Tennessee. As he reported at the end of the letter to his brother, the division returned to Chattanooga on the evening of the Battle of Missionary Ridge, after giving up pursuit of the fleeing enemy. After a day's rest, however, the troops again were on their way. The days of leisurely regrouping after a victory were over; Grant, now in overall command, drove his troops hard, in contrast to Buell and Rosecrans; and Colonel Sherman had little time to write. There were no letters from November 19 until December 21, while he and his men marched to Knoxville and back. Finally, a year behind schedule, a Union army was going to rescue East Tennessee from the Confederates. Many, but not all, of the region's citizens were glad to be rescued.

Before the Battle of Missionary Ridge, Bragg's army had been weakened substantially, when Longstreet, reluctantly but at President Davis's insistence, left Chattanooga to retake Knoxville from Burnside. Grant's intelligence led him to believe that Burnside was hard pressed to hold out against Longstreet, and after the battle of Missionary Ridge he immediately sent an emergency force of twenty-five thousand men to the rescue.

The rescue mission consisted of W. T. Sherman's troops and Granger's Corps, which included Sheridan's division. Their provisions and clothing were inadequate for a winter trek, but Burnside's danger seemed acute. They went "with two days' rations, without a change of clothing—stripped for the fight, with but a single blanket or coat per man, from myself [General Sherman] to the private."[1]

Colonel Sherman maintained his diary through the Knoxville expedition and described the logistics of the forced march.[2]

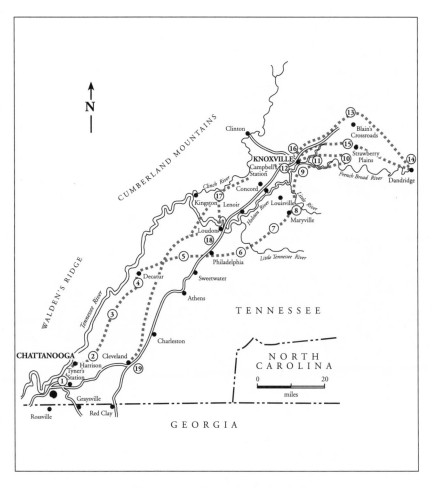

Knoxville Campaign, November 1863–April 1864.
Legend: 1. 11/28; 2. 11/29; 3. 11/30; 4. 12/1—Decatur; 5. 12/2; 6. 12/3–4;
7. 12/5; 8. 12/6; 9. 12/7–11; 10. 12/12–15; 11. 12/16; 12. 12/17; 13. 12/18–1/15;
14. 1/16–17; 15. 1/18–19; 16. 1/20; 17. 1/21–26; 18. 1/27–4/20; 19. 4/21.

Saturday, November 28, 1863

Marched at 1 o'c P.M. up the Tennessee (so side). Went into camp at dark across Chickamauga.

Sunday, November 29

Marched at 9 A.M. and reached Harrison at 2½ P.M. and went into camp ½ mile beyond; made 7 miles. clear and cold.

Monday, November 30

Marched at 3 o'c A.M. Very cold and freezing, and reached the Hiawassic River at 2 P.M., and crossed by means of flat boats. Marched 23 miles. Found many Union people who cried for joy to see the Yanks. Encamped on east side.

Tuesday, December 1

Marched at 10½ A.M.; reached Decatur, Tenn. at 3½ o'c. Found many Union people today. Drove the rebs out of the town. Camped on farm owned by Silliard, rebel of the first water. Most all Union people on the route today; Decatur secesh.

Wednesday, December 2

Left Decatur at 6 A.M. Marching on Kingston Road, made 14 miles and camped. Plenty of meat in hands of reb citizens which was taken. Fine farming country.

Thursday, December 3

Marched at 6 A.M. on Loudon Road; passed through Philadelphia at noon. Left Loudon Road here and took Morgantown Road. Made 17 miles. Fine farming country and many Union people came out to greet us.

Friday, December 4

Remained in camp today 4 miles from Morgantown, waiting for bridge to be built across Little Tennessee River by 15th Army Corps. Longstreet reported still in front of Knoxville. Weather fine. Good farms all through this country. Army subsisting off the country.

Saturday, December 5

Marched at 7 o'c A.M., crossed the South Tennessee River at 12 noon and made 16 miles. Camping at the Brick Mill on Morgantown pike. Rich country. All rebels through here.

Sunday, December 6

Marched at 7 A.M. on direct road to Knoxville. Passed through Maryville at 12 noon, a secession town. 15th Army Corps occupies this place. News here Longstreet gone from Knoxville into Virginia. Camped at 1½ o'c P.M.

Colonel Sherman and his men had come in a forced march through cold and snow to rescue Burnside, to destroy Longstreet, and, finally, to make East Tennessee safe. What they found was that Burnside appeared not to need rescuing, that Longstreet had departed, and that there was no one left to harass the loyal East Tennesseeans. It was, to say the least, an anticlimax.[3]

Longstreet, after having been detached from Bragg's troops in Chattanooga to retake Knoxville, had attacked Burnside at Fort Sanders on November 29, probably motivated by the news that General Sherman's force was on the way. He was repulsed and by December 5 had retreated back into Virginia. Burnside, who had reported that he was almost out of food, appeared better provisioned than the new arrivals, welcoming General Sherman with a sumptuous turkey dinner with all the trimmings.[4] Sherman was exasperated and after dinner started back with his troops to Chattanooga, leaving Granger to support Burnside in whatever mopping up had to be done.[5]

Colonel Sherman and his troops had no turkey dinners; as he indicated in his diary, they were concerned primarily with finding food, forage, and shoe leather:

Monday, December 7

Marched at 8½ o'c. Crossed Little River at Rockford at 12 noon. Went into camp at 8 P.M. one mile from Knoxville; made 15 miles. Men on short rations, very tired and shoes worn out. Burnside's forces in pursuit of rebs; learned nothing of their whereabouts.

Tuesday, December 8

Remained in camp; sent 88th (Regiment) to Waylands Mills and took possession of same to grind grain for the Brigade as we now have to live off the country.

Wednesday, December 9

In camp all of today. Visited Knoxville; very fine town. Shows that armies do not improve the condition of towns or the inhabitants thereof.[6]

Thursday, December 10

Remained in camp today. Received orders at noon to march on Kingston and call in all detached parties. At 12 midnight orders were countermanded.

Friday, December 11

In Camp all day. Rec'd orders at noon to send out and take possession of Brabson's Mill and Keenan's Mill on French Broad River in Sevier County.

Saturday, December 12

Marched this A.M. at 7 for Brabson's Mill. Sent 88th to Wayland's Mill. Went into camp at 4½ o'c P.M. ½ mile from Brabson's Ferry & 18 miles from Knoxville on French Broad River.

Sunday, December 13

Took possession of Brabson's Mill. Sent 74th Ill to Keener's Mill 4½ miles down the French Broad [River]. Sent 22nd Ind to Atchley's Mill on Little Pigeon River. Also sent into the country for wheat, corn, etc.; parties successful. 88th Ill at Wayland's Mill, 7 miles.

Monday, December 14

Gathering grain and meat for the Command today. Mills all running. Got a raft of lumber today and commenced building a boat for ferry.

Tuesday, December 15

Col. James B. Kerr, 74th [Illinois], took possession of Bowman's Mill 2½ miles from Keener's Mill. Found 4000 lbs. flour there. Found flat boat partially built; ordered it finished. Rec'd orders to return to Knoxville this eveng. at once.

Wednesday, December 16

Finished boats today and loaded them with what flour & meal we had collected and shipped it to Knoxville. Brigade marched at 10½ o'c A.M. Made 12 miles and bivouac'd for the night. Very heavy rain during the night.

Thursday, December 17

Marched at 7 A.M.; roads very bad. Arrived at Knoxville at 11 A.M. Ordered to take cars to McMillan's Station by Gen'l. Forster [*sic*]. Issued shoes to the men today. Bivouacked at 12½ A.M. Cars & march 17 miles today.

Friday, December 18

Left McMillan's Station at 7½ A.M. and reached Blanes' [*sic*] X Roads at 11 A.M., joining the Div at this place and went into camp. "Big scare all gone."[7]

With the "big scare all gone" and Longstreet's Confederates out of the picture at least temporarily, Colonel Sherman finally had a little time for letter writing. On December 21, he wrote a short note home:

> Blane's Cross Roads, Dec. 21, 1863
>
> Dear Father, Mother, Sisters, Brother:
>   I yesterday received letters from you all. I have not heard from you before for nearly a month, and they came like a sunbeam to me in this out-of-the-way country. I have time to write only a few lines since the express leaves for Chattanooga in a short while. All I can say is we gave Bragg a sound whipping at Missionary Ridge, and the 88th and my brigade on that day did its whole duty. I will say here that my brigade captured the battery which had the guns Lady Breckinridge and Buckner in it, Col. Harker to the contrary notwithstanding.[8] He admits as much. From the battlefield we were sent to the relief of Burnside at Knoxville, making rapid and fatiguing marches to accomplish this object. We are here watching for Longstreet and living off the country. The weather is very cold and the men are only half clad.
>   I am well and hope soon to write you that the war is over for this winter, as we are all worn out with marches and fighting.
>   My love to you all.
>
> Write me, Frank

Overcoats, tents, and shoes were in short supply; many of the soldiers were wearing moccasins cut from their blankets. Finally General Sheridan's wagon train with supplies, including winter clothing, got through, but it was intercepted by Gen. John G. Foster, who had succeeded General Burnside, and the supplies were distributed to all the forces instead of just to Sheridan's men. That left Sheridan's troops not much better off than before, so Sheridan sent for another wagon train.

This time his quartermaster, Capt. Philip Smith, disguised the stores in the wagons with straw, making it appear that the wagons carried only forage and thus enabling the train to pass Foster's inspection. Sheridan later wrote, "On Smith's arrival we lost no time in issuing the clothing, and when it had passed into the hands of the individual soldiers the danger of its appropriation for general distribution, like the preceding invoice, was very remote."[9]

Colonel Sherman's next letter included a copy of the recommendation for his promotion, with the wish that it be kept "as an heirloom for my family."

Blane's X Roads, Dec. 23rd, 1863

Dear Father:

I enclose [for] you a copy of a recommendation made by Major General Sheridan, endorsed by General [Gordon] Granger [now in command of the Fourth Corps], and addressed to General Thomas, urging my promotion to the rank of Brigadier General. To have received from such thorough soldiers and distinguished officers such a testimony of their regard and esteem is in itself a gratification and reward equal to the receiving of the appointment and commission from the President. For I assure you, officers who meet their approbation and come up to their standard of what is required to make a competent soldier and commander at the present time are few and far between, especially those in the volunteer services and not educated at West Point to the profession of arms. I feel that I have done my duty since I entered the army, and if I am promoted it is because I have honestly and worthily earned it by long and tried service. I wish this recommendation kept as an heirloom for my family.[10] You can show it to whom you please, for I desire that my friends who stood by me in times past shall see that their confidence in my ability was not misplaced, and that I received from my commanding generals testimonials which many officers would give a year's service to obtain. General Sheridan told me that General Thomas promised to forward it to Washington and to urge on the President my promotion.

We are out here twenty miles from Knoxville watching Longstreet and supporting Burnside's [actually, now Foster's] army, which was driven back to this point last week. Some think that a battle is inevitable before we can settle down for the winter; others think differently, and I confess I do not know what to think. One thing I do know, I am heartily tired of the campaign in East Tennessee and wish we were back in Chattanooga, where we belong. We have had so far very fine but cold weather since we came into this country, and were we all provided for staying here, it would not seem so irksome to us. We are out of the way for getting news or mail from America, nor have we any facilities for writing or sending letters home. Our army has been worked and fought nearly to death and must rest to recuperate its strength. What we most need we are not likely to get. Love to all; kiss the children for me.

Your son, Frank

In his next letter, Colonel Sherman recapitulated the events of Missionary Ridge and the pursuit of Longstreet:

Blane's X-Roads, Jany 10, 1864

Dear Father:

In spite of the weather and the inadequate supplies my health is good. I have so far passed through the perils of the battlefield and the accidents incident to a soldier's life during active operations without a scratch. In this respect I have been peculiarly fortunate, and after a few more battles if I come out safe I shall consider myself almost bulletproof.

[B. F.] Taylor's description of the Battle of Missionary Ridge,[11] which I received yesterday from Martha, is the most truthful one I have seen and does not do more than is due to the brave officers and men who braved that terrible hill under a storm of iron and lead which I trust it may never be my fortune again to be called upon to lead brave men to encounter. Life was not worth a fig when we started on that journey into the valley of death. But having passed through its dark shadows and gained the crest of that ridge unharmed, it was full of new charms, for had we not been rejuvenated by the ages which had passed over us whilst stumbling forward through its noisome vapors laden with death? Many a brave, true, and noble spirit was left behind to mark the terrible journey. Peace to their ashes. The nation mourns them dead on the field of honor. That night, the 25th of November last, repaid me for all the privations and toil which I have passed through in the service of my country. I cannot describe my feeling. Such elation and exuberance of spirit filled me that I must give them vent, and I joined the men in their shouts of victory. The feeling uppermost in the minds of the men was that Chickamauga had been avenged.

A few hours of delay to reorganize the troops and get a hasty cup of coffee, and we were on the heels of the beaten foe and forced them to take shelter wherever they could find it, abandoning everything that in any way would retard their flight. Two days we followed them and then we were recalled to be placed on the track of Longstreet; without rest or proper rations we commenced the march on Knoxville to relieve Burnside. In seven days it was accomplished. A hundred and forty miles were marched and four rivers crossed over, and the 4th Corps was at Knoxville; Longstreet and his "pups," as his men style themselves, were in full retreat toward the North Carolina mountains.

This feat of an army moving without supplies and gleaning its subsistence from a country already drained of its products will stand as one of the most brilliant on record. And the result, what of that? I wish I could say that it was disastrous to the enemy. Finding that he was not pursued, Longstreet marched leisurely some sixty or eighty miles from Knoxville, and then encamped his "pups" and awaited events. Two days passed, and a tardy pursuit commenced by our forces resulted in their being sent to the right about in double-quick time by the advance of the enemy's cavalry to reconnoiter and see what we (i.e., Burnside's [or Foster's] army) were about. [W. T.] Sherman in the meantime considered the campaign over, and marched his troops back to Chattanooga, and we (the 4th Corps) expected to do the same thing. But no, Longstreet was turning on his pursuers, and we were double-quicked to this place to stay the advance of the destroyer.

Well, we have been here since the 16th of December, and nobody knows where the enemy is. Our condition is anything but enviable. On half rations; no shoes, hats, shirts, socks, pants, or coats; without tents or blankets; the earth frozen six inches deep and covered with snow—that sums up in brief the comforts of the men who were at Chickamauga and Missionary Ridge, and no prospect of relief. Is loyal East Tennessee worth the sacrifice? I say No, and the prayer of every man and officer of the 4th Corps is that we may be ordered back to Chattanooga. I am very well myself, and if we are allowed to go into camp where the men can be made comfortable, I shall apply for a leave to come home. Love to all and write often.

Good-bye, your son, Frank

In his next letter, Colonel Sherman described another frustrating march:

Flat Creek, Tenn., Jany 18th, 1864

Dear Father:

I have just come in off of one of the most fatiguing marches that ever an army has been called upon to perform. On Friday, the 15th, we broke up our old camp at Blain's Cross Roads and took up our line of march for Dandridge on the French Broad River, which we reached on Saturday at noon. Our object was to get forage and subsistence from the country, as we had eaten out the area about us for thirty miles. This movement brought us up close to Longstreet's whole army.

On Saturday afternoon the enemy drove in our cavalry to within musket range of our camp, so I had to move my brigade to keep from being run over, which I did by throwing out a line of skirmishers in front of my line of battle. I ordered a charge made, and away went the boys over our cavalry and drove the Rebs back a mile before we stopped, having to march over open ground into timber, in which the Reb skirmishers were posted, and under artillery fire as well. We had a loss of two wounded; night closed the fight and we went back to camp.

Sunday all was quiet until 3 P.M. when a scattering fire from the pickets told of the advance of the enemy. This continued for an hour, gradually increasing until 4:30, when the fire on the skirmish line had become very rapid, and the sounds of the Rebels and our own men could be distinctly heard. The artillery on both sides opened about this time, and for an hour we had what is called a heavy skirmish fight, which lasted until darkness. It was evident that Longstreet intended to give us battle today if we should stay and accept it. We did not so choose, nor were we prepared to fight a battle. We had gone to get something to eat for our men and animals; we did not have all our forces there, and it would have been folly to fight two or three to one.

The consequence was we were ordered to fall back to Strawberry Plain, and to get away without loss we had to make a night march. We left Dandridge at 8 P.M. and arrived here at 10:30 this morning, having marched twenty-three miles[12] over as bad roads as ever I saw. I am nearly worn out, as are the men. They fell out of ranks through exhaustion in squads of ten, fifteen, and twenty at a time, lying down in fence corners in the mud. When I got into camp I did not have over 300 men of the Brigade who kept up. The men have not had enough to eat for a month and have been exposed to weather so cold as to make ice an inch thick during the night. It is the hardest march that they were ever called upon to perform. The whole move was wrong and should not have been attempted, but Potomac generals run this Department, and in my mind account for the whole thing.

How we are to subsist our troops and keep alive our animals I have no idea. Our men get now from the commissary three-sixteenths of a ration daily of flour, a full ration of fresh meat and half a ration of coffee and sugar. This is sumptuous fare for Uncle Sam's boys, and the old man expects long marches and hard fighting from them, and that, too, in midwinter without sufficient clothing. Don't you think the boys ought to respond to so careful a parent in all of his demands when he is so kind and good?

I am very well with the exception of fatigue. My love to Mother and to all at home, and to Ellen. Kiss the babies for me, and good night.

Your son, Frank

Sheridan shared his subordinate's frustration with this expedition and with General Foster. He wrote of the snow in Strawberry Plains, from which "the thin and scanty clothing of the men offered little protection, and while in bivouac their only shelter was ponchos. . . . there was not a tent in the command."[13]

In his next letter, Sherman told his mother how pleased he was to have received a letter from her:

Kingston, Tenn. Jany 24th, 1864

Dear Mother:

Your letter of the 14th came to hand today and took me completely by surprise and made my heart bound with joy to find you had so far been restored to health as to make the effort of writing me. You will see by the heading of this letter that I am somewhat ubiquitous, since we were ordered into East Tennessee to force it from the incubus of Rebel armies. Well, we have done everything else but accomplish this object. We have marched and frozen, gone naked and dirty, been hungry and fought, and all as yet to no purpose. We were forced to retreat from Dandridge after fighting Longstreet for two days. We fell back on Knoxville, but had nothing for our men to eat, and so we were ordered down here to subsist on the country. I got here yesterday and have not yet had time to get anything in, and so we have nothing but dried beef to live on, which the men call dried on the hoof.

As we fell back the Rebels pursued with their cavalry to within four or five miles of Knoxville, where there was some sharp skirmishing. That is about all that it will amount to, in my opinion. They cannot invest the place for the want of something to eat, as they are also obliged to subsist on the country, and God knows the people of this country are having a hard road to travel. By spring there will not be enough left in the way of corn and meat to feed a sparrow in all Tennessee. How they will manage to make a campaign is beyond my comprehension. We shall see what we shall see. My brigade is busy at work providing and building winter quarters, as we expect to remain here until the spring opens sufficiently for campaigning purposes, which will be three months hence.

You speak of my letter to Martha in which the word "humbug" was frequently used and think I must have had the blues; well, I have had them ever since we have been in this Department. Subsequent events have shown that my fears were correct, and we have for the future the same brilliant strategy before us that we have had in the past with nothing to cheer us on but the military blunders which have consistently characterized the campaigns in East Tennessee. I heard unofficially yesterday that our Corps had been assigned to this Department; I hope not, for there is neither honor, glory, nor success to be gained for the Union cause in it. In fact I am discouraged and disgusted and am half inclined to leave the service if we are to be kept here. We are not half-equipped—no medical stores, no rations, no transportation, no organization.

Old Rosey's boots would do more for the success of our cause than the present head which is trying to lead us. With a general like Rosecrans to command this Department, victory would be organized before we moved out of our camps. But now we are sent out without any definite plan and go wandering over the country objectless and aimless—run into a hornets' nest and get out of it the best way we can, disheartening the men and breaking down all discipline and soldierly qualities. Every soldier wants to feel confidence in his officers that he can't be whipped. When that feeling is gone you have a mob for an army. Well, I will say nothing more on this subject, only that I have no faith.

I sent home to Father the recommend which Generals Sheridan and Granger gave me to General Thomas to be forwarded to Washington. I begin to think there is no promotion for me if such papers will not bring it. I will tell you, Mother, that if the President will not appoint me a brigadier general after those papers reach him, it is my opinion that my country does not need my services any longer as an officer, and I shall offer my resignation and come home to my wife and babies. I will no longer remain in a service that rewards not for merit but for the influence which the recipient may have to dispose of.

I am pleasantly situated here in a Rebel house and have a large and well-furnished parlor to myself. Love to you and to Father, and kiss the babies for me.

Your loving son, Frank

The colonel may have been pleasantly situated, but his mood was anything but pleasant when he wrote his next letter, to his brother-in-law Bill:

Kingston, Tenn., Jan. 29th, 1864

Dear Bill:

I am sorry to say that after all the hardships and exposures of the season (the most inclement known for many years in this region), we have made an utter failure to accomplish what we were sent here to do. Longstreet with his army still occupies a portion of East Tennessee, and we like cravens were forced to relinquish a large tract of country to his minions for want of a head that could or would listen to wise counsel. We, the 4th Corps, the men who assaulted Mission [sic] Ridge, the veterans of the Army of the Cumberland, had to fall back in disgraceful retreat, who knew not before what it was to turn our backs upon an enemy. There is a fearful responsibility resting somewhere which will have to answer for the mismanagement which has characterized every movement of our Army in the Department of the Ohio since the siege of Knoxville was raised.[14]

In his next letter, Colonel Sherman again complained about the lack of mail, but his harshest complaints were directed toward his commanding officer, Gen. John G. Foster, who would be relieved on February 9:[15]

Loudon, Tenn., Feby 6th, 1864

Dear Father:

I have not received any letter from you or home in some time. I hope you are all well and there is no reason why some out of the many of you should not write and let me know what is going on in Chicago. I write so many letters to all of you and get one in return for every half dozen written. It strikes me that I should receive more than I send off.

I have written to Ellen today to come here and join me if possible; if not, to stop in Chattanooga until she can. Lieutenant [James A.] Jackson of my staff who is home on leave will soon return, and I have written Ellen and him to come together. I have also written to Chattanooga for a pass, which I have no doubt will reach her in a day or two after my letter. I wish you to pay the school bills for my children as they come due, and I will remit the amount when I receive my pay. I expected to get a leave as it had been promised me and get home through this month, but that, like so many things promised, has been indefinitely postponed, and I have had to give up my excursion and anticipated visit to you. You can now expect me when I arrive and not before.

After being dragged all over this part of the seat of war and worn it threadbare, we have been allowed finally to settle down in what they call winter quarters. My brigade was first ordered to Kingston, there to remain for the balance of the winter. We were there just a week when a big scare was got up and we were ordered toward Knoxville to repel the enemy, who was (presumably) marching in force on that lonely spot of loyal Tennessee. Whilst on the march it was discovered that the enemy was quietly enjoying himself some forty miles distant in winter quarters, and my order of march was changed to Loudon.

Well, here we are, busy preparing new quarters to abandon, I suppose, for some new point when [another scare] disturbs the slumbers of our vigilant command and opens afresh the wound which has so disabled him [General Foster] that he has to be relieved from active field operations. Every officer and soldier in our Corps will throw up his hat when he is relieved, for I do not know one, from the highest rank to the lowest, who is not disgusted with our movements and has [not] lost all confidence in the present head of the Department of the Ohio. To characterize what has been done as puerile and imbecile is using moderate terms. But the country and the people are gulled and swallow the pill that disability from wounds received in service is the cause of the withdrawal of General Foster from the active command of the U.S. forces in this quarter.[16]

General [John M.] Schofield is to be his successor. I hope that he has common sense; if he has all will yet be well.[17] Any man is better than the present one. We ought to have Old Rosey here; he would soon bring order out of the chaos that surrounds us. Never since I have been in service have I seen troops so badly treated and their wants and needs so little cared for as in this department. I took up a paper this morning and read that the Army of the Potomac is to be supplied with oysters whilst this army is starving on less than half a ration.

I had hoped ere this time to have heard something about my promotion. I have sent you papers such as few colonels receive from their commanding generals, and of which I feel proud, but, as kissing goes by favor, [they] will be of little use to me unless someone with influence takes them and presses my claim in person on the Secretary of War and the President. I have been brigadier with the rank of colonel for a year now and can justly urge my claim. With such testimonials as I have sent you, at the commencement of this war I could have been commissioned major general. Well, so be it, I do not propose to complain, but shall endeavor to perform all of my duties to the best of my ability so long as I wear the livery of my country.

Love to all, your son, Frank

By February 13, the new winter quarters in Loudon had not yet been "abandoned," as Colonel Sherman had expected, although he was almost forced to abandon his own house. He wrote:

Loudon, Tenn. Feby 13th, 1864

Dear Father:

We are very comfortably settled here in winter quarters. If we are allowed to stay here for a month or two we will be in good fighting and marching trim again. My regiments are all in log houses of their own construction, and I have tonight taken possession of one which I had built. I feel almost as if I was at home, so like living does it look.

12 o'clock midnight. After commencing to write this, I felt weary and went to bed and to sleep. How long I had slept I know not; at all events I woke to find my new home on fire, from the fireplace. Fortunately I had a pail of water and succeeded in checking the flames with it until I could get help to put it out. In a few minutes more I should have had trouble getting my few effects from the building, as it is built out of dry pitch pine logs and would burn very fast. Well, this is the last time I have been under fire. I am now sitting up writing and watching to see if I got it all out.

Yesterday the [railroad] cars came through from Chattanooga to London [Loudon] for the first time. We now have rail communication all the way to Chicago, and I expect we shall soon have plenty of rations and can begin to accumulate [supplies] for the coming campaign.

General Sheridan expects to get a leave of absence to visit his home, and before he returns he will visit Chicago. I would be glad to have you to call on him and show him all the courtesy which the good and brave officer is entitled to. You will find him a perfect gentleman and a thorough soldier.

General Foster is gone and [Gen.] Schofield has quietly taken his place, and as yet we have not had any scares under his rule. I think we shall have military movements that will amount to something when we do move.

[Feb.] 14th: This morning I was agreeably surprised by a visit from Adjutant General [Lorenzo] Thomas who is on his way to Knoxville. I liked very much what little I saw of him, a pleasant, affable gentleman, without any of the affectation or stiffness which mark so many of the old officers of the regular army.

I have sent for Ellen to come on here and stay with me whilst we remain at this place. The paymaster is here and will pay to December 31st. It is my opinion that we will not be paid until the first of July next as there will not be funds, because it has taken so much to pay for bounties to "veteran volunteers."

Love to all, your son, Frank

Col. Sherman's diary for that day is as terse as usual.

Feby 14, Sunday. St. Valentine's Day. No valentines came. Cloudy. Gen. [Lorenzo] Thomas called upon me.

He wrote rather petulantly to his wife on Valentine's Day, apparently after having discovered that he would not long be enjoying his new house:

Loudon, Tenn., Feby 14, 1864

My Dear Wife:

I have no idea when this will find you. I write, however, to tell you that Captain McClurey[18] could not get a pass for you at present, because an offensive movement is about to take place. I am discouraged trying to get to you, or of getting you with me, as it seems as if there is to be no rest or anything else allowed us except to go, go, go on some wild goose chase and starve our way through the best we can. We have had three mails and not one letter from you or any of our family. I am going to stop writing home and keep a regular debit and credit account, giving you all line for line and word for word in my answers so as not to be in debt to any of you. I will simply be just and honest on the score of letters.

Two divisions of the 14th Army Corps I understand are under orders to leave Chattanooga today. Their supposed destination is Knoxville. If such is the case we shall soon be on the move again and this time Longstreet will have to leave the state or risk a battle. The weather has been very fine for campaigning, and the roads are dry and hard so that we can move artillery anywhere. God knows I would be glad to have our present unsettled state of affairs brought to some conclusion.

If you cannot get to Chattanooga you had better stay where you are for the present, as you will find it difficult to get through. Again are all my hopes and dreams of having you with me and a short season of peace and quiet dashed to the earth. It seems as if Grant and his generals are all sitting on nettles and cannot remain quiet long enough to get one good day's ration ahead for this army. I hope they have everything needful to make a successful campaign, but I confess I am unable to see it. It is well that I cannot, I suppose. Still I have enough of the soldier about me not to like to see our men sacrificed and exposed to hardships for nothing as has been done heretofore.

Everything is done so differently from what Rosecrans did. No one seems to look after the details as he did and know if the men are properly equipped and supplied. All the attention to the condition of the Army has passed away, and we are ordered here and there, and have to go with such as we have. This way of doing weakens the efficiency of the army and takes from it that esprit de corps which was so prominent in the Army of the Cumberland under Rosecrans.

As to East Tennessee and its people, we are thoroughly disgusted with them. Their patriotism is in their pockets and their supreme selfishness. As to their fighting qualities as soldiers, they are counted amongst the poorest soldiers in our army. This fact grows out of having very poor officers. They need never talk to me again about the close and penurious Yankee from New England; a loyal East Tennesseean can beat them and give them two in the game.

Love to all, and kiss the children for me.

Your loving husband, Frank

On the same day he wrote his mother, still complaining about the lack of letters from home:

Loudon, Tenn. Feby 14th, 1864

Dear Mother:

This is Sunday and St. Valentine's Day. How many happy hearts there will be among you at the reception of the written and printed messages which will be sent in accordance with the time-honored custom on this day. I too am looking for a valentine from home in the shape of the letter which shall bring me tidings of your well-being. Two mails have come to us and not a letter for me. Letters are an event; we look for the mail and examine its contents with great eagerness and anxiety, and great is our disappointment if there is no letter to reward us.

We have been having beautiful weather for nearly a month, so warm we scarcely needed a fire at night, which has made it very pleasant soldiering. We are now in winter quarters after the winter is over. I have built for myself a log house which makes me feel like I am again living like a white man. It is a one story structure, fourteen by twenty feet inside, and it has a floor in it, two doors, and six light windows, and there is a fireplace attached to the gable end. Now, all this is rough and comfortable and is, in fact, a better house than nine-tenths of the people of this country live in. I wish you could drop in on me for an hour or so and see the brightest side of a soldier's life. How long we shall be permitted to stay and enjoy the fruits of our labor is an enigma; I hope until we can get thoroughly rested and the army built up and equipped.

The Rebels are making extraordinary efforts to fill up the ranks of their army so as to be ready to meet us in the spring. Young or old are not spared, but are dragged from their homes and a musket thrust into their hands. Men, women, and children are fleeing north from their homes and seeking protection within our lines. Rebel soldiers desert by the hundreds, many of them offering to enlist in our army. Tales of suffering and woe, of outrages and cruelty, told by these miserable refugees surpass belief and would not be entitled to credence were it not for the fact that they come from all directions and are told substantially alike by refugee and deserter. There is a heavy load of misery and sin which will have to be answered for by the arch-traitor and all of his abettors.

Today it has been trying to rain. I wish it would and raise the rivers which at present are very low and make it difficult to supply the army.

I suppose my wife will be on the way toward Chattanooga and this place long before this will reach you, and my only fear is that we shall be moved from here on some reconnaissance or other duty which will prevent her coming to me.

Love to all, your son, Frank

Mrs. Sherman's train ride from Chicago started on February 21 and did not end until March 4. Two days after her arrival, Colonel Sherman wrote to his mother:

Loudon Tenn, March 6th, 1864

Dear Mother:

Ellen arrived here Friday evening, March 4th, after many adventures and obstacles which she was able to overcome by her perseverance, and took me completely by surprise. How long I shall be able to have her with me [I don't know]. She is as well as could be expected after being twelve days on the way from Chicago. The trunk and contents I received all right; accept my thanks for the goodies therein contained, for they came at an opportune moment, whisky and all I assure you.

Everything is very quiet here at present. Longstreet is *non est,* and our generals are puzzling themselves over his disappearance. He has left forces at Bull's Gap to cover his movements, and a portion of our army is at Morristown watching. My brigade is scattered, and I now have only two reg'ts with me. General Sheridan is absent on leave and will probably visit Chicago before he returns. I wish you could see him.

As soon as our veteran regiments return I expect we will take the field.[19] God *grant* that sufficient ability may guide the councils of those who hold

[our] destinies [so that] before this year shall end this cruel war shall come to an end.[20] There is a probability that this may be accomplished if president-making in the north does not interfere. God speed the right for us. I hope our lives as soldiers battling in a just cause will not be sacrificed to the moves of party power. When we have won back to loyalty our whole people and country it will be time to consider party and not until then. What say you and what says father to that? I know he will say amen.

I received a letter from Mr. Ryder[21] tonight, which was read with great gratification. Tell him we are debarred from all participation in lectures or religious exercises as all our chaplains have left us. You can also say to him that they are no loss. Some of us will, however, live to once more come under the influence of civilized life and our homes. Love to all; kiss the babies for me.

Your loving son, Frank

Colonel Sherman finally was granted a twenty-day leave and left for Chicago on March 14, ten days after his wife had arrived at the end of her marathon train ride. He left her behind, presumably in the house that was twenty by fourteen feet, with two doors and six windows. We do not know why she remained in Tennessee; perhaps he thought that he could travel faster alone and that a round trip to Chicago would exhaust her completely. We also do not know what she thought about spending her husband's three-week leave alone in his quarters, but she was happy to see him upon his return on April 4, as he said in his next letter to his father:

Loudon, Tenn, March [actually April] 5, 1864

Dear Father:

I arrived here last night worn out, having been eight days on the way from Chicago. I found Ellen well and glad to see me back, as she had found it very lonely during my absence. I have no news to write, as I find everything as I had left it. There are rumors of our moving ere long, but I do not believe we shall move for a month yet. The weather here has been very capricious since I have been away. There have been heavy falls of snow and rain; roads are impassable, and the rivers are high. All this is not favorable for movement.

I expect we have lost General Sheridan for good; report says that he is to have command of the Cavalry of the Potomac Army. All regret to lose him from amongst us, although he takes with him the best wishes of every officer and soldier who has served in his command.

Love to all, your son, Frank

The regret was reciprocated. General Sheridan left on March 24, "without taking any formal leave of the troops I had so long commanded. I could not do it; the bond existing between them and me had grown to such depth of attachment that I feared to trust my emotions in any formal parting."[22]

Colonel Sherman probably would have been unhappy with anyone who replaced Sheridan, but he might have been less unhappy with someone from the Army of the Cumberland. Instead, Sheridan's replacement came from the Army of the Potomac,[23] and Sherman's indignation was evident in his next letter:

Cleveland, Tenn., April, 1864

Dear Father:

I arrived here on the 21st [of April]. Here we found a new Division commander in Major General John Newton, who was sent out from the [Army of the] Potomac for that purpose. I cannot say that I am very favorably impressed with him. He is a Virginian and a graduate of West Point. General [Oliver O.] Howard, our Corps commander, is also of the Potomac army and a native of Maine. With him I am very much pleased, as he looks the soldier and a gentleman.

The changes thus made in our Corps and our Division, bringing strangers amongst us, is not to our liking. I do not know as we have any choice in the matter; we certainly have not been consulted as to whether we would prefer our old and loved commanders with whom we have fought and endured to those [of whom] we know naught. We have no right to expect that we should be consulted, and if the good of the service demands these changes we are too good soldiers to complain. Our likes and wishes we cannot help.

We had a sad accident in our Regiment when crossing the Tennessee River at Loudon. Lieutenant [John T. D.] Gibson, commanding Company D, fell from the railroad bridge into the river, a distance of eighty or ninety feet, and was killed. The current was very swift, and swept his body away. Every effort was made to recover it and men were left behind to search for the body, but all to no purpose. Lieutenant Gibson was a worthy officer and leaves a large family in Chicago to mourn his loss. I understand that they are not in very good circumstances, being dependent on his pay to live. I would like something to be done for them. You can find out how they are situated and bring the matter before the Board of Trade [the sponsor of the 88th Illinois] so that they may never come to want. Lieutenant Gibson before entering the service was in business on Lake Street in stoves and tinware.

I have made an application to General Sheridan to take me on his staff. As yet I have not heard from him. The probability is that he cannot do so, if so disposed, as my rank is such as to preclude me from serving with him in that capacity.

I am not feeling very well since my return as I am troubled with the asthma. The little march we made from Loudon here, a distance of fifty-five miles, almost used me up. I fear I shall have to seek detached service where I can be quiet and not exposed to the rigors of a campaign or, failing that, resign and come home, neither of which do I wish to do unless compelled by failing health. If I could get six months of rest it would do me good.

The weather is very warm, and the roads in good condition; everything points to active operations before many days or weeks have passed. Troops are constantly arriving. I also expect as my reward to be sent back to the regiment, this being consequent from the changes. I shall never take command of my regiment again; it is in good hands now with two field officers.

Love to all, your son, Frank

It is not clear just what Frank did expect—certainly not a subordinate position in the 88th Illinois. His comments no doubt reflect his bitterness at his anticipation of being deprived of the command of his brigade.

Ellen was still with her husband at Cleveland and remained there when the army began its spring campaign into Georgia, heading for Atlanta. With Lincoln up for reelection in the fall and the nation tired of the war, the administration badly needed a significant success to head off the antiwar politicians. Capturing Atlanta would provide such a success, so the invasion of North Georgia was crucially important.

10

Invasion of North Georgia: Spring, 1864

The army assembled for the invasion of North Georgia was really three armies. The largest, the Army of the Cumberland under General Thomas, included the IV Corps under General Howard, which included General Newton's division and Colonel Sherman's brigade. The next largest was the Union Army of the Tennessee, under Gen. James B. McPherson; and the smallest was the Army of the Ohio, under Gen. John M. Schofield. Altogether, there were between 100,000 and 125,000 men.

This immense force was under the overall command of Gen. William T. Sherman. Sherman was not only a superb strategist, he was also a master at arranging for his troops to be supplied. He left little to chance, and, with him at the helm, Colonel Sherman's men did not suffer the privations they had endured earlier under Buell, Rosecrans, and Foster.

The Union forces were opposed by from 75,000 to 90,000 men, primarily from the Confederate Army of the Tennessee, which, after the disaster of Missionary Ridge, had retreated, still under Bragg, to Dalton, Georgia. There, finally, Bragg was replaced.

Bragg's successor was Gen. Joseph E. Johnston, a controversial figure before, during, and after the campaign in North Georgia. Historians disagree about Johnston's qualities as a general. Some believe that in North Georgia he engineered a masterful withdrawal of an outmanned army; others think that he was overly cautious and too often backed away from opportunities to strike significant blows against the Union forces.[1] Johnston's defenders make a strong case for him, and from what he said in his May 29 letter to his father, Colonel Sherman seems to have held a favorable view of Johnston's skill as a commander.

Starting early in May, General Sherman moved his troops into Georgia,

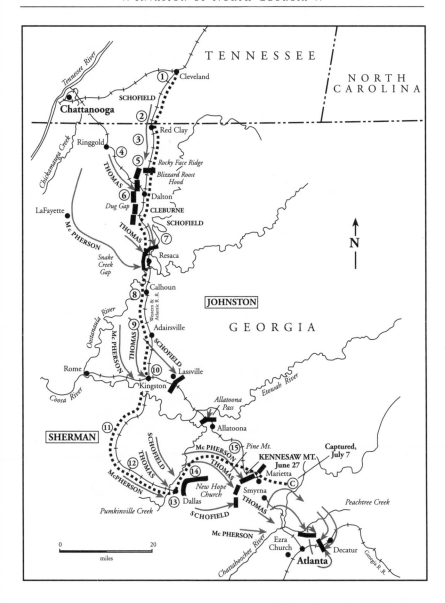

North Georgia Campaign.
Legend: 1. 5/2—Cleveland; 2. 5/3—Red Clay; 3. 5/4—en route; 4. 5/5–6—Catoosa
Springs; 5. 5/7–12—Rocky Face Ridge; 6. 5/13—Dalton;
7. 5/14–15—Resaca; 8. 5/16—Calhoun; 9. 5/17—Adairsville;
10. 5/18—22—Kingston; 11. 5/23; 12. 5/24; 13. 5/25–31; 14. 6/1–4; 15. 6/5–10.

repeatedly attacking or threatening to attack along a line roughly following the Western and Atlantic Railroad line. Outnumbered, Johnston for the most part retreated until, by the end of May, the Union forces were more than halfway to Atlanta. During his retreat, Johnston either had chosen, or had been forced, to engage in a battle at Resaca, as well as a number of smaller but hard-fought engagements. Colonel Sherman participated in several of these latter engagements. He wrote no letters until the end of May. Perhaps he had no time for writing, or maybe the "blues" he complained of on the Knoxville expedition remained with him, as the likelihood of his promotion had diminished with Sheridan's transfer. His diary for the first three weeks in May records his progress from Cleveland, Tennessee, to Kingston, Georgia:

[May] 2d Monday 1864

Everything got ready to move on Dalton from Cleveland.

3d Tuesday

Marched at 12 n., followed on Dalton R.R. Encamped at 6 P.M. at Red Clay. Made 13 miles.

4th Wednesday

Marched at 7 1/2 o'c; made 8 miles and went into line of battle at Murray's house 5 miles E of Ringgold on Chickamauga Creek.

5th Thursday

In camp at Catoosa Springs. No movement and all quiet . . . 12 miles N from Dalton.

May 6th Friday 1864

In camp at Catoosa Springs all day.

7th Saturday

Marched 4 A.M., our Div on left. Firing at T[unnel] Hill 9 A.M. Went into camp at 2 o'c. Slight skirmishing on the right.[2]

8th Sunday

Fight on Rocky Face 10 A.M.[3] Left camp and moved by the left one mile and formed brigade. Moved at 12 n 1/2 mile to left and massed. Camped for the night.

9th Monday

Moved on to crest of Rocky Face ridge; remained here during day. Col Harker's brig'd on right. Heavy skirms. Moved off ridge at 9 o'c back two miles to Gap and camped.

10th Tuesday

6 A.M. rec'd orders to move forw'd ¾ mile. 9 A.M. marched on to Rocky Face; connected on right with Col H[arker], on left with Gen'l Schofield.

May 11th Wednesday 1864

Relieved Gen'l [George D.] Wagner's Brigade 10 o'c on front of Rocky Face. Slight skirmishing all day; no other movements.

12th Thursday

Wagner & Harker withdrawn this A.M.; 1st brigade left to hold the ridge.[4] 11:30 A.M. enemy moving to our left—inf'y, art'y, & cav. 6 P.M., moved back.

13th Friday

Got into Dalton at 8 A.M.; enemy gone. Advanced my line to rebel signal station. Shelled by our own people. 2d Mo. on the advance; marched in pursuit at 12. Made 12 miles and came up with the enemy.

14th Saturday; Battle of Resaca

Broke camp at 7 o'c, moved 3 miles & went into position at 2 o'c. Went into action relieving Harker's Brigade. Loss not heavy. Remained at enemy's works till dark.[5]

15th Sunday; Battle of Resaca

Commenced to be relieved at 9 A.M. by Wagner's brigade. [My] brigade went into reserve. At 11 o'c enemy made demonstration on our front. All quiet till morning.

May 16th Monday 1864

Enemy left his works and fell back this A.M. to Calhoun, seven miles. Harker's brigade in the advance. Skirmishing with the enemy's rear guard.

17 Tuesday

Resumed the march at 6 A.M.; 1st brigade in advance. Skirmished and drove rear guard of rebs back to Adair[sville] where they made a stand. My brig. heavily engaged until night. Loss 167 men.

For Colonel Sherman's brigade, the action on the road from Calhoun to Adairsville was the bloodiest engagement in the North Georgia campaign. As Castel described it, Sherman's brigade, in the van of Howard's Corps, fought a running fight with Gen. Joseph Wheeler's Confederate cavalry, who were covering Johnston's retreat. Wheeler's cavalry built log barricades across the road every half-mile or so, as they made sequential stands. By skirmishing around Wheeler's flanks until he would withdraw, Sherman's troops slowly worked their way down the road until they arrived at the outskirts of Adairsville, where they met artillery and heavy sniper fire. Colonel Sherman rode back to tell Howard that he had "encountered a Rebel division behind substantial earthworks, with cavalry and a battery. Howard doesn't believe it, says that Sherman is only opposing a part of a brigade, and orders him to go forward. Sherman returns, but not only cannot go forward but has a hard time holding his position, and his brigade suffers a large number of unnecessary casualties."[6] Finally Howard saw the shellfire, realized the strength of the enemy, and prepared to attack, but by that time it was almost nightfall, and Howard held off until morning. During the night, however, Johnston decided that his position was not strong enough, and by morning he was gone.[7]

18 Wednesday

Entered Adairsville at 9 A.M.; enemy gone. Halted here until one o'c. Marched 6 miles on [toward] Kingston & halted for the night.

19 Thursday; Battle of Kingston

Marched to Kingston. Enemy supposed to be in force three miles out on the Armstrong farm; whole army put in position. Some firing. Went into camp at 9 P.M.

20 Friday

This A.M. recd orders to camp for the day which we did.

May 21 Saturday 1864

No movement this A.M. of troops. Still in camp. Relieved today from command of brigade by Genl Nat Kimbal.

Although Colonel Sherman apparently led his men effectively in battles at Rocky Ridge, Dalton, Resaca, and Adairsville, he again—for the fourth and last time—lost the command of his brigade, this time to a much more senior officer, Gen. Nathan Kimball.[8] Colonel Sherman became a staff officer, as he states in his diary, and remained a staff officer throughout the rest of his active service:

22 Sunday

Appointed Chief of Staff by Genl Howard comdg 4th A.C. Assumed my duties today. Enemy supposed to be at Alatoona entrenched.

23 Monday

Corps moved at 12 M., Genl Wood in advance. Crossed Etowah Run at [indecipherable]. Moved to Stilesboro and camped 12 midnight. No enemy in our front today.

24 Tuesday

Moved to Burnt Hickory, 20th Corps in advance. No skirmishing. Very dusty and warm. Rained tonight quite hard.

25 Wednesday

Corps moved at 9 AM for Dallas. At 3:30 we crossed Pumpkinville Creek. Genl Hooker engaged the enemy at 5 oc P.M. and drove them back 1½ miles.[9]

May 26 Thursday 1864

Corps put in position on left of the Ackworth Road. Left swing around Genl Wood and crossed Bresson [?] creek & camped for the night.

27 Friday. Battle of Picket[t']s Mill

Genl Wood's Division relieved this A.M. by genl Stanley's div. Genl Wood was formed for column of attack supported by Genl Johnston [Richard

W. Johnson] 14th Corps. [At] 10:55 Genl Wood moved to turn R flank of enemy; heavily engaged for 3 hours. Loss heavy—1500.[10]

28 Saturday

Enemy still in force in our front; heavy fighting at 10 am A.M. Newton's front. Genl McPherson heavily engaged during day on the right.[11]

29 Sunday

This A.M. all quiet along the lines. Sunday night Enemy made demonstrations on Genl Newton's front. The night passed in a series of alarms. No breakfast this A.M.

On this day Sherman wrote his first letter home in almost six weeks:

near Dallas, Ga. May 29th, 1864

Dear Father:

This is the fourth day we have been fighting here. The rebels fight very obstinately and tenaciously, fortifying their position strongly. Notwithstanding we are slowly but surely pressing them, and they are losing as many men as we. The issue is not as yet certain that we shall be able to destroy their army and close the rebellion in the west. So far they have held their positions just long enough for us to get ready to give them the finishing touch, when they pull up and under cover of night retire to some new point. This tactic is the best one they can adopt and works our troops with harassing marches and continual exposure which, if followed up, in time will break us all down.

The weather is very hot and dry, and twenty days' steady fighting and anxiety is enough to test the quality of the best troops in the world—and those we have. Our losses have been tolerably heavy, say ten thousand from all causes since we commenced this campaign, and yet we have not fought any decisive battle. That is yet to come—I hope will soon be over as we all want rest.

I have been relieved from command of my brigade by General Kimball one week ago today, after leading them through three engagements, the last one before Adairsville, where I fought from 6 A.M. until dark, driving [the rebels] before me eight miles from Calhoun to Adairsville, and finally bringing up at three P.M. upon the entire rear guard of the Rebs under the immediate supervision of General Joe Johnston himself.[12] I could get no help, as no one of our general officers would believe there was much force in my front, so I held what ground I had taken and repulsed one charge which the Rebs made. The Brigade fought splendidly that day, my loss being 167 men killed

and wounded. When I was relieved I had lost nearly four hundred men at
Dalton [May 13], Resaca [May 14–16], and Adairsville [May 18].

Colonel Sherman, now a seasoned veteran, was less critical of his superiors
in the North Georgia campaign than he had been in earlier days. Perhaps it was
maturity as an officer; perhaps he respected General Sherman more than the
targets of his earlier criticisms; perhaps he was just too tired and discouraged at
the loss of his command.

At the time, Colonel Sherman did not know that he had had his last command as a line officer. He considered the staff positions he held for the rest of
the war to be inferior to positions of command. Without much enthusiasm,
he described his new job in the latter part of his May 29th letter:

> I am now chief of Corps staff, with General Howard, who is now com-
> manding the Fourth Corps. I felt very much chagrined and hurt to be sent
> back to my Regiment at such a time as this, as no one would know why such
> a thing was done. The reason given me by General Thomas was that I was
> the junior colonel commanding a brigade and therefore must give way to
> general officers. I am under great obligation to General Howard for giving
> me a position on his staff, which is looked upon by many officers in my
> position as being more desirable than the one I had (I don't think so). I may
> resign and come home after this campaign is over; that is my present feel-
> ing. I have been Colonel and played Brigadier to my satisfaction, and unless
> I can be secured in some position that belongs to me, I will not serve any
> longer as a chink to be put in and pulled out at pleasure.
>
> Love to all; kiss the babies for me, your son, Frank

Not only were the Union troops tired from their three weeks of almost continuous action, but also they had outstripped their supply trains. General
Sherman, too, was waiting for reinforcements and for the rebuilding of the
bridge across the Etowah River. So, as usual when things were quiet, Colonel
Sherman's diary entries were brief and fragmentary. On June 7, he wrote to his
mother about the progress of the Union army toward Atlanta:

> Acworth, Ga June 7th, 1864
> Dear Mother:
> Since this campaign commenced we have been almost continually fight-
> ing, although the two armies have not as yet been joined in grand battle
> throughout their whole length and breadth at the same time. The rebs have
> fought entirely upon the defensive, so far falling back from their chosen
> positions as fast as we can find and turn them. The country we are now in is
> densely wooded and broken, with thick undergrowth, which makes it very
> difficult to fight in and determine where to strike.

The enemy left their last position Saturday night after holding us in check in continuous fighting for ten days [in the Dallas and New Hope Church area]. Had they stayed twenty-four hours longer we would have been ordered to assault them along our line, their right flank having been turned. Sunday morning found them gone, and to this writing we do not know whether they have stopped at or near Marietta or crossed the Chattahoochie River six miles north of Atlanta, where they have the last ditch that covers the heart of the Confederacy.

There has been considerable hard fighting up to this time, and the losses on our side have been heavy, but that of the Rebs I believe to be equal to ours. Whilst we have lost nothing in morale, that of the enemy is falling sensibly; in this is our greatest victory so far. The weather is and has been very hot for the last three weeks, and I hope that soon, very soon, this campaign will be closed and the old flag proudly floating from the Rebel heart (Atlanta) which I believe will be before the 4th of July next. Amen.

For myself I have been up to this time well. My regiment has suffered considerably, having lost twenty-five percent of its men in killed and wounded since the first of May. They have fought nobly and bravely in all the actions so far. Near Dallas the 88th was under continuous fire night and day for ten consecutive days without being relieved. Trees three and four inches through were cut off by bullets and fell to the ground in their front. . . . [13]

On June 13, it was his father's turn to hear from Frank.[14] He spoke of his new position as chief of General Howard's staff as

a very honorable and responsible position, one which will be of benefit to me in a military point of view, although I shall not be able to make any reputation which would tend to secure that which I so much desire, i.e., promotion.

The weather has been very bad for the last ten days, and our army is literally mud-bound. Nevertheless we manage to do a little fighting every day to keep up our interest and our patriotism. Whilst I write the heavy boom of cannon and the rattle of musketry tell of war and traitors close at hand . . .

The 88th Illinois boasts now of having a hundred and sixty muskets to take into action, and that is all that is left of the second Board of Trade Regiment.[15] Chicago should be proud of this Regiment that never left the field of battle without orders and then in good order. The men are in splendid spirits and condition, and when the hour of trial comes will give such an account of themselves as will satisfy the country that they have done their full duty. If we fail it will rest on our generals and not on our men.

Ellen is still at Chattanooga and well when I last heard from her. Give my love to the children when you see them. Also to all at home. May this

campaign bring peace to our country and unite those who have been separated beneath the rooftree. I am well. Good-bye.

Write often to your son, Frank.

There are no further letters until June 27. Colonel Sherman wrote in his diary
of the events of the previous two weeks, as Johnston's army continued to fall
back toward Atlanta:

Tuesday, June 14th, 1864

Our lines were moved forward & to the left ½ mile. Opened artillery
at 11 A.M. Rebel Gen'l. [Leonidas] Polk[16] killed on Pine Top. Rebels left
their works on Pine Ridge during the night.

Wednesday, 15th June

Ordered to make assault on Rebels at 2 P.M. [near Lost Mountain],
Gen'l [John] Newton in front, [Gen. David S.] Stanley next, and [Gen.
Thomas J.] Wood next. Advanced at 3 P.M. in column; doubled 5 rebels
out. [Col. Luther P.] Bradley, in com'd of skirmish line, advanced and
drove rebel skirmishers before us and into their works. Loss small. Went
into position at dark, Newton on left and Stanley on right.

Thursday, 16th

Morning: enemy in our front, strongly entrenched. Moved our lines
forward during the day to within 350 yards. Skirmish fire severe.

Friday, 17th of June, 1864

Enemy gone from their works. Pressed forward and engaged their skirmishers very heavily, shoving them back slowly. At dark charged across
open field and effected a lodgement in the timber beyond. 11 o'c P.M. Rebs
charged our lines and at 1 o'c A.M. also; both assaults repulsed. Commenced raining at 3 o'c A.M. very hard. Loss small.

Saturday, 18th June

4 o'c A.M. skirmish line pushed for'd; at 8 o'c charged and drove enemy
from their pits, capturing a few prisoners after hard fighting. At 10:30
Newton's Div. [Colonel Sherman's old cohorts] charged and took enemy's
first line of works and held them. Heavy skirmishing and fighting during the day. Heavy rain.

Sunday, 19th of June, 1864

Enemy left his works and fell back during the night. At 6 A.M. Gen'l. Stanley's Div. ordered in pursuit, Col. [William] Grose's brigade leading. Came up with the enemy at 7 A.M., engaging him sharply and driving him back across Nose Creek. Gen. Stanley's Div. on the right, Gen'l. Newton on the left, Gen'l. Wood in reserve. Night closed the fight. Casualties light. Rained all day.

Monday, 20th of June, 1864.

The morning opened with skirmishing along the lines and kept up til 4 P.M. Gen'l Woods Div. placed in position on the right of Gen'l Stanley relieving Gen'l Williams Div. at 5 o'c A.M. At 4 P.M. made demonstrations along the lines and gained considerable ground on the Rebels. At 6 P.M. Enemy chg'd to regain lost ground & were repulsed by Gen'l. [Walter C.] Whitaker's Brigade, and again at 9 P.M. with heavy loss. Col. [Isaac M.] Kirby's skirmishers were driven in at the same time. Our loss light in Stanley's Div.

Tuesday, June 21st, 1864

Gen. Newton's Division relieved by Gen'l [John H.] King's Div. 14th A.C. and moved to the right to relieve [Gen. John W.] Geary's Div. 20th Army Corps this A.M. At [indecipherable] Stanley and Wood charged a bald hill in their front and made good a lodgement, taking 18 prisoners and fortifying it under a hot Artillery fire. On the right Gen'l. Newton advanced his lines 400 yards and held the ground. Rebels kept up a strong artillery fire, shelling our lines vigorously all day. Loss of the Corps small today. Rainy all day.[17]

Wednesday, June 22d, 1864 [Battle of Kolb's Farm]

Morning opened without rain. Skirmishing brisk along the lines. At 5 P.M. Stanley's Division moved to the right of Corps and relieved [Gen. Daniel] Butterfield's Division, 20th A.C. At 6 P.M. Rebels [of Stevenson's division] assaulted Gen'l. [Alpheus S.] Williams' Division, 20th A.C., [which drove the rebels] back in confusion. Lines advanced during the day.

Thursday, June 23rd, 1864

Light skirmishing during the day until 4 P.M., [then] opened on the Enemy's lines with 40 pieces Artillery for 15 minutes. At the close our skirmish lines advanced and tried the Enemy's works, taking some prisoners. They were found too strong to assault. Our main lines on the right were advanced 300 yards. This closed operations for the day. Our loss considerable.

Friday June 24th 1864

No movements today. All is quiet along the lines.

Saturday June 25th 1864

Army rested today . . . weather very *hot.*

Sunday June 26th 1864

No movement today, rest being the order.

Monday June 27th 1864 [Battle of Kennesaw Mountain]

At 8 o.c. A.M. we attacked the enemy by forming a column; Genl Newton's Div led, supported by Genls Stanley and Wood. Our troops were repulsed after a gallant attempt to carry the works in our front with considerable loss. Gen'l Harker was killed; Lt Col Chandler killed & Col Silas Miller wounded. Our troops came back in good order to our works. No more fighting today.

In a June 27 letter to his father, Colonel Sherman described the Union defeat at Kennesaw Mountain. Until this time, General Sherman's pattern in North Georgia had been to outflank the enemy and force him to withdraw to protect his rear. Apparently Sherman believed that a frontal attack with his superior numbers would succeed at Kennesaw Mountain because it would have the advantage of surprise.[18] The assault failed, however, and, although the Union forces eventually took over the area, the casualties were 2,000 Union men, including Gen. Daniel McCook,[19] and only 450 Confederates. Colonel Sherman described the battle and mourned the loss of Lt. Col. George W. Chandler, his successor as commander of the 88th Illinois Regiment:

Kennesaw Mt., Ga. June 27th, 1864

Dear Father:

This morning at eight o'clock our army assaulted a Rebel works at three different points in front of our lines. Schofield's 23rd Corps attacked on the right; Howard's 4th Corps on the center; and McPherson on the left. I am sorry to say that we did not break through the enemy's lines at any of these points. The battle lasted two hours when we were forced to withdraw; in fact we were handsomely repulsed, and that, too, with severe losses in both officers and men in the 4th Corps. What the losses in the other two Corps are I have no way of knowing.

The 2nd Division [John Newton's, formerly Sheridan's] led the attack for the 4th Corps, and as a consequence suffered severely.[20] Amongst the killed are General C[harles] G. Harker, commanding the 3rd Brigade; Lieutenant Colonel [George W.] Chandler, commanding the 88th Illinois; and many more officers and men. I have had the body of Lieutenant Colonel Chandler embalmed and sent to Chattanooga, there to be put in a burial case and shipped to Chicago by express.

The 88th is met with a loss that is irreparable, and Chicago may well be proud of him who has been taken from us—a true soldier, a gallant officer, and a pure man. He has laid down his life in defending the right against treason and its abettors. Our city has not sent out a better or a more earnest patriot to help restore the laws and regain order throughout our broad and beautiful land. A nation should mourn when such a spirit as his is called from our midst.

Major [George W.] Smith is now in command of the Regiment, which numbers about one hundred and twenty-five muskets, and that is all that is left of the noble 88th, the Second Board of Trade which came out with me as its Colonel in September 1862. It has poured out its blood like water on every battlefield from Perryville to this place. Never has she failed to do her duty, and that duty has always been where bullets fell the thickest. All honor to those men and to her gallant commander who fell on today's fatal field.

I do not wish you to think we are whipped—far from it. We did not succeed in what we undertook, but we have gained materially in ground. Our lines and the enemy's are now not to exceed seventy to a hundred yards apart, and as a consequence sharpshooting is very brisk. We shall probably make another attack upon the enemy tomorrow, which will be crowned with success, although it will cost us dear in valuable officers and soldiers.

We have the worst country to fight in I ever saw. The forest has a dense and complete tangle of undergrowth which fills up the space beneath the large timber. The land is broken into hills, knobs, mountains, valleys, ravines, swamps, etc. When we make an advance you cannot see the length of a regiment, and as a consequence our lines become deranged and often one portion of a brigade will break off and get lost from the other in going three or four hundred yards.

Love to all, your son, Frank

Despite the victory at Kennesaw Mountain, Johnston's position was precarious. Threatened by Sherman's return to his flanking strategy, he again retreated, toward the Chattahoochie River, the last natural obstacle before Atlanta. The Union army followed, through the thick undergrowth that made the going difficult and provided concealment for enemy pickets, as Colonel Sherman was soon to find to his dismay.

11

GUEST OF THE CONFEDERACY: SUMMER, 1864

Colonel Sherman was soon to confirm through his own experience the ease with which contact with friendly forces could be lost in the difficult Georgia terrain. The letter of June 27 is the last for some time from Colonel Sherman, but entries in his diary continue his story:

Thursday, June 30th, 1864

No movement today and no skirmishing on the picket lines, our men and the Rebs having made a compact not to fire unless an advance is ordered.

Friday, July 1st, 1864

Everything quiet along the lines until evening when our batteries opened for ½ an hour with feeble response from the Johnnies.

Saturday, July 2nd, 1864

Nothing doing today. Some demonstration with artillery.

Sunday, July 3rd, 1864

Enemy left his trenches last night and fell back four miles below Marietta towards Atalanta [*sic*]; a large number of prisoners taken during the day. Enemy in position at Neil Dow with works prepared. Slight skirmishing towards night. Gen'l Stanley in advance today.

Monday, July 4th, 1864

The day commenced with artillery and picket firing. At 11 o'c A.M. Gen'l Stanley charged his skirmishers and took rebel skirmish pits, moving over open ground. Newton and Wood did the same. Nearly two hours' hard fighting; loss less than 100.

Tuesday, July 5th, 1864

Enemy left his works during the night and fell back toward the Chattahoochie River, where they had very strong works evidently prepared. 4th Corps, Gen'l [Charles R.] Woods' Div leading, took the pursuit at 7:00 o'c A.M., forcing the enemy across the Chattahoochie River at 12 N. Went into camp at Case's Ford[1] with Atalanta [*sic*] in plain sight from Signal Hill.

Wednesday, July 6th, 1864

Morning opened with artillery fire and reconnoitering to find a place to lay pontoon bridge. Weather very hot and dry.

If November 25, 1863, at Missionary Ridge was the high point of Colonel Sherman's career, certainly July 7, 1864, was the low point. His diary succinctly records the unhappy event:

Thursday, July 7th, 1864

Captured this A.M. on General [John] Adams' front, C.S.A., and put in confinement in Atalanta in an enclosure of half an acre with a dirty barrack building as a lodging place. Was courteously treated by Confederate officers with whom I came in contact. I found five officers and sixty men confined here as prisoners of war.

The Confederate soldiers who captured Colonel Sherman thought that they had General William T. Sherman, and whisked him off to Gen. Joseph E. Johnston's headquarters, where their captive's true identity was quickly established—amid, one may assume, considerable disappointment. General Howard wrote in his autobiography that Colonel Sherman

suddenly came upon the Confederate skirmish line and was captured. He could hardly realize where he was when he saw the rifles aimed at him, and heard a clear-cut command to surrender. As his name was Sherman the rumor ran through the Confederate army that the terrible "Tecumseh" had been captured.

Colonel Sherman, an active, intelligent, and healthy man, full of energy, had aided me greatly during this trying campaign. No officer could have been more missed or regretted at our headquarters than he. Our picket line was completed, but this did not relieve us from the chagrin caused by the loss which slight care might have prevented.[2]

General W. T. Sherman wrote in his memoirs that "[b]etween Howard's Corps at Paice's [*sic*] Ferry and the rest of Thomas's army . . . was a space concealed by dense woods, in crossing which I came near riding into a detachment of the enemy's cavalry; and later in the same day Colonel Frank Sherman, of Chicago, then on General Howard's staff, did actually ride straight into the enemy's camp, supposing that our lines were continuous. He was carried to Atlanta, and for some time the enemy supposed they were in possession of the commander-in-chief of the opposing army."[3]

Colonel Sherman did not appreciate the Confederate cuisine, as he indicated in the next day's diary entry:

Friday, July 8th, 1864

The rations furnished are insufficient and of poor quality, consisting of corn meal, a little fresh beef, less salt, with no cooking utensils.[4] Weather very hot. Cannonading plainly heard this evening at the front. Citizens are leaving.

Saturday, July 9th, 1864

Nothing unusual today. Sent letter to Mrs. S. by Major [Henry A.] Rogers of 9th Tenne[ssee], C.S.A. Rec'd orders to leave for Macon in the morning. No chance to escape.

July 10th, 1864

Left Atlanta this A.M. for Macon. Arrived at 1 o'c and ushered into camp of Federal officers as prisoners of war.[5] Found over fifteen hundred here, mostly from the Potomac army. But few officers rec'd from Sherman's army at this point.

Monday, 11th, 1864

Was placed in command of the camp being the senior officer present. Day hot. Very monotonous. No faith to be placed in Rebs.

Colonel Sherman was back in command, but hardly the one he had been looking for. On July 11, Richard Realf, the adjutant of the 88th Illinois, wrote to Mrs. Sherman:[6]

Dear Mrs. Sherman:

I am sure that amid your sorrow at the capture of your husband you will be glad to learn this intelligence which I today on the march received from a most trustworthy source and which I hasten to convey to you. One of General Howard's scouts returned yesterday from the enemy's lines where he saw and recognized Colonel Sherman, who it appears fell into the hands of a Rebel Brigadier, name not known, with whom in other days he had been acquainted. This general treated him very courteously, allowing him the limits of the town and making him as comfortable as a prisoner could possibly be. No doubt he will be removed from Atlanta, but I trust the influence of his friend will secure him exemption from a great many inconveniences and privations. It is midnight and we march early in the morning. You will, therefore, I know excuse the hastiness of this note.

Believe me to be, most sincerely yours,
Richard Realf

The adjutant also wrote to Colonel Sherman's father:

The manner of [Colonel Sherman's] capture was after this wise. The 4th Corps at that time constituted the left of the army, the 14th Corps connecting with our right. The left division of that Corps received orders to gain ground to the right, which movement, of course, broke the continuity of our line. General [Absalom] Baird, commanding the division to which I have alluded, did not, it seems, notify General Howard of the withdrawal of his pickets, so that a gap between the pickets of the two corps necessarily intervened. The next day Colonel Sherman was sent out to extend our picket line to the right, thus filling up the interval, and it was while on the line of this gap that he was surprised and taken prisoner, together with his orderly.

I am glad to be able to state that he fell into the hands of a certain General Nelson of the Confederate Services,[7] with whom Colonel Sherman had formerly been acquainted. This general treated him very well, restoring his pistol and making him as comfortable as a man deprived of liberty could possibly be made. I do not suppose he will remain long in Atlanta, because we Yankees are going down there soon, but I trust that wherever they remove him the influence of his friend will be of use and benefit to him in mitigating the discomforts of prison life . . .

Be good enough to acquaint Mrs. Sherman with the contents of this letter and give her my kindest regards, as well as my sincere condolence with her in her sorrow and grief over the capture of her husband. I am so much indebted to her for so many hours of social intercourse, and to the Colonel for so many evidences of esteem and friendship, that I have the right to sympathize with both in their present misfortunes.

For yourself and the Colonel's mother accept also my sympathy in your loss which is, however, only temporary, for I trust that before long we shall have driven this iniquitous rebellion to the wall, releasing not only your dear son, but the sons and brothers of ten thousand desolate homes that are silent for lack of the dear voices that are hushed in captivity.

Sincerely, Richard Realf

The picture of Ellen Sherman that emerges from Colonel Sherman's letters is of a relatively passive, compliant wife who "made no waves." This impression is contradicted, however, by her vigorous and effective efforts on the colonel's behalf once he was a prisoner. In addition to many letters she wrote attempting to promote his exchange and several interviews with officials in Chicago, she went to Washington to interview Secretary of War Stanton and possibly President Lincoln as well.[8] On July 11, four days after her husband's capture, Mrs. Sherman wrote to her father-in-law, presumably from Chattanooga, about the plans she was already making to secure her husband's release:

I suppose you received the telegram from me notifying you that Frank is a prisoner of war. I know nothing more than the telegram stated, that he was captured on the 7th with his orderly while on reconnaissance. I have telegraphed to General Howard to learn if possible if he was wounded when taken, but have received no answer yet. I shall write to him today and remain here a few days for his answer.

I am very anxious to get home now, as I shall proceed at once to have a special exchange effected for him if it is possible. I have sent a letter to the front to be sent out to Frank by the first flag of truce with the faint hope of its reaching him. I wish you would see Mr. Arnold.[9] He can tell you what steps will be necessary to be taken to effect this exchange. I think if we persevere we can accomplish it without much delay.

Prisoner exchanges had been fairly frequent during the first part of the war, but the procedures broke down somewhat when the two sides differed about exchanging black soldiers. Although Grant opposed exchanges, since the Confederacy was short of troops and he did not want to do anything to strengthen the rebel army, many exchanges were carried out, usually with the help of politicians. Nevertheless, in attempting to arrange the colonel's exchange, Mrs. Sherman had a formidable task ahead.

In the meanwhile, Frank was not enjoying his captivity. More from the diary:

Tuesday, 12th July, 1864

Bo't of Rebs 1 pail, $12.50; plate, $5.75; knife & fork, $8.50; 1 yd muslin, $5.75; soap, $9.50; toothbrush, $5.00/ $47.50. Roll call & counting of the prisoners at 8 o'c A.M. Messing with Capts [Henry] Hescock & [Benjamin F.] Campbell of 36th Ill. This camp guarded by Ga militia.

Wednesday, July 13th, 1864

Rec'd one tin cup and 3 ears of corn, $5.00. The life here is becoming intolerable, shut up as we are amongst so many and our movements circumscribed. All sorts of reports about 'exchange' and the movements of our army come to us of the most absurd character. Weather very hot. Tobacco, $1.25.

Thursday, July 14th, 1864

Gave order for $53.25 to settle sutler's bill of sundries to date. Rumors that this camp will be moved to another point farther south. Bo't of sutler 1½ yds of toweling 9.75—common bagging. Dixie is but a shell.

Friday, July 15th, 1864.

Bo't 1 pt molasses $3.00. Same today as yesterday. In afternoon had a fine shower. Many rumors afloat about Grant & Sherman & big raid by Early into Maryland and on Washington

Saturday, July 16th, 1864

Monotony! Monotony! Rations issued today per man to last five days consist of about one lb of meat, 5 pts meal, 3 table spoons of salt, ½ pt molasses, 90 to 120 beans, rice, and vinegar. Weather very hot.

Sunday, July 17th, 1864

Change of prison commander today, Col [George C.] Gibbs relieved by Lieut [Samuel B.] Davis, C.S.A.[10] Have a severe cold. Considerable trouble about making good the count of prisoners.

Monday, July 18th, 1864

Reb authorities found tunnel this A.M. at roll call and filled it up.[11] Report of Art'y heard yesterday to the north of us.

Tuesday, July 19th, 1864

Tobacco 6.50, salt 4.00, jug 5.00, 3 qts molasses 18.00, onions 5.00 / 38.50. Rumors of raid by Fed Cav on Montgomery, Columbus, & Andersonville where our prisoners of war are confined. Weather extremely hot. Some excitement in Macon.

Wednesday, July 20th, 1864

No papers allowed in camp today. Ordered that only two Confed for one Fed dollar be allowed. Also reported Grant dead. What the news is we know not.

Thursday, July 21st, 1864

Death of Gen'l Grant a canard. Reports of a raid by our cav'y on Columbus etc. was confirmed today, also that [W. T.] Sherman & Hood have been fighting. Results not known to us. We believe Rebs were whipped.

Friday, July 22nd, 1864

This A.M. 24 officers from Army Potomac rec'd as prisoners of war, Col [Samuel J.] Crook[s] 22nd NY amongst them.

Saturday, July 23rd, 1864

Battle reported to have been fought yesterday between Sherman & Hood. Rebel accounts say Sherman was whipped with loss of 22 cannon and number of prisoners, that Gen'ls [James B.] McPherson, Giles Smith, and [John B.] Hood were killed.[12] Not believed here in camp. Rumor that Atlanta had fallen.

Sunday, July 24th, 1864

Very severe cold with asthma. Weather very cold, especially at night. Rebs jubilant over "Hood's victory."

Monday, July 25th, 1864

Last night very cold and uncomfortable. Asthma growing upon me. Nothing new today.

Tuesday, July 26th, 1864

Rec'd orders to be ready to go to Charleston, S.C., tomorrow night. 600 officers go at the same time on the same train. Weather cool.

Wednesday, July 27th, 1864

This A.M. warm and cloudy with disposition to rain. Have orders to move to Charleston today at 4 P.M. Rebs evidently fearful of a rescue by our raiders.[13]

Colonel Sherman wrote a brief autobiographical sketch after the war, in which he said of his captivity at Macon:

The stockade, which enclosed about two and a half acres of ground, had an old building inside it which was the only shelter furnished by the rebel authorities [for 1600 Union officers],[14] except a few shanties erected by the prisoners out of refuse lumber graciously permitted the d——d Yankees, without proper shelter from the climate, no blankets, poor water, insufficient food and no chance for bathing and cleanliness . . .

The rations issued to the prisoners, during the stay I made at this delectable resort as a guest of the Confederacy, consisted for each person of one quart of cornmeal, unbolted; one pint of sorghum molasses, in a state of fermentation; four ounces of bacon with bone, and one tablespoon of salt to last three days. For cooking a group of twenty men was allowed a Dutch oven ten inches in diameter, three inches deep. Twenty pounds of wood were provided for this purpose—all things considered we were not a happy family.

The above comments about the Macon prison were deleted from the rest of Colonel Sherman's autobiographical sketch after he died in 1905 when it was quoted in the Loyal Legion's memorial to him, with the following justification: "Inasmuch as our present beloved Commander-in-Chief of the Army and Navy [President Theodore Roosevelt] boasts of being of the half blood with our then enemies,[15] and because of the latter's good behavior and loyal citizenship for the past forty years, your committee has omitted the harrowing experiences of [Francis T.] Sherman."[16]

After twelve hours' delay, Colonel Sherman was transferred with most of his fellow prisoners to Charleston. His diary describes an interrupted trip:

Thursday, July 28th, 1864

Left Macon at 4 A.M. for Charleston. 50 officers and 2 sentinels put in common boxcar. Weather intolerably hot. Arrived at Savannah junction at 5 P.M. and changed cars at 6 P.M. On the move again. At one A.M. jumped from cars and escaped with Col. [Henry M.] Hoyt, 52nd Ohio;[17] Lt Col [Thomas J.] Thorpe, 12th [probably 19th] NY Cav; & Major [David] Vickers, 4th NJ Cav.

Friday, July 29th, 1864

Traveled about all night and made poor progress. At daylight camped in a swamp near R.R. for the day. Started at 6:30 P.M. to find the coast. Traveled due south until near 12 o'c when we were caught by means of hounds by Capt. Curry of the slave catchers when within five miles of the coast (near the Edisto River). Were well treated and marched back to Adams' Run on Charleston & Savannah R.R. and held under guard.

Escapes from Confederate prisons were frequent. It was much more difficult to get back to the Union lines than to escape, however, and most escapees were captured, often with the aid of bloodhounds. By the end of the war, the Confederates, not wanting to share their scanty provisions with prisoners, became less effective as guards and permitted more escapes.

Saturday, July 30th, 1864

At 12 o'c N. today were placed on the cars and sent to Charleston, the birthplace of rebellion. Arrived at 2 o'c P.M. and put into Charleston City Prison. Officers in charge of prisoners very courteous. Tents were issued for our comfort.

Sunday, July 31st, 1864

During night mosquitoes very troublesome. Slept very well being nearly worn out from fatigue consequent upon my attempt to escape. Firing can be distinctly heard from our batteries as they batter away at [Fort] Sumpter [sic]. Weather very hot. Prospect of being moved today to more comfortable quarters. 87 officers escaped from the cars on the trip from Macon to this city. 33 of them have been recaptured to this date and bro't here.[18]

Monday, Aug'st 1st, 1864

The 50 officers sent into Charleston to be placed under fire were yesterday exchanged and start home tomorrow A.M.[19] A full list of names was yesterday made out of the prisoners of war held at this point. Wrote home yesterday for the first time since my capture.[20]

Tuesday, Aug'st 2nd, 1864

Gen'l Stonewall [Stoneman] reported captured today with 500 men. Several of the exchanged officers called upon us this evening and left sundry articles among us. They leave in the morning for Hilton Head. No other news.

Wednesday, Aug'st 3rd, 1864

Full of promises and but little execution of them are the Rebel authorities. Shells fell into this city during the day and night quite rapidly and within a few hundred yards of our present place of confinement.

Thursday, Aug'st 4th, 1864

Not moved today from this inferno. Am very unwell today; feel an attack of billious fever coming on. [Major] Gen'l [Edward] Johnson, Reb, looked in upon the prisoners (Yanks) today. He is just exchanged.

Friday, Aug'st 5th, 1864

Sent protest today to [Major] Gen'l [Samuel] Jones, com'ding C.S. forces at Charleston, against keeping us in the Charleston jail yard amongst felons as no proper place for prisoners of war.

Despite this protest, Colonel Sherman stated in his autobiographical sketch that "the Rebel authorities treated prisoners of war confined at Charleston with more consideration and humanity than was ministered in any other prison where it was my misfortune to be confined."[21]
To return to the diary:

Saturday, Aug'st 6th

Health of the prisoners becoming very bad from our confined and exposed condition. I learn that we are not to be moved to better quarters because of bad treatment of C.S. officers by Gen'l [probably John Gray] Foster as reported by them whilst off Charleston. Any excuse is sufficient for Rebels to be barbarous.

Sunday, Aug'st 7th, 1864

Retaliation upon us is the order of the day by the Rebs for the alleged bad treatment of their officers by Gen'l Foster. Rations issued today are

1½ oz of lard, ½ oz salt, and one loaf bread. No sign of moving to better quarters as promised.

Monday, August 8th, 1864

Rations sent in to be issued today: rice, lard, & salt, all so poor as to be unfit for use. P.M. sent a protest to Capt [William J.] Gayler. Capt Raymond, inspector of prisons, said we would be moved today.

Tuesday, Aug'st 9th

Nothing new today, nor were we moved. Hot and sultry.

Wednesday, Aug'st 10th, 1864

News today of the fall of Fts Gaines and Powell in Mobile Bay. At one o'c we were moved to new quarters in the workhouse, which are far preferable to Charleston Jail.[22] 400 in all to be thus moved. Weather very hot.

Roper Hospital, Charleston, S.C. Courtesy of Library of Congress.

Thursday, Aug'st 11th, 1864

No movement of prisoners from the other jail today. Rumors that "we all" are to be exchanged soon.

Aug'st 12th, 1864

Rebels act very singular in regard to their prisoners. No wood or cooking utensils are furnished us.

Saturday, Aug'st 13th, 1864

At daylight were moved to the Roper Hospital building to make room for 300 Federal officers from Macon, Ga, Gen'l [George] Stoneman being amongst their number. Weather very warm and produces a lassitude and relaxation of the system.

Sunday Aug'st 14th, 1864

2 oz of bacon, ½ oz of salt, pint of meal as ration. This afternoon Col [Henry M.] Hoyt, Capt [Austin] Pendergrast USN, and a number of others were notified that they would be exchanged on the 15th.

Monday Aug'st 15th, 1864

Same ration as yesterday. Were placed on our parole today not to leave certain limits. 6 officers exchanged.

Tuesday Aug 16th, 1864

Nothing new today. Weather warm and it is very dusty. The fire from our bat'ys bright.

Wednesday Aug 17, 1864

Same as yesterday. Officers disposed to try and keep clean in person and quarters.[23]

Thursday Aug 18th, 1864

One officer was fractious, but came down. Very hot day.

Friday 19th, 1864

Nothing new or important today.

Saturday, Aug'st 20th, 1864

Water gave out today. New cistern opened in medical college building. Officers stole blankets, etc.

Sunday, Aug'st 21st, 1864

Rainy today, which is very acceptable. Maj D[avid] Vickers, 4th NJ Inf'y, caught stealing blankets and sent to Charleston Jail.

Monday, 22nd Aug'st

Weather very fine today. Great indignation amongst officers against Major Vickers.[24] No exchange news.

Tuesday, 23rd, 1864

Our people commenced shelling the city again today. Weather very warm. Symptoms of sickness amongst officers.

Wednesday, Aug'st 24th, 1864

Heavy shower of rain with wind today. Poor rations of rice issued us. Heavy cannonading tonight, supposed to be at blockade runner.

Thursday, Aug'st 25th, 1864

Nothing of importance today. Our bat'ys shell the city with fuse shells entirely.

Friday Aug'st 26th, 1864

Same as yesterday

Saturday, Aug'st 27th, 1864

Today 2d anniv'y of 88th Ill. This P.M. a violent wind & rain storm.

Sunday, August 28th, 1864

A bright beautiful day. At 3:30 P.M. piece of shell fell into a part of the quarters occupied by our officers. No one hurt. Shelling very lively for the past week. Med officers to be exchanged this week.

Monday, Aug'st 29th, 1864

Weather fine. Major [Francis] Pruyn paroled and goes north for an equivalent this A.M. Report that Grant & Sherman falling back.

Tuesday, Aug'st 30th, 1864

No truth about Grant & Sherman. Weather very hot & sultry. Today piece of shell killed Negro woman. We are guarded by militia.

Wednesday, Aug'st 31st, 1864

Today closes the summer months. Have been two months a prisoner of war. Our life is monotonous. The officers are demoralized and apparently all self-respect has left them, judging of their actions. The shelling of the city is kept up with vigor. This evening the weather changed & became very cool. I have the asthma and a feeling of debility.

Thursday Sept. 1st, 1864

Cool and delightful day. Rumors of exchange. That is all.

Friday, 2d Sept, 1864

Learned that 600 rebel officers [are] at Hilton Head. Exchange stock very active. In the evening piece of shell fell into the yard; no one hurt.

Saturday, 3d Sept, 1864

This A.M. several officers were taken out to be exchanged on flag of truce boat. 4 officers were taken through; the rest were returned. Our hopes for an immediate exchange are dashed. Weather cool. Asthma on me.

Sunday, Sept 4th, 1864

City shelled severely today. Rebs refused to allow divine service to be held at the hospital.[25] Weather comfortable.

Monday, Sept 5th, 1864

Very warm today. Money was rec'd from Richmond for our officers. Reported change in prison command.

Tuesday, 6th Sept. 1864

Heavy rain last night. Rec'd call from Col [Henry D.] Clayton of Jno Morgan's com'd with his sister. Very hot and close.

Wednesday 7th Sept, 1864

Two months this A.M since my capture. Two years ordinarily would not seem so long. Weather cool and squally. Sisters of Mercy came in and bro't peaches & grapes.[26]

Thursday 8th Sept, 1864

Clear weather but cool. No news of import this day. Rebs very despondent over Atlanta.

Friday 9th Sept, 1864

Learned yesterday that there is a strong conservative party growing up here & many are shaping their course for the advent of Yanks. City shelled as usual.

Saturday 10th Sept, 1864

Clear and cool. The Governor's proclam. of S.C. called out all patriotic citizens of Charleston as the Grand Militia to defend the State and die in the last ditch. Special exchanges are made.

Sunday, 11th Sept, 1864

Very hot. No incident worthy of note.

Monday, 12th Sept, 1864

Hot. The fall of Atlanta & peace party of the North occupy the Southrons [sic].

Tuesday, 13th Sept, 1864

Yesterday some 7,500 of our men from Andersonville were bro't here and confined in the race course for safekeeping. No news. Am unwell with severe cold.

Wednesday, 14th Sept, 1864

Very hot. A few cases of yellow fever reported in the city.

Thursday, 15th Sept, 1864

The weather very hot and dry. Shelling the city not so lively for three days.

Friday, 16th Sept, 1864

Rec'd letter from home today, the first since my capture, dated Sept 1st. Talk of moving us back a mile and out of fire.

Saturday, 17th Sept, 1864

Large fire today one block from our pris. Whilst it was burning shell was thrown very lively, bursting near and over the fire. One piece of shell tore through roof of pris and into room, grazing one man [Lt. Morris C. Foot] slightly.

Sunday, 18th Sept, 1864

Another fire this A.M. Dull, very dull and tiresome this life.

Monday, Sept 19th, 1864

An incident pleasant and unexpected occurred today. Mr. J. T. Welsman of Charleston gave me $2000 to be loaned to the officers asking only a due bill for same payable when convenient.[27]

Tuesday, Sept 20th, 1864

Anniversary of Chickamauga. Positive information on exchange of naval officers. Weather cloudy and sultry. Yellow fever in the city and spreading.[28]

Wednesday, Sept 21st, 1864

Rec'd a letter from my dear wife dated the 10th of July. Also learned that my prospects for exchange are good. Weather very hot.

Thursday, Sept 22d, 1864

Good news. Was informed that I was exchanged. Wrote father today. Very hot.

Colonel Sherman's hopes to be back in the Union were not to be realized for another two weeks. The clipped and terse style of the diary suggests his frustration but doubtless does not begin to reveal the extent of his feelings about the delays.

Friday, Sept 23d, 1864

Flag of truce today. Captains [David B.] McKibbin and [J. H.] Smith went out on parole for exchange. Was informed by Captain Gayer [William J. Gayler], Provost Marshal, that I was exchanged and would leave in the morning.

Saturday, Sept 24th, '64

Did not get away this A.M. A large mail and many boxes came in by flag of truce yesterday. Weather extremely hot. Capts. [Benjamin] Campbell and [Henry] Hescock, captured at Chickamauga, will be exchanged. Special order for me to go to Richmond. Decided to go that way and let Colonel [Milton] Montgomery 25th Wis. go to Sherman's army via Macon.[29]

Sunday, Sept 25th, 1864

58 officers of Sherman's army were taken out from amongst us this A.M. and started for Georgia to be exchanged. Weather very cool. I expect to be sent via Richmond today for exchange.

Monday, Sept 26th, '64

Left Roper Hospital at 5 o'c A.M. and went to Columbia depot. Train left Charleston at 6 o'c A.M. Changed cars at Branchville; country level and swampy with heavy pine timber. Arrived at Columbia 7 P.M. Changed cars for Charlottesville.[30] Weather clear and cool; trouble with the asthma.

Tuesday, Sept 27th, 1864

Arrived Charlottesville 7 A.M. Ch'ged cars for Greensboro, arrived at 2 P.M. Changed cars again for Danville; arrived at 6 o'c P.M. Changed cars again for Richmond. Weather cool. Cars and rolling stock poor.

Wednesday, 28th Sept, 1864

Arrived at Richmond 10 o'c A.M. Went to com[mander] of exchange, Colonel Oldild [*sic*].[31] Was informed that my equivalent had come through; was placed in Libby [prison]; ration pint of soup, beans, and ¼ loaf of bread.

Thursday, Sept 29th, 1864

Breakfast ration at Libby: 8 oz bread and 4 oz of fresh boiled beef without salt. Two meals pr day issued to the Federal officers. This is called treating prisoners of war properly. Great excitement in the city of Richmond today, as troops passed out toward Deep Bottom or Drury's [Drewry's] Bluff. Alarms & bells were rung, and the Minute Men turned out. Citizens with their baggage coming into town. Can see shells bursting about 5 miles distant. All workshops closed, and the men sent to front.

Friday, Sept 30th, 1864

Firing of cannon distinctly heard today & with great rapidity. The Yanks evidently are trying to get into Richmond. Our officers captured yesterday and bro't here say that they (the Yanks) took one or more lines of works and a fort with 13 guns. In the prison all is excitement at the prospect of release. Weather rainy.

Saturday, Oct 1st, 1864

Rainy during the morning. About 11 o'c A.M. cannonading could be distinctly heard at different points around the city. Apparently most intense excitement prevailed towards night amongst the citizens. After dark campfires could be seen all around, supposed to be Yanks.

Sunday, Oct 2d, 1864

At 2½ o'c A.M. the officers were taken from Libby and sent away south. The city is quiet today and myself and Lieutenant Wakeman, 2d N.Y.

Art'y, are the only officers left in prison. A long, lonely, and dreary day. I hope the truce boat will be up tomorrow.

Monday, Oct 3d

Fifty-eight officers captured at Petersburg on Saturday last was [sic] bro't in today and a large number of enlisted men. Everything seems to be quiet all around Richmond.

Tuesday, Oct 4th, 1864

This A.M. at 3 o'c 58 naval officers were bro't to Libby from Charleston for exchange. No news of a truce boat.

Wednesday, Oct 5th, 1864

Truce boat came up last night with a large number of Rebel wounded. It will be here some two or three days. Have not been notified myself as yet, although exchanged.

Thursday, Oct 6th, 1864

No information given me today that I would be taken off on this truce boat, which goes back [to Union held territory] tomorrow. Cloudy and cool.

Friday, Oct 7th, 1864

Three months this A.M. since I was captured. At 9 o'c A.M. was ordered out of Libby to go on truce boat for exchange. At 2 o'c P.M. was once more under the Stars and Stripes on board hospital steamer *George Leary.* Sundry drinks were taken by released officers. 600 sick and wounded men were bro't down with a no. of officers, Col DeSand and Lt Col [Francis A.] Walker, 2d Corps,[32] amongst the prisoners. Our truce boat stops at Aiken Landing on James River. Weather warm.

Colonel Sherman was finally free, but it took him almost a week to get home after still more frustrations, such as failing to see Secretary Stanton and taking the wrong train.

Saturday, Oct 8th, 1864

Left Aikens Landing this A.M. at 8:00 for Annapolis. Arrived at Bermuda 100s at 10 o'c at Fortress Monroe. Very cold and windy.

Sunday, Oct 9th

Arrived at Annapolis this A.M. & reported to Col [Adrian R.] Root, com'dg Parole Camp who gave us orders to proceed to Wash[ington].

Monday, Oct 10th, 1864

Left Annapolis at 6 A.M. Arrived at Washington 9 A.M. and reported to Col [William] Hoffman, com'g of prisoners. Went through all the offices at Washington and left for home at 8:30 P.M. via B. & O. RR. Could not see the Sec'y of War. Weather very cold.

Tuesday, Oct 11th, 1864

Arrived at Belle Aire at 5.30 P.M. Took wrong train and run out to Belmont on Central Ohio Ry. Returned to Bellair at 10 o'c and started right. Stopped at Wellsville until 3:20 A.M. when train took me to Alliance.

Wednesday Oct 12th, 1864

Regular train on P., Ft. W., and C. had left Alliance. Took way (?) train to Crestline and arrived at 12 o'c M. Remained here until 10 o'c P.M. Weather very raw and cold.

Thursday, Oct 13th, 1864

Train delayed during the night, making us two or three hours behind. Have met with a series of delays since I left Washington. Arrived at Chicago at 12 noon today & *home.*

There is no record of the celebration of Colonel Sherman's homecoming; presumably more "sundry drinks were taken," and Ellen Sherman's efforts to secure her husband's exchange were duly appreciated.

Two days later, the Chicago Tribune reported the colonel's "Release from Southern Bondage." After describing his captivity, the reporter commented that "Colonel Sherman is by no means strong in body. He has suffered, as his attenuated frame too plainly tells, but his eye is as bright as ever and his voice has lost none of its old decision. . . . Though physically unfit for exertion, he yesterday yielded to the solicitation of his friends, and visited the Board of Trade, where he was received with defeaning cheers."[33]

Colonel Sherman spent the next three months at home, as far as is known, recuperating from his prison experience. The only other note in the 1864 diary is dated Dec 21st and briefly comments that he had received pay to Nov. 30th of $375.88.

12

ROAD TO APPOMATTOX:
SPRING, 1865

Although the war evidently was drawing to a close and Colonel Sherman often had spoken of resigning from the army, he now showed no sign of wishing to resign or even to stay in Chicago any longer than necessary. Before he was released by the Confederates in October 1864, he wrote to his major supporter, General Sheridan, concerning his imminent deliverance and his wish to join Sheridan's command.[1] Sheridan's reply was dated October 27, 1864:

> Dear Colonel:
>
> Yours of the 10th came duly to hand, and I am indeed gratified to hear of you being liberated. Although it is many months since my transfer from the old Division, I hold it and its officers in kind remembrance, and often look back with satisfaction and pleasure to the many happy hours passed with it. Hescock's exchange was applied for by me on several different occasions but without success, and I am rejoiced to hear that it has at last been effected. Poor fellow, I am advised that he suffered terribly during his confinement.[2]
>
> I shall do all I can to procure your advancement and shall endeavor, should the opportunity offer, to have you transferred to this Department. Remember me to Mrs. Sherman and to your parents, and believe me to be,
>
> Yours truly, P. H. Sheridan, Major General

This may sound like scant encouragement, but General Sheridan apparently was only being cautious. It took him a while, but by the end of January he had worked something out, and Colonel Sherman was on his way, albeit even more slowly than on his trip home from prison. While the southern railways were in much worse shape than their northern counterparts, the latter had suffered greatly from overuse and limited maintenance during the war years. The colonel wrote in his diary:

Monday, January 23

Left Chicago at 10 P.M. via P. Ft. W. & C. RR. for Washington and to join Gen'l P. H. Sheridan. Weather cold and snowy.

Tuesday 24

Arrived Ft Wayne at 5:30 A.M. Locomotive run off track at depot. Left Crestline at 2:00 P.M.; three locomotives used up to this place. Very cold. Arrived at Alliance at 6 P.M., ran up 4 miles and lay on side track until 3 A.M. 25th. Series of mishaps and delays all day.

Wednesday, January 25, 1865

Got into Pittsburg at 9:30 A.M. 13 hrs behind time. Trains gone; none until 4:30 P.M. Left Pittsburg at 4:30, supper at Latrobe. Engine broke at Johnstown. Car axle broke and left; another car wheel broke. Behind time as usual.

Thursday 26

At Harrisburg 5:30 A.M.; left at 7:45 A.M. on No. C'trl R.R., ran 8 miles, found passenger train off track. Arrived at Baltimore 4 P.M. and left for Wash at 6 P.M.; arrived at 9 P.M. Weather very cold. Went to Willard's Hotel.

Friday 27

In Washington saw Senator [Henry] Wilson of Mass. and M.Cs. [Isaac N.] Arnold and [John F.] Farnsworth on matter of retaliation in kind on Reb prisoners of war. Met Lt Col [Pennock] Huey, 8th Pa Cav, who has just been paroled.

Saturday, January 28, 1865

Left Wash at 8:15 A.M. for Winchester Va, Gen'l Sheridan's HdQs, on B&O R.R.; arrived at 6 o'c P.M. Was cordially received. Everything very quiet here and weather very cold.

Sunday 29

Lounged about all day, had a sleigh ride in the afternoon with Gen'l S. through the town of Winchester which is very much dilapidated and worn by the actions of war.

Monday 30

Very quiet day. Weather warm and show of rain.

Tuesday, January 31, 1865

The day closed with a grand party and dance at HdQs. Very brilliant for the field.

Wednesday, February 1

Today review of the Cav'y of this Division, the finest display I have ever witnessed. Assigned to duty today as Acting Inspector Gen'l of this Army.

Thursday 2

Change my quarters to Mrs Miller's with Capt Q Neave. Not as yet entered upon the active duties of my position. Everything should be bright for me but feel that I am out of place. What to do; poor health keeps me down and anxiety for my family keeps me despondent.

Friday, February 3, 1865

Feel miserable; no occupation for mind or body. Guerillas fired into train from Harper's Ferry. Have done nothing in assuming my new duties.

To what extent Colonel Sherman's despondency reflected a delayed reaction to his captivity, disappointment because he could not obtain a field command, frustration at failing to secure a promotion, insecurity in the new situation, or response to family troubles is hard to tell; probably all of these factors played a part. However, the next day, when Colonel Sherman wrote to his father, he revealed much less about his depression than he had in his diary. Perhaps he was feeling better, or perhaps he hesitated to let his father know how badly he felt.

Winchester, Va., Feby 4, 1865

Dear Father:
 I reported to General Sheridan Saturday, and was received by him in

the most cordial manner. He told me he could not give me a command at present, but offered me the position of Inspector General of this military Division, which I, of course, accepted. General Sheridan then telegraphed the War Department to have me ordered to report to him for assignment to duty. That order I received this morning and am now installed on his staff as Acting Assistant Inspector General of this Army.

General Sheridan has a very large territory [the Middle Military Division] under his command, embracing the Departments of West Virginia; the Middle Department, comprising Maryland and the District of Columbia; and the Department of the Susquehanna, taking in the State of Pennsylvania. There is no regular Inspector Department organized at these Headquarters, and I am really at a loss to know whether there will be one or not.

General Sheridan wants me to give my view upon the subject. I do not care to undertake the labor connected with its organization but suppose I shall have to do something in that line. Well, it is a very responsible position, as the Inspector General is expected to know all about the troops, their organization, equipment, discipline, and position. When once I get fairly to work I have no doubt that I shall be able to perform my duty creditably. Shall try anyway. To make things more embarrassing I am amongst strangers, nor am I posted in the particular duties of the position.

The weather has been very cold here, but at the same time capricious. I have written Ellen all my observations since my arrival here. Nothing new has transpired, one day being very much like another in its routine. The troops are all in winter quarters, and no active work [is] likely to be required of them for some time to come unless the Rebels take the initiative, which is not likely, as they have been so severely punished during the summer and fall campaign by Sheridan.

There was a cavalry review the other day which was the finest display in that line I have ever witnessed. The talk that General Sheridan would be assigned to command the Army of the James in [Gen. Benjamin F.] Butler's place he does not believe. It requires an active and bold man to protect this frontier, and he is the only man who has been successful at the task.

Love to all, your son, Frank

On February 24, still at Winchester, Colonel Sherman wrote to his parents concerning their health—the specifics are unclear—and he went on to try again to persuade his father to stay away from politics:

[You] will have to be careful and leave the cares of business and office to others. Surely you have had enough of honor from the citizens of Chicago, and as rotation in office is a democratic principle, you should give way to some other deserving aspirant for the honor of the mayoralty, especially as the position has become a sinecure. The patriotic Republicans thought that

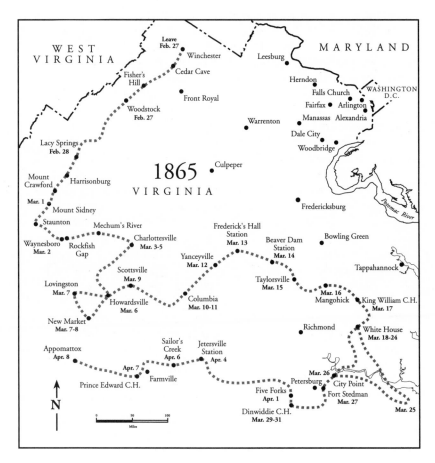

Appomattox Campaign.

Chicago was not capable of electing its own officers, as I understand, and have therefore so arranged it that the [Cook] County could control the City—*pro bono publico.*[3]

My advice to you, though unasked, would be to leave public life and try to recuperate your health by travel, new scenes, change of climate, and diet. Take a short sea voyage and visit pleasant places. You are in a position to do so, you and mother both. It will, I am satisfied, be beneficial to both, and you ought not to neglect anything so important as your health. You have both taken big and little pills, solutions bitter and sweet long enough to test their efficacy in restoring health. Now try my prescription and give nature a chance to recover its healthy tone. If I can do anything about going away, write me and I will do it.

My own health is none the best, and I begin to feel prematurely old. The remnants of my southern fever still cling to me, and are not thoroughly out of my system. I have had one chill since I came here; I am taking quinine, and that has kept it off.[4]

The weather has been very cold and disagreeable here, with more snow than I have seen for years. Frozen hard one day, next all splash and slop. The snow has now nearly disappeared under the influence of sun and rain. I am tired of it and will heartily rejoice when Dame Nature once more puts on her mantle of green.

Mayor Sherman as usual was disinclined to take his son's advice and continued to campaign for another term as mayor.

There are no letters extant from the colonel about his next six weeks' activities, but he did keep up his diary, as Sheridan's troops marched south to join Grant. Gen. W. T. Sherman, in North Carolina tracking down Gen. Joseph E. Johnston, was short of cavalry and had requested Sheridan's help; Sheridan, however, sensing that the end was near and that the action would be in Virginia, wanted to be there; and Grant went along with his wish. Colonel Sherman's diary records the relentless progress of Sheridan's ten thousand cavalrymen and accompanying artillery through Central Virginia toward Appomattox:

Monday, February 27, 1865

Left Winchester at 7 o'c A.M. and marched to Woodstock 30 miles. Passed over the battlegrounds of Cedar Creek and Fishers Hill. Weather fine; frost not out of the ground.

Tuesday 28

Left Woodstock 5½ A.M.; passed through Mt Jackson at 11 o'c A.M. Two

miles south threw pontoon bridge over Shenandoah River in one hour
& 10 minutes. [Gen. George A.] Custer [commanding the 3rd Division]
lost one man drowned in fording. Went into camp at Lacy Springs;
marched 27 miles.

Wednesday March 1

Left Lacy Springs at 7 A.M., passed thro' Harrisonburg at 10 A.M. At Mt
Crawford saved bridge which rebs set on fire; captured 25. [Gen. Thomas
L.] Rosser in command of rebs; Col [Henry] Capehart's Brig'd in advance.
[We] ran the Rebs thro' Mt Sidney and across the Middle River where we
went into camp.

Thursday, March 2, 1865—Battle of Waynesboro

Entered Staunton at 8 A.M. & left at 1 P.M. Custer div. moved to
Waynesboro; captured 1165 pris, 78 officers, 17 ps art'y, 150 wagons with
loss 1 man killed, 12 wounded. Rained all day, roads in horrible condition. Reb Gens Early, [Gabriel C.] Wharton, [Robert D.] Lilly, & Rosser
escaped; part of their staffs taken.

Friday 3

Left Waynesboro at 11 A.M. and crossed Blue Ridge at Rockfish Gap. Capt'd
trains here + 5 ps Art'y, which was destroyed by burning at Greenwood. Roads
in awful condition from rains. Bridge over Mechums River (very fine one)
burned; forded river. Pushed on and arrived at Charlottesville at 11 o'c P.M.;
Custer's div came in at 4 P.M. without opposition. Rained all night. No trains
up; rear column 15 miles back.

Saturday 4

Remained in Charlottesville today. Nigs plundered the town, encouraged
by the solid citizens. Expected University to be burned at once; not done.
Found 1000 stand of arms + 3 guns; all destroyed. Bridge at Rivanna River
burned; track torn up and rails bent. Soldiers very orderly. Stopt at Mrs.
[D. T.] Shreve's. Weather fine.

John B. Minor, professor of law at the University of Virginia during the Civil
War, wrote in his diary on March 2, 1865, that "most persons think that they
(Union forces) will destroy the University. I am not of that opinion, but I cannot avoid much anxiety in consequence of so many having a contrary impression. Last night . . . the Faculty deputed the chairman, Dr. [Socrates] Maupin,

Colonel [Thomas L.] Preston (the Rector), and myself *ut capiat Universitas nil detrimenti*[5] by soliciting a guard [from the Union command, to protect the University]." They were successful in this mission, and in his diary entry of March 5, Professor Minor wrote, "In the course of the day we were visited by Capt. [Thomas W. C.] Moore of Gen. Sheridan's staff, at the instance of the General, to express his determination to preserve the University unharmed . . . In the afternoon the University was searched by order of Gen. Sheridan, under the direction of Col. Sherman . . . They were as civil as possible and of course found nothing contraband."[6] The colonel's version was recorded in his diary:

Sunday, March 5, 1865

Remained at Charlottesville to rest and for the trains. Plenty of forage & prov'ns in the country. Visited the University today to look for Concealed Arms. Citizens here intensely secesh but polite & courteous. No depredations of moment committed. Weather spring like & warm. Burned excess of baggage and otherwise lightened up the wagons.

Monday 6

Marched at 6 A.M. on two roads: one column to Howardsville, the other to Lovingston. Went into camp on Rock Fish River, 150 ft. broad. Burned R.R. bridge and tore up track. Made 25 m[iles]. No enemy of any force to oppose us. Roads better, our way being between the Blue Ridge and [indecipherable] mountains. Fine defensible country; valley narrow but rich for agriculture.

Tuesday 7

Marched at 6 o'c A.M., crossed the Rock Fish at 7 and arrived at Lovingston at 12 N. Column under [Gen. Wesley] Merritt destroyed Jas. River canal for a distance of about 40 miles and camped at New Market. Custer's Div went into camp at Arrington Sta. R.R. bridge over the Tye River burned and track destroyed. Weather fine and road improving. Large amt of cotton and stores destroyed. Made 20 miles.

Wednesday, March 8, 1865

Crossed from Arrington Station to New Market. Destruction of canal complete. Column moved on Lynchburg. No opposition so far. Destroyed R.R. bridge over Buffalo River and 6 locks on Canal. Commenced raining at 5 o'c P.M. and rained all night. Large amt of tobbaco [*sic*] burned at New Market.

Thursday 9

Left New Market at 6 A.M. and arrived at Howardsville at 11 A.M. Very warm. Canal effectively destroyed at this place. Roads in very bad condition. Rebel scouts to be seen on the south side of the James River watching our movements. We moved upon the tow path from Howardsville to Scottsville, arrived at 4 P.M. Made 25 ms.

Friday 10

Marched at 6:30 A.M.; arrived Columbia at 2 P.M.; made 24 miles. Col. [Charles L.] Fitz-Hugh's brigade occupied the town at 5 A.M. of the 9th capturing 3 scouts, canal boats & supplies. Cannot cross the James River, all the bridges being burned from Lynchburg to Richmond. Made Hdqs at Mr [William] Galt's house, a wealthy Scotsman—owns 3800 acres.

Saturday, March 11, 1865

Remained at Columbia today bringing up the trains and resting the horses. Crossed on aqueduct over Ravenna [Rivanna] River. Rebel cavalry in plain view on opposite side of the James; we crossed a small party over last night and ran them out. A warm and fine March day dries up the mud. Fitz Hugh brigade gone to Goochland.

Sunday 12

Marched at 6 o'c A.M. towards Louisa C.H. on Va Central R.R. Delayed in getting on the right road. Crossed Bird's Creek at Bowles' Mill and moved on Yanceyville on the South Anna [River]. Arrived at 4 P.M.; ford too deep, crossed lower down and camped on Goodings' place near gold mine. Barren country; roads good & weather fine.

Monday 13

Marched at 6 A.M. to Colesville Station on Va Central R.R. Track torn up and burned to Beaver Dam. Two trains caught at Gordonsville. Tobacco works burned at Frederickshall Station & Depot and $150,000 tobacco destroyed. Made hdqs at Dr. Pendleton's house. Marched 13 ms; Weather very fine; roads good; Country not very productive—timber pine.

Tuesday, March 14, 1865

Custer's Div went to Ashland Station on Fred'burg R.R. to destroy bridge over So Anna River; [Gen. Thomas C.] Devin's div to No Anna on same mission. Hdqs. moved to Beaver Dam station on Va Central R.R. 10 miles. Roads good, weather fine, country poor. Station burned and track torn up. No enemy to be heard of although within 20 miles of Richmond. Large numbers of ducks following.

Wednesday 15

Moved to Taylorsville 6:30 A.M. R.R. bridge over Little River & So Anna on Va Central and Fred'burg Roads. Custer's div at Ashland; two Divs of enemy Inf—Longstreet's Corps—in his front. Some skirmishing; loss slight; no intention of fighting. Weather cloudy and warm. Marched 30 miles; went into camp at Mount Carmel. Honest men tired out. Poor country.

Thursday 16

Moved from Mt Carmel at 7 A.M. and camped at Mangohick, making 16 miles. Roads sandy and good. Rained during the night. On the 14th came near capturing Early who with his Adjt Genl + 50 men were journeying towards Richmond. His escort dispersed and Adjt captured. Today the whole cavalry force were put on one road to go to White House, the Raid being over. I am glad.

Friday, March 17, 1865

Left Mangohick Church at 7 A.M. & moved towards White House between the Mattapong and Pamunky Rivers. Passed Aylettsville at 10 A.M. on the Mattapong. Arrived King William C.H. at 2 P.M. Roads very good; heavy rain during the night. Country poor, covered with pine & oak timber. King Wm C.H. old place. Made 20 miles.

Saturday 18

Marched to White House on Pamunky River 8 miles. Found transport with forage and supplies for the troops. Made hdqs on Steamer Metamora. Will stay a few days to refit. Weather very fine. Caught some shad.

The Army of the Shenandoah remained in White House for a week for a sorely needed rest: "Despite the dearth of enemy opposition, the grueling march to White House had taken its toll on Sheridan's cavalry. Hundreds of men were unarmed and unhorsed; others were reduced to riding captured Rebel mules. More than two thousand cases of hoof rot were reported among the horses, caused by weeks of slogging through mud."[7]

On March 25, the cavalry broke camp, and on the next day General Sheridan, accompanied by Colonel Sherman, went to General Grant's headquarters at City Point for consultation about the next moves. The plan was for Sheridan's cavalry to go around Richmond and Petersburg to cut the last remaining rail link, which would permit Lee's army to join up with Johnston's in North Carolina. Colonel Sherman wrote in his diary with ponderous sarcasm of the departure from White House:

Saturday 25

Cav'y Corps moved for City Point this A.M. All transports and Gun boats left the Pamunky River & White House. Again it became a desert after having been the seat of luxury, elegance & refinement. Arrived by steamer at Fortress Monroe 7 o'c P.M.

Sunday, March 26, 1865

Steamer broke down and anchored in James River. Sent troops up to City Point. Haled tug and towed up. Arrived at 6 P.M. Went to Gen. Grant's Hdqs and stayed. President Lincoln and lady there. Went up the River on Excurs.

This brief encounter probably was the only time Colonel Sherman saw President Lincoln at close range. Grant had asked Lincoln to visit the troops at City Point. Although he had not invited the difficult Mrs. Lincoln to accompany her husband, she insisted upon joining him and created some embarrassment by her suspicions. The president reviewed the troops within earshot of firing from the battle lines nearby.[8]

Monday 27

Left City Point at 12 and went to Hancock Station near Petersburg. Some firing along the lines. Weather fine. All the cavalry Army of the Potomac under Gen'l Sheridan. Rebels repulsed by ninth Corps on Saturday; took 3000 prisoners.

Colonel Sherman's March 27 entry refers to the Battle of Fort Stedman, a desperate surprise attack by Gen. John B. Gordon's division, ordered by Lee in an effort to break out of the Union trap. The Union troops indeed were surprised, but the Confederates could not withstand their counterattack. With that defeat, Lee's last chance of avoiding a full-scale retreat was lost.[9]

Wednesday 29

Command marched from Hancock Sta at 6 A.M., passed Resaca (?) Sta at 9 A.M., at Rowanty Creek 11 A.M., rebuilt bridge (delay of four hours). Head of column arrived at Dinwiddie C.H. 5:30 P.M. 2d div. Cavy Genl Crook in advance

Thursday 30

Weather bad, heavy rain. Skirmishing with enemy all day long towards Five Forks by 5th & 6th cav of Gen Devin's command. Losses high. Custer's div in reserve with wagon train. Roads impassable. Capt'd 30 prisoners.

Friday 31

Rain this A.M; clear at noon. [Gen. George] Crook's Div engaged with the enemy on Stony Creek under [Gen. George E.] Pickett. 1st Div engaged. In afternoon enemy crossed Stony Creek turning our right and cut off [Gen. Henry E.] Davies' Brig. 2nd Div, Cav'y Corps. Night closed with enemy close up in our front at Dinwiddie having forced back the Cav'y two miles; losses not known. Custer Div. came up at night. Rebs outnumbered us; we got out of Ammunition.

Saturday, April 1, 1865

Enemy withdrew during the night across Stony Creek and Gravelly Run and took position on White Oak Road. Custer at Five Forks. Enemy composed of Pickett's, Busford's [probably Thomas T. Munford's], and [Robert E.] Johnston's Divs of Inf'y and Fitz Lee's Cav'y. 5th Corps under [Gouverneur K.] Warren reported [to Gen'l Sheridan] at 6 A.M. Cav'y—1st Div on the right; 3rd Div on the left; 2d Div in reserve—were pushed out and forward. The enemy pickets covering Stony Creek and Gravelly Run were driven to the main lines of the Rebs posted parallel with the W[hite] O[ak] Road. 5th Corps were moved up and massed at Church. At 4:30 P.M. moved for'd to assault the enemy whom we struck upon their left flank. When night closed the enemy were broken and driven in confusion with 5000 prisoners in our possession [and] all their artillery. [Ranald] Mackenzie's Cav'y Div operated on the right of the Inf'y with great success. Gen'l Warren relieved at 6 P.M.[10] Our loss slight.

Sunday 2

Cavalry under [Gen. Wesley] Merritt struck the So. Side R.R. at Port's house[11] at 11 A.M. and tore up track. Enemy's cav'y in position at Port's; they moved off by their right flank on farm road by Spain's house. Our advance was checked at the Namozine road at Dr. Brauder's. Pickett's Div crossing the [Appomattox] river at Exeter Mills. Slight skirmishing during the day and at sunset until dark.

Monday 3

Cav'y in pursuit on River Road. Many prisoners taken from [Gen. Ambrose P.] Hill's Corps that were cut off near the Appomattox River [by 5th Corps]. 3 pcs of Art'y left by the enemy on cross road to Namozine Road. Passed Namozine Church at 4 P.M. and went into camp at Mrs Cousins 5 o'c P.M.

4th

Inf'y moved at 6 A.M., crossed Deep Creek at 11 A.M. Passed Jackson house at 1 P.M. at junction of road to Amelia C.H. & Burksville. Passed Mt. Parkinson on main road to Jetersville, 3½ miles distant, at 4 P.M. Arrived Jetersville at 6 P.M.; troops went into position. Enemy under Lee at Amelia C.H.

5th

At 12 M. 2nd Corps came up to Jetersville and went into position on left of 5th Corps. Gen. Davies' brigade of Crook's cav'y moved on enemy's flank via Paineville and captured 5 pcs. art'y & 200 prisoners and burned 150 wagons, including Gen'l Lee's Hdqtrs. Genl Meade came up at 4 P.M. Genl [John I.] Gregg's brigade struck by the enemy and driven in: lost 50 men captured. Enemy cav'y made reconnaissance late in the afternoon; Col. [Hugh H.] Janeway, 1st N. J. Cav'y, killed. 10 o'c P.M. Genl Grant came up to our Hdqtrs, also to 6th Corps. Enemy believed trying to escape.

6th

Inf'y moved towards Amelia C.H.; Cav'y towards Deatonsville, Genl Crook in advance. At 10 A.M. discovered enemy's train moving on road parallel to our own on the right. Crook and Merritt were ordered to attack at once; 6th Corps ordered to report to Sheridan. At 4 P.M. advance of 6th Corps came up and was immediately formed and moved on the enemy's rear. Lively skirmishing until we reached Sailor's [sic] Creek, where they made a stand. Sharp fighting took place for an hour when a charge was made which resulted in the capture of all the force opposed to us, between 10 and 12,000 men. Custer took 4 pcs. of art'y; 7 battle flags; and Genls. [Richard S.] Ewell, Custis [Lee], [Seth M.] Barton, DeFoe [probably Dudley M. DuBose], [James P.] Simms, [Montgomery D.] Corse, & [Joseph B.] Kershaw. 300 wagons were burned, loaded with stores of all kinds. Marched 12 miles.

7th

Moved to Rice Station and came upon Genl [Edward O. C.] Ord's troops. Cav'y were pushed to the left crossing Briery Creek & Sand River, passing through Prince Edward C.H. to Buffalo River and camped for the night [after] marching 18 or 20 miles during the day.

8th

Cav'y moved through Prospect Station and Ferguson's Mountain to Appomattox Station. Custer's Div in advance struck the enemy at the Station, capturing a R.R. train loaded with supplies, 20 pcs art'y, 100 wagons, and 1000 prisoners. Heavy fighting all done by Custer's. Loss slight.

April 9

Wilmer McLean House: R. E. Lee surrendered the Northern Army of Virginia to U. S. Grant, Lt Genl Comdg U.S. Forces, at Appomattox C.H. At the time Lee sent in his flag of truce the 5th, 24th, & Cavy Corps were moving forward to attack and became partially engaged. 5th Corps captured a small brigade in the town. Genl Sheridan & Staff [including Colonel Sherman] rode into town and met Genls Longstreet, [John B.] Gordon, [Cadmus Marcellus] Wilcox and others. Hostilities were suspended. Genl Grant met Genl Lee and terms of capitulation agreed upon. Enemy's troops to be paroled; Officers to retain their side arms and private property and give personal paroles. Rebs taken by surprise at our appearance in their front with Infty and Cavy.

10th

Moved from Appomattox C.H. toward Prospect Station at 8:00 P.M. Final act of the war took place on the part of the rebels in turning over their public property to Generals [John] Gibbon, 24th Corps, [Charles] Griffin, 5th Corps, and [Wesley] Merritt of the Cavalry Corps, Commissioners on our part to see that the terms of the Capitulation were carried out in good faith. Arrived in camp at Prospect Station at 5 oc P.M. Rain during the night.

This is the last notation in Colonel Sherman's wartime diary. Although he commented in the diary on action in the Appomattox campaign at Five Forks, White Oak Road, Namozine Church, Jetersville (Amelia Springs), Sayler's Creek, and Appomattox Station,[12] the nature of his duties as inspector general during the last phases of the war is unclear. However, on May 16, 1865, General Sheridan reported to the Secretary of War on the operations of his command from Winchester to Appomattox, stating:

I have the honor to bring to the notice of the War Department the gallant conduct of the following officers and to recommend them for promotion . . .

[*inter alia*] Col. Francis T. Sherman. . . . to be Brigadier General of Volunteers by Brevet (for great services) during the Cavalry Expedition from Winchester to the James River, from Feb. 27th to March 27th, 1865, and for distinguished services at the battles of Dinwiddie Court House, March 31st, Five Forks, April 1st, Sailors Creek, April 6th, and Appomattox Court House, April 9th.[13]

13

NATIONAL TRAGEDY AND PERSONAL
DISAPPOINTMENT: SPRING, 1865

Possibly to console his protégé for his failure to be rewarded with promotion, General Sheridan chose Colonel Sherman for a special mission shortly after Lee's surrender. Sheridan's order explains the assignment:

> Cavalry Headquarters, April 13, 1865.
> Special Field Order No. 19.
>   Colonel F. T. Sherman, AAIG, is hereby ordered to proceed to Washington, D.C., with a detachment of 52 (fifty-two) officers and men of this command for the purpose of presenting to the War Department colors captured from the enemy by them in the recent engagements.
>   The Quartermaster Department will furnish the necessary transportation.
>   By command of Major General Sheridan.[1]

Now, at last, as the war drew to a close, Colonel Sherman was about to confront his nemesis, Secretary Stanton, with evidence that he deserved to wear the star to which he so long had felt entitled. Finally he would have a place in the sun at the War Department, which had so consistently turned down recommendations for his promotion.

But it was not to be. The letter he wrote to his father is brief but poignant:

> Washington, D.C., April 17, 1865
> Dear Father:
>   I started from Burksville on the South Side Railroad on Thursday morning of last week, having been selected by General Sheridan to present to the War Department fifty-one [*sic*] battle flags taken by the Cavalry from the

enemy at Five Forks, Sailors' Creek, and Appomattox Court House during the recent brilliant campaign which ended in the surrender by Lee of the Army of Northern Virginia. I arrived in Washington to find it laboring under intense excitement and overcast with gloom and grief at the tragic and foul deed which ended in the death of the President.

I anticipated a grand time in presenting these trophies of the prowess and gallantry of Sheridan's men. As yet I have been unable to learn when I can deliver my charge, or how they will be received, publicly or privately. Nothing will be done, I am assured, until after the funeral.

The whole nation one week ago was ablaze with joy and rejoicing over our victories and the prospect of peace. Today the nation mourns a calamity which overshadows all our past successes and leaves the future dark and uncertain. May God direct and guide us through the evil clouds that are settling down upon us as a people and bring us safe into the sunshine beyond. I can think of nothing else and write only what fills the mind to the exclusion of all other thoughts. Woe, woe unto the people who resort to the assassin's dagger.

I am well, much better than I expected to be. Outdoor work agrees with me, and together with the excitement does not leave time for getting sick.

Love to all, your son, Frank

Colonel Sherman's disappointment was soon matched by disappointment of another kind for his father. The victorious end of the war, with its affirmation of the administration's policies, and sympathy and outrage about the assassination of President Lincoln, greatly strengthened the Republican party's appeal. Unfortunately for Mayor Sherman, local Chicago elections were scheduled four days after Lincoln was assassinated, and the mayor was soundly defeated.[2] There is no record of condolences or comments offered to his father by Colonel Sherman. Almost a week later, Frank wrote his mother a rather formal note:

Washington, D.C., April 23, 1865
Dear Mother:

I have delayed writing you for a long time. My excuse is the want of an opportunity, and the active duties that have fallen upon me since I left Chicago and joined General Sheridan. It is different being with the Cavalry than with the Infantry, as the greater portion of the time we are not in communication with any person or have any mail facilities.

I am now here with fifty-one battle flags captured by Sheridan's command during the recent campaign, which ended with the surrender of Lee and his army to Grant. Tomorrow I present them to the War Department, and after that is over start immediately for Petersburg, where our headquarters are. I hope I shall find them still there when I arrive. I expect General Sheridan will have marched before I can reach them, as there is something for the Cavalry to do which has suddenly come up. I suppose it to be in consequence of the disapproval by the War Department of the terms granted by General [William T.] Sherman to [General Joseph E.] Johnston and the order for renewal of hostilities at once.

I believe that General Sherman has ruined himself. He certainly has made a great and grave mistake. The assassination of President Lincoln has produced a feeling in the Army which will find vent on the battlefield that will not tend to ameliorate its horror if we ever come into collision again. Such to a great extent is the feeling of the men and their officers. I had hoped that the last battle had been fought, and that no more blood would have to be poured out upon the altar of freedom. Woe to the Johnnies if they do not now throw down their arms. They need not look for favorable terms if they continue to fight from desperation, for that will be the only reason for their continuing in arms against us.

I saw General Lee when he came to meet General Grant to surrender. That was a glorious day and sight. My opinion is that I shall see Johnston's army taken. It is only a ride of one hundred and fifty miles. I also think that General Sheridan will have a very active part in that performance, as well as a very high command.

My love to you all. Kiss the children for me, and write again all of you—write me—why don't you?

Frank

Colonel Sherman finally got to present his flags, but not to Secretary Stanton. The presentation was anticlimactic, following as it did upon Lincoln's assassination, and Secretary Stanton apparently did not attend the ceremony.

After Appomattox, General Sheridan and the cavalry proceeded to Petersburg in anticipation of being demobilized. The "something which has suddenly come up" was the news that Lee's surrender had not ended the war and that, because General Johnston's army was still fighting, the Union cavalry was ordered to proceed to Greensboro, North Carolina.

They got only as far as South Boston, Virginia. On April 24, the day after Colonel Sherman's last letter was written, General Sherman was ordered to demand General Johnston's surrender within forty-eight hours, on the same terms as Lee's surrender to Grant. Two days later, at Bentonville, North Carolina, Johnston surrendered, and Sheridan's forces retraced their steps.[3]

There are no letters from the next two months, during which Colonel Sherman continued on General Sheridan's staff. After Johnston's surrender, Sheridan was ordered to New Orleans to expedite the surrender of Confederate Gen. Kirby Smith's forces. General Grant denied Sheridan's request to delay his departure from Washington for a week in order to participate in the Grand Review of the Union Army, and Colonel Sherman probably accompanied General Sheridan. Otherwise, surely he would have described the Grand Review in a letter to his father.

By the time Sheridan and his troops arrived in New Orleans, in late May, Kirby Smith had surrendered. Sheridan was put in charge of the Fifth Military District, with instructions to carry out the terms of the Reconstruction Acts in Texas and Louisiana, which meant working with southern politicians. But politics was not his strong point; he was "a classic example of the good combat soldier who finds it nearly impossible to shift from the aggressive and physically dangerous theatre of war to the area of politics."[4] His solution to the problems of government in the South was to replace civilian officials with military officers, thus anticipating the Reconstruction Act of March, 1867, which placed the South under comprehensive military rule. In the late summer of 1867, President Johnson, who favored a more conciliatory policy, replaced Sheridan as military governor.[5]

Colonel Sherman was Sheridan's provost marshal general, charged with keeping order. In Reconstruction, his sympathies were with those who recommended a repressive policy, and he fitted in well with his chief's views. He wrote little, however, about his work in New Orleans; reading between the lines, one gets the impression that he, like Sheridan, would have preferred a more traditional military role.

Colonel Sherman's first letter from New Orleans was written to his mother. This letter was taken up with a histrionic discussion of an unfortunate family quarrel and its effect on the colonel and his wife; the details of the quarrel are not known, but its substance can be inferred from the letter:

New Orleans, La., June 27th, 1865

Dear Mother:

I received a letter from Father, date June 3rd, and answered it immediately.[6] In it he says that I almost broke your heart in consequence of language I used in a former letter expressing my surprise that he should deem it necessary to give me notice that he would not consent to the leasing of the house, at present my home for those I hold dear and near to me. He also thinks, as expressed in his letter, that Ellen, my wife, has influenced me against you all and made me ungrateful to my best friends, coupled with ingratitude to you both. God forgive me if I have written aught that could thus be construed by either of you. My conscience acquits me of any such intent. I may have been hasty in what I wrote at that time, as I only had a few minutes to write in and did not even read it over. I thought, and still think, that many of Ellen's faults were magnified and her speech and acts taken for facts when they were only the result of loneliness and discontent caused by our separation. I thought and still think that these things might have been overlooked and allowances made for her under the circumstances. If Ellen was wrong, certainly it would not mend the matter by a stern disapproval of the same, and thereby raise an antagonistic force in her.

We are none of us perfect and least of all am I, but, Mother, of all my faults ingratitude towards you or Father is not one of them. I was in hopes

Mrs. Francis Cornwall Sherman. Collection of C. Knight Aldrich.

that this would never be charged against me. That Ellen ever endeavored to influence me against you by word or deed does not rest in my memory. That she had complaints is true, and the burden of them was at being left alone and away from me to care for herself and the children without my protecting arm to screen her from invidious remarks.

Father speaks of her being at Mrs. Bronson's; it was unfortunate that she went there. What could she do? Aunt Mary would not have her, but took others to board. Aunt Jerusha would not have her after saying she might come, and for some unassigned reason turned her away. You could not have her because your house was full, and she and Martha [Colonel Sherman's sister] do not agree. Somewhere she must seek asylum, a place to lay her head during my absence. I don't know why Father cites Josh[7] in his letter and calls her conduct and treatment of him 'disgraceful.' That part looks like a desire to hurt my feelings. The conduct cited never made any difference in the friendship which has always existed between Josh and myself.

Father says you cannot ever feel again towards Ellen as in the past. Ellen was entirely ignorant of that letter, nor did I intimate in any way to her that I should write about what Father said to us that morning when I left home last. Mother, I have never spent so many unhappy hours before as I have since that time, and I now feel most miserable to think I did not keep within my own bosom the feelings which I gave vent to in that unfortunate letter.

I would rather a thousand times feel myself hurt than give you one moment's pain or trouble. I have the same feeling for Father. I now see my fault and most bitterly repent me of it. I feel that I am an outcast from your affections, me and mine. You whom I have so loved and revered and still love and revere. My future is all a blank to me; I am at sea drifting, I know not whither. I had looked forward to the time when I should return to you all and to a home which would make me happy and contented with all around me.

Forgive me, Mother. Forgive Ellen who is my wife. Forgive, for we all need forgiveness. You can at least be kind until I can find some way of caring for my family. And now adieu. Give my love to all at home, and believe anything but that I have been influenced against my family and best friends, or that I have been ungrateful, or that ingratitude is among the faults of your ever loving and affectionate son,

Frank

Perhaps it is just as well that "that unfortunate letter" no longer exists, although one's curiosity is piqued. It would be surprising if three years either living with in-laws, or leaving three children with in-laws while she went off to war with Frank, did not strain Ellen's relationship with his parents. She probably let off steam to Frank, assuming that he would keep it to himself. In any event, what is said and implied in the colonel's letter makes it easier to understand why Ellen was so compliant with her husband's wish that she be in Tennessee rather than in Chicago with her children—and her in-laws.

Whatever the cause of the family turmoil, Colonel Sherman seems to have been ambivalent about his role in it. He was both apologetic and defensive, and was torn between loyalties to his parents and his wife. Clearly it was not only political differences that created problems between father and son.

In his letter to his father two days later, however, Colonel Sherman did not mention the family troubles; instead, he was back with his old preoccupation—his promotion to brigadier general.

14

END OF THE QUEST: SUMMER, 1865, AND AFTER

In his June 29 letter, Colonel Sherman still seemed convinced that, if only his father and others at home would express themselves in the right places, his promotion would be assured.

New Orleans, La., June 29, 1865

Dear Father:

I have written to John Wentworth asking him to do what he can for me at Washington in the way of getting me appointed as full Brigadier. General Sheridan told me this morning he would recommend my appointment at once. Failing that he would have me assigned to duty under my brevet rank.

I feel certain that I can get this appointment—if my friends can be induced to do anything on my behalf with any vigor. Governor Yates, Governor Oglesby,[1] Wentworth,[2] and others of the State delegation to whom I am known would write letters in my favor if the matter were called to their attention. I have written this to you to show what my chances are of substantial promotion and continuance in the Army if this appointment is secured for me.

The weather is very hot here and I am nearly roasted but manage to exist some way. There is no news of importance to relate.

What is left of the old 4th Army Corps arrived here last week en route to Texas. My opinion is that Maximilian will be making a European tour within a year, a living monument to the Monroe Doctrine. Napoleon may frown and show his teeth but he will not bite—if he does his fangs will be drawn without the use of chloroform.

Give my love to Mother and all at home, and believe me I am ever your son,

Frank

On July 1 Colonel Sherman's letter clarified the reason for his feeling of urgency at that time about the promotion:

New Orleans, La., July 1st, 1865

Dear Father:

Yours of the 20th ult. was received yesterday and read with much pleasure. In regard to your inquiry as to how the muster out of the 88th would affect me, I reply as follows:

The muster out of the 88th throws me out of service unless I am assigned to duty by special order of the War Department, according to my brevet rank, in which case I would draw the pay and emoluments of a brigadier general. General Sheridan told me he would get an order from the War Department as above stated and also forward a recommend for my appointment to the full rank of brigadier general.

My duty and jurisdiction as provost marshal general of the Military Division of the Southwest are various, covering all permits for trade, passes, and regulations for the police and convictions of abuse within the military lines of this division. I have also supervisory direction of all departmental, district, and army provosts throughout the command under direction of the general commanding.

For instance, I have now in my possession the Archives of the State of Louisiana, taken at Shreveport from the Rebel Governor [Henry W.] Allen, including all papers, books, etc., of the different Departments of the State's correspondence with Rebel authorities in Richmond during the rebellion. There is a large amount of State and City of New Orleans bonds deposited with the Auditor for banking purposes, school fund, etc., amounting to nearly four million dollars. Besides that I hold nearly one million dollars of Confederate notes and notes issued by the State of Louisiana. All of the above is in my possession as Provost Marshal General. You will see by the above that I hold a very responsible position, one of importance and trust.

I have no doubt but that I shall get my appointment and retain my position in the army, provided my friends at home will do half as much for me as my general.

There is no news here of import to relate, only it is hot, hot, hot, with any amount of mosquitoes thrown in as a blessing.

Love to all, your son, Frank

The next letter makes it clear that, for his mother, at least, the family conflict was still a problem.

New Orleans, July 18th, 1865

Dear Mother:

Your letter of the 8th of July has come to hand and read by me with pleasure and pain. I regret exceedingly having been the cause of giving you one moment's pain or sorrow. With you I believe that it is better that the past should be buried and driven from our remembrance. Let the sun break through the clouds of sorrow and bring back warmth and health, refreshing us with new light and brightness for the past obscurity. I hope that never again will I be the cause, directly or indirectly, of giving you or Father one moment's pain. Now I will say no more upon this subject, but let it drop, never more to be spoken of by me, truly grateful for your love and forgiveness.

There have been changes in our military divisions since I last wrote home. Ours is no longer the Division of the Southwest, but the Division of the Gulf, with the States of Florida, Mississippi, Louisiana, and Texas for its geographical boundary. This military Division is the most important one in the U.S., covering as it does the southwestern frontier, including that bordering upon Mexico.

Yesterday I received a dispatch from the Adjutant General's office at Washington that I was mustered out of the service on the 20th of June last. I showed the telegram to General Sheridan, who requested me to stay with him for the present and I shall do so. The General immediately telegraphed to Washington to have me made a full brigadier as he required me to remain with him. This dispatch was sent to General Grant. I think that will bring the appointment. When it comes, the General told me, he should make me Chief of his Staff.

Dear Mother, it is with pride that I write you this. To have earned the confidence and friendship of so eminent a soldier and gentleman and to be placed in such a responsible position, a position sought after with eagerness by graduates of West Point, is not often the fortune of volunteer officers. I feel that I have been highly honored and distinguished by General Sheridan and will try to merit a continuance of his kindness and trust which he has reposed in me. The weather continues very warm, and the sun's rays are very fierce. I keep out of the sun as much as possible. The nights are improving and are not quite as hot as they have been.

If I remain in the army and attached to General Sheridan's staff I [will send] for Ellen and probably the children to join me here this fall. I have a very fine furnished house assigned to me as quarters with all the conveniences about it that one could ask for. It is one of the best built and furnished houses that New Orleans can boast of. This arrangement will be very pleasant for us, and I think beneficial to the health of us all.

I now close with love to all at home. Kiss the children for me, and remember me to Ellen, and believe me, I remain, as ever, your true and loving son,

Frank

Meanwhile General Sheridan had been trying hard to secure his protégé's promotion. On July 4, he signed a letter written by his aide:

Mr. Edwin M. Stanton, Secretary of War, Washington, D. C.
Sir: I have the honor to respectfully request that Brevet Brigadier General Francis T. Sherman be appointed to the full rank of Brigadier General of Volunteers.
General Sherman, as Colonel of the 88th Illinois Volunteers, served with distinction as a Regimental and Brigade Commander in the Army of the Cumberland and since his appointment upon my staff has served to my satisfaction. His regiment . . . has just been mustered out of service and as I am very anxious to retain him in his position as Provost Marshal General of this military division I would earnestly urge his appointment. I am, Sir, very respectfully,
Philip H. Sheridan, General Commanding[3]

Two weeks later the promotion had not come through, and on July 17 Sheridan wrote a note in his own handwriting to Col. F. S. Bowers in the Adjutant General's Office: "The Regiment of which Bvt. Brig. Gen. Francis T. Sherman was Colonel is mustered out. He is my Provost Marshal. I want him as my Chief of Staff. I have applied for his full promotion. Please help me in this matter or at least have him put on duty according to his Brevet rank. P. H. Sheridan."[4]

Finally, on July 21, 1865, four days from the date of the above letter and just over three months after the war ended, Colonel Sherman achieved the goal that had eluded him for at least two years: Secretary Stanton's resistance gave way, and Colonel Sherman was promoted to the full rank of brigadier general. The quest was over; he could wear his star.

Frank's father apparently had attempted to intervene personally with Secretary Stanton on his son's behalf and had received a blunt rebuff. Ironically, the attempted intervention probably took place after Sherman's promotion had been approved. This is a touching episode. Unless he was using a great deal of denial, Mayor Sherman, as an experienced politician who knew much more about politics than his son did, must have anticipated the kind of reception he would get from Secretary Stanton. So, he probably made the trip against his better judgment. Stanton was a brilliant, well-organized, obsessive worker of impressive mien, who was famous for his abrasiveness and irascibility. He had been a Democrat—he was Buchanan's attorney general, and tried to put some iron into that vacillating president at the time the Union was falling apart—but he was well known to have no patience with Peace Democrats or anyone who trafficked with them, and he held grudges.

So what could the former mayor hope to get out of the long trip to Washington and the confrontation with a man who held all the cards and certainly was going to be anything but sympathetic? Was it a gesture to make up to Frank for his son's frustration about promotion, or to heal the breach within the family? Or was he simply making a final effort, with the war over, to get for his son the star that he wanted so badly? There the defeated mayor sat, hat in hand in the secretary's anteroom, waiting to be humiliated. And all for naught; the general already had his star, "all due to General Sheridan," as he said in his next letter.

New Orleans, August 14, 1865

Dear Father:

Your letter of July 28th from New York came to hand this morning and contents noted. I regret exceedingly that you were put to so much trouble and inconvenience in Washington on my account, nor am I surprised at your proper indignation at the reception you met with there. You now know why so many people are down on Mr. Stanton; it is because of the ungracious manner with which he receives people who approach him.

You will know before this reaches you that I have received my appointment to the full rank of Brigadier General of Volunteers, having written to Ellen to that effect. It is all due to General Sheridan who telegraphed to General Grant for my promotion and got it. I thank you, however, for what you would have done for me and have done. I cannot see what the Secretary could expect to gain by being so discourteous. I hope the rest of your trip will be sufficiently pleasant, and that you and Mother, Martha and George, will have enjoyed your visit east so as to obliterate the disagreeable part of it.

I expect to be made Chief of Staff, as the General told me he should give me that position. I have made arrangements to live in the same house with the General and have Ellen with me. It was his request that I should do so. I have written to Ellen to be ready to come on here the 1st of October as it will be safe for her to do so at that time. The children will be sent to some good school where they will learn and be well taken care of this winter; I would have them here if there were any good schools here.

I just now read your letter to General Sheridan, and he inquired if you had not shown General [W. T.] Sherman some courtesies when [he was] in Chicago. I told him you had. He remarked that that would explain the treatment received by you from the Secretary of War.

Will write again soon. It is most infernally hot here; never experienced such weather before.

Love to all, your son, Frank

The following excerpt from the now General Sherman's letter of August 30 to his mother shows perhaps a little insight into the implications of the Washington visit:

I suppose the visit to Washington was not as pleasant as it might have been, and especially to Father. The Secretary of War does not like the name "Sherman" and to that name Father must credit his reception from that high functionary.[5] I have got my promotion, and no thanks to Stanton for it. General Sheridan and General Grant could not well be refused, and so it came to pass that I am Brigadier General.

This has been the most infernally hot summer that I ever experienced, and so say the oldest inhabitants of New Orleans. There is no ice in the city, the supply having been used up. What we shall do here I do not know if none arrives in a day or so from Boston. I have been suffering terribly with the prickly heat, which covers my body all over, and even my face. I never would scold a child again that cried when the d——n stuff was out.

I would like to feel that I had a home to go to for me and mine when by the vicissitudes of fortune and the uncertainty of my present position I should require it . . .

I have no doubt but that General Sheridan will retain me with him as long as he can, but the day must come when all volunteer officers will be mustered out of the service no matter what their rank and record. If an army is retained by our country it must necessarily be a standing one and regularly organized. If the Monroe doctrine is to be sustained and Maximilian driven out of Mexico—which I am confident will be done—it will retain in service those of the volunteers who have not been mustered out until that is accomplished and our political faith as a nation vindicated.

The heat in the New Orleans summer may have been a factor in steering General Sherman's thoughts towards the time when his military career must come to an end. More significantly, Sheridan apparently did not make him chief of staff, perhaps because of his status as a volunteer, or possibly because Sheridan recognized that his own tenure as a military governor was fast coming to an end and he was not in a position to make more appointments at the chief of staff level.

Meanwhile, it is not clear whether Francis Sherman accompanied General Sheridan on his mission to the Mexican border for a display of strength against the troops that the French Emperor Napoleon III had sent to Mexico to bolster Maximilian. Generals Grant and Sheridan would have liked to cross the border and help out the Mexicans under Juárez, particularly since they felt that the emperor had supported the Confederacy, but the State Department was opposed to any show of force that might alienate the French.

In his letter to his mother of September 12, General Sherman remained bitter about what he perceived as insufficient backing at home for his promotion:

It makes me happy to learn that your visit East has been beneficial to you all but more happy still to receive your congratulations on my promotion. I believe we all of us now know who has been my firm and steadfast friend [Sheridan]. I feel no less pride than you do in the fact that I am not beholden to my numerous Chicago friends for my present position in the Army.

I have sent you today two pictures of myself taken here by Captain [James S.] Ransom. I hope they will be satisfactory to you. One of these pictures I wish you to give to Father [-in-law] Vedder, the other to yourself.

. . . If we should have a war with Mexico I shall probably remain in service until it ended. If there is no war I may be mustered out at any time, as it is the policy to reduce the Army to the smallest possible limit and reduce the expense of the national government. Who can tell what will occur in the next six months? One thing is patent to me; the French and Austrians will have to get out of Mexico, gracefully if they will, forcibly if they must.

I hope to see you and father down here this winter . . .

The next three letters are concerned primarily with the sale of a house that General Sherman's father apparently had bought for him, and with reiterated invitations to his parents to spend the cold months with him in New Orleans. On September 30, the new General Sherman wrote to his father in response to a proposed business opportunity:

The proposition to enter into partnership with Uncle Alva in the lumber business I must own took me completely by surprise. That it would be advantageous to me in a pecuniary way I have no doubt. . . . However tempting the offer I am constrained to decline the alliance for the following reasons:

First, through the exertion and influence of General Sheridan, I have but just received an appointment to my present grade in the army;

Second, this grade was solicited in my behalf from General Grant by General Sheridan because I could be useful to him, and duty and gratitude demand alike that I should not hastily leave where such disinterested friendship and appreciation had been shown me by so distinguished and able a gentleman.

Third, I feel, therefore, that under the circumstances I am only doing simple justice to myself and my honor not to accept the proposition of you and Uncle Alva for the present.

Do not think that I do not appreciate the offer and the kindness and interest that you have so generously manifested for my welfare in this matter . . . now, if I could have until March next to accept or decline it might be different. Long before that time events which are now on the horizon will determine whether the service of volunteers will be required in Mexico. This I give you as a private reason. If the matter can wait for a short time I will give you a direct answer, yes or no. I don't want you or Uncle Alva to be under a misapprehension in regard to this business. I will say that the chances are that I will not be able to go into it for the reasons named. I hope that they will be sufficient, Father, and that you appreciate my present position.

One may infer from this letter that Frank Sherman did not want to resume the dependency on his father for his employment that he had escaped through being in the army. If he could not remain in the army, he wanted to make it on his own.

By October 20, Ellen had arrived, and General Sherman, now content—well, almost content—with his new rank, wrote to his mother:

> General Sheridan has placed at [Ellen's] disposal his elegant turnout whenever she desires to ride or to go about the city . . .
> I am glad the photographs I sent pleased you. As for the 'Star' I have not found that it is burdensome and could if urged carry another alongside of it without feeling any physical disability from its weight. Well, I am satisfied and content as it is.
> I have been afflicted with the asthma lately severely in connection with a prevalent fever called the "dengue," but am better.[6]

A week later, on October 27, Frank Sherman wrote to his father, employing his accustomed heavy-handed sarcasm:

> Everything is quiet from a military point of view. There is some political agitation as the state election draws nigh; it takes place on the 6th of November. There is every indication that the so-called Democrats will elect their ticket. These Democrats have fought us at home and in the field for the past four years trying to subvert the Government and erect their bogus affair upon the ruins. Failing in that, with the defeat of their armies, they have become suddenly, through the amnesty oath and the President's pardon, the most loyal people in the country and eager to administer the State and National Governments for the glory of free institutions and filling their empty pockets from the State and National Treasuries.
> It is wonderfully pleasant to look on and see the patriotism displayed by these immaculate gentlemen of the south, the mirror and soul of chivalry, whose whole aim and object is to sustain the President in his recon-

struction policy, and who claim that they are the persons who can enter into his view entirely and carry out his wishes in this great task. To have been traitors, to have used the wealth and talents at their disposal for the breaking up of the old Government, seems to be the greatest qualification which a man can put forward for position and appears to be more deserving of reward from those in authority in Washington than those who spilled their blood freely to maintain the integrity of the Union.

This is the last of the wartime letters. Brig. Gen. Francis T. Sherman was mustered out of the army in February 1866. Like many former officers, he appears never quite to have recovered from his experience of command. He lived a restless life after that, dabbling in several enterprises with indifferent success. He remained in Louisiana until the spring of 1867, trying unsuccessfully to run a sugar plantation in Jefferson Parish, a few miles south of New Orleans, and losing his entire investment of twenty-five thousand dollars.[7] In August 1867, he was appointed postmaster for the city of Chicago by President Andrew Johnson, but that post lasted only a year, because President Grant appointed a Republican in his place. After his father died in 1870, Frank took over part of his father's duties at the Sherman House and at about the same time started a manufacturing business. Both enterprises were wiped out the next year by the great Chicago fire. Although the Shermans received only 15 percent of the insured value of the hotel, they rebuilt, only to lose the new building during the financial Panic of 1873.

The closest General Sherman came to his old glory was immediately after the fire, when he was chosen by General Sheridan, whose headquarters then were in Chicago, to command volunteer troops who had been mobilized to halt looting. When the fire began, Sheridan had just returned from hunting buffalo on the western frontier. At the height of the conflagration, he ordered several buildings blown up to save other buildings behind them. On October 9, while the fire was still raging, Sheridan was asked by a group of citizens, led by City Prosecutor Thomas W. Grosvenor, to place the city under martial law. Sheridan agreed, and martial law was proclaimed by Democratic Mayor Roswell W. Mason on October 11. Sheridan called in six companies of regular troops from Kansas and at the same time authorized the enlistment of one thousand volunteers. The volunteers were called "Sheridan's Guards" and were commanded by Gen. Francis Sherman.

The Republican governor, John M. Palmer, perhaps believing that he should have been in charge of martial law, was highly critical of Mason for letting federal troops patrol the city. He was even more critical on October 20, when Theodore Treat, a nineteen-year-old volunteer, shot and killed Grosvenor, the prosecutor who had called for martial law, apparently mistaking him for a looter. Governor Palmer sought without success to have General Sheridan, Mayor Mason, Treat, and General Sherman all indicted for murder. Three days later, the volunteers disbanded, and Frank Sherman's last military command came to an end.[8]

In 1872, Sherman was elected to the Illinois House of Representatives as a Democrat, but he soon found out that he was not a politician by temperament and served only two terms. In 1876, at age fifty, he led a party of four on horseback on a trip to the Arizona and New Mexico territories. This trip was made at the request of the 57th Illinois Infantry Volunteer Regiment, which was looking for a site for a colony for its surviving members.[9] For General Sherman, this trip in some way may have represented a return to his military life, as he wrote in his diary that he felt like a new man:

> The climate is unexceptionable and healthy, the atmosphere being dry and pure. The hills are covered with a growth of dwarf cedar and fair pine of small size. There is plenty to sustain animal life, except water. As a consequence of the lack of water there are no cattle or sheep in these ranges which are otherwise so well adapted for grazing. There is no game of any kind.
>
> The hills with their grand perspective and charming scenery are untenanted and given over to solemn silences and grandeur only disturbed by occasional muleteer and ox-drivers as they halloo and crack their whips at their teams. When they have passed nature resumes its sway. Every day brings to light some new beauty and delight to view. I feel like a new man renewing my age under the invigorating influences that surround me. We have discomforts, but they are more than compensated for by the novelty of our situation.
>
> . . . 12 o'clock midnight is the time when this was written by the light of a camp fire whilst on guard duty over our stock and plunder, all we have to take us through the long journey yet before us.
>
> At this lonely vigil thoughts of home and the loved ones there arise, and the wish to be with them tugs at the heart strings. Also to know that they are well, and thinking of the husband and father now and then . . .

Frank Sherman and his crew spent much of their time on this trip looking for water, which may have reminded him of the Perryville campaign in 1862, but they could not find a suitably irrigated spot for the 57th Regiment. In his diary note of September 30, 1876, Frank wrote, "What a waste and desert it is . . . Millions of the human family could be made happy and rich in its healthful climate. All this and more but for the want of one element, water. Its only inhabitants now are the wild beasts. This must surely be so for some wise purpose, past human ken. Well, I enjoy the scene and take in deep draughts of the beauties and sublimities of nature . . . One needs no other society."

Sherman remained in Tucson for a while after the party dispersed, hoping

Francis Trowbridge Sherman, circa 1875. Collection of C. Knight Aldrich.

at last to make his fortune. Unfortunately, he was no more successful this time than he had been in his search for gold in California in 1850 or his attempt to run a sugar plantation in 1866 and 1867.

One letter to Ellen, dated October 29 from Tucson, is all that we have about his stay in that frontier town. It sounds familiar themes; Frank still was troubled about the lack of mail, and he still was optimistic about advancement:

It seems to me that I should have received more letters than have come to hand. . . . I know, my dear wife, that you are making a brave struggle to get along, and that many discouragements and impediments are in your way. To remove them is my hope and wish, but I fear that it cannot be accomplished in this territory for a long time to come, unless I have some capital to start with. . . . [General Sherman then discusses at some length the discouraging results of his exploration of opportunities in farming, mining, and milling] . . . Of course, we could not live in Tucson at present unless I had a government office that would pay, say Governor or Marshal or Collector of Customs, which might be, provided Tilden is elected.

Samuel J. Tilden, the Democratic candidate for president in 1876, came close to being elected. A week after this letter was written, he received a quarter of a million more popular votes for president than his Republican opponent, Gen. Rutherford B. Hayes. Hayes, however, received one more electoral college vote than Tilden, and with that vote went the last chance for a political appointment for Frank Sherman. He returned to Chicago and in 1879, in partnership with his brother-in-law, started a company, Sherman and Marsh, to make and sell barbed wire. It did not do well, and Frank lived the rest of his long life in relative obscurity and in straitened circumstances.

His last contact with Sheridan was in October 1880, when he went to New York to testify at the Warren Court of Inquiry. On April 1, 1865, Sheridan had relieved Maj. Gen. Gouverneur K. Warren of his command of the 5th Corps following the Battle of Five Forks for being too slow in deploying his troops, and Warren—and the Court of Inquiry—thought that the accusation was unwarranted. Sherman's testimony apparently was not too helpful to either side; in it he "characterized Warren's demeanor as having been 'earnestly impassive,'" which led to some "sharp if fruitless exchanges [with Warren's counsel] to clarify what he meant."[10]

In 1890, the Shermans moved to Waukegan, Illinois, the home of Ellen's family. Frank had become ill with valvular heart disease, which, together with his continuing asthma, made him an invalid for the last fifteen years of his life. In the fall of 1905, he contracted pneumonia and died on November 9, not quite two months before his eightieth birthday and shortly after his and Ellen's fifty-fourth wedding anniversary. According to the memorial adopted by the Military Order of the Loyal Legion of the United States, he died "poor in prosperity and purse, but rich in character and honor."[11]

General Sherman had been receiving a pension of twelve dollars a month; after his death, Ellen sought to receive a larger pension on the basis that her husband had died of a service-connected condition. According to the pension records, "Mrs. Sherman is in needy circumstances. She has no property or other resources. Her husband, in his lifetime, was in receipt of a good salary, but he was generous and liberal to his old comrades and at his death left nothing . . .

it is believed that the distinguished services of the soldier and the widow's ne-
cessitous circumstances merit a more liberal allowance."[12]

Ellen's claim at first was denied, but she persevered until, through a Special
Act introduced by an unidentified member of Congress[13] and approved on
March 1, 1907, she was granted a pension of thirty dollars a month. She enjoyed
her dollar a day for only a brief period; she died on December 30, 1907, at the
age of seventy-eight. She was survived by two daughters, Ella Sherman Marsh
and Lulu Sherman Aldrich (my grandmother); two sons, Francis Cornwall
Sherman II and Eaton Goodell Sherman; and six grandchildren, one of them
my father, Louis Sherman Aldrich.

NOTES

Abbreviations

NA National Archives, Washington, D.C.

OR U.S. War Department, *The War of the Rebellion: A Compilation of the Official Records of the Union and Confederate Armies,* 70 vols. (Washington D.C.: Government Printing Office, 1880–1901).

Preface

1. From "Sheridan's Ride," a once popular poem written by Thomas Buchanan Read (in Thomas Buchanan Read, *Sheridan's Ride* [Philadelphia: J. B. Lippincott Co., 1892]) about the Cedar Creek victory; the poem was used for recruiting and by the Republicans in the 1864 election. When Sheridan, at his headquarters near Winchester, Va., heard of a Confederate breakthrough at Cedar Creek, he turned his horse's head and, "with a slight touch of the spur . . . dashed up the turnpike and was off . . . [on] the black charger, Rienzi. A magnificent animal, seventeen hands high, the horse was a gift to Sheridan from the men of the Second Michigan Cavalry." David Dixon, *Hero of Beecher Island* (Lincoln: Univ. of Nebraska Press, 1994), 46.

2. Colonel Sherman was 5 feet, 11-1/2 inches tall and weighed 170 pounds.

3. Charles L. Francis, *Narrative of a Private Soldier* (Brooklyn, N.Y.: Wm. Jenkins & Co., 1879), 67.

4. Although Mayor Sherman was against slavery, he was not always for slaves. In the fall of 1862, supported by the City Council, who thought that freed slaves might take jobs away from white citizens, he turned down an army request to cooperate in seeking employment in Chicago for slaves liberated by the Union armies. Clarence W. Alvord, ed., *Centennial History of Illinois* (Springfield, Ill.: Illinois Centennial Commission, 1920), 3:334.

5. Historian James McPherson observes that "sometimes the Victorian idioms in which soldiers expressed their patriotism become almost cloying . . . [but] what seems like bathos and platitudes to us were real pathos or convictions to them"; James M. McPherson, *For Cause and Comrades—Why Men Fought in the Civil War* (New York: Oxford Univ. Press, 1997), 99–100.

6. "Mail call was the brightest part of a soldier's day—if he received a letter from home. If he did not, his spirits sank" (McPherson, *For Cause and Comrades,* 132).

7. Colonel Sherman's letters and diaries are in the library of the Chicago Historical Society.

8. Although I have been able to identify most of the men Colonel Sherman mentions and correct the spelling of their names (for example, he wrote Confederate Colonel Ould's name as "Oldild"; see ch. 11, n. 31), a few have defied identification. These unidentified men appear in the text with rank and surname only, as "Captain DeSand," not "Captain John DeSand."

1. A Chicago Innkeeper and His Son

1. Two Democrats fought the election of 1856 in Chicago, because the Whig party was no longer strong enough to run a campaign in the city and the Republicans had not yet developed a base of support. In this election, it was alleged that more votes were cast than there were eligible voters—Chicago's reputation for crooked elections began early. Bessie L. Pierce, *A History of Chicago* (New York: Knopf, 1940), 2:213.

2. George P. Upton and Elias Colbert, *Biographical Sketches of the Leading Men of Chicago* (Chicago: Wilson, St. Clair Co., 1868), 625–26.

3. In the 1841 mayoral election, Sherman defeated his Whig opponent, Isaac R. Gavin, by a vote of 460 to 419; Pierce, *History of Chicago,* 1:421.

4. Ibid., 2:213.

5. Upton and Colbert, *Biographical Sketches,* 626.

6. Unsigned editorial, *Chicago Daily Tribune,* Apr. 15, 1861.

7. Pierce, *History of Chicago,* 2:254.

8. In an 1833 treaty, the Potawatomies, along with the Ottawas and the Chippewas, had ceded 5,000,000 acres of land to the United States for about $1,000,000, paid in annuities. As Moses and Kirkland put it in 1895, "the time had come when the necessities of the white race demanded these vast tracts for the superior uses of civilization" (John Moses and James Kirkland, History of Chicago, Illinois [Chicago: Munsell & Co., 1895], 1:92).

9. Upton and Colbert, *Biographical Sketches,* 625. In 1834 education in Chicago was limited to a few "family" or "subscription" schools. Public schools officially began in 1835, although three years later the average term was still less than six weeks (Pierce, *History of Chicago,* 1:269). It is not known whether Francis T. Sherman went to school or was taught at home by a private tutor or, perhaps, by his mother. Neither his mother nor his father, however, could spell or write as well as he could.

10. Bucket Company No. 1 provided a bucket brigade of 25 volunteers and 160 buckets. See Alfred T. Andreas, *History of Chicago* (New York: Arno Press, 1975, 1:223).

11. Robert T. Sherman Jr., ed., *Letters from the Gold Rush* (Chicago: Privately published by R. T. Sherman, 1980), 2.
12. Ibid., 14.
13. James M. Woodman, ed., *Portrait and Biographical Album of Lake County, Illinois* (Waukegan, Ill.: Lake Publishing Co., 1891), 674–75.
14. From the collection of Robert T. Sherman Jr., Glenview, Ill.
15. Andreas, *History of Chicago*, 2:161.
16. The Mechanics' Union Association was not so much a trade union as an organization for the social and cultural benefit of its members. It developed the Mechanics' Institute, which promoted adult education through a museum, library, lectures, and fairs. Pierce, *History of Chicago*, 1:288–89.
17. On Sept. 4, Colonel Wilson wrote to the adjutant general that his regiment was "full and ready for mustering into service. Where shall I consolidate them? To whom shall I apply for subsistence, transportation, etc.? Companies are now stationed in Ind., Ill., and Mich. Regiment is numbered 1249 rank and file." Office of Adjutant General, Volunteer Branch, 1861 Letter File, NA, G-80.
18. U.S. War Department, *Combined Service Records of Military Units in Volunteer Organizations, 1861–65,* 1862, NA, M-594, Roll 27. Camp Douglas originally was a training center; later it became a military prison. Eisendrath, in writing about Camp Douglas, says that "the Mechanics' Fusileers [*sic*] were among the first in camp." Joseph L. Eisendrath, "Camp Douglas," *Journal of the Illinois State Historical Society* 53, no. 1 (1960): 37–63.
19. Arlo Guthrie, father of a captain in the regiment, wrote on Dec. 27, 1861, to then Secretary of War Simon Cameron, that "the regiment had generally signed a petition for Wilson's removal, and that they now understand that Col. Wilson has gone to Washington with a petition signed by the men for his retention in command; they state that if he has any such thing it is probable that the heading has been removed and another substituted . . . there are very few if any one of the soldiers (privates) who would wish in any way to be under his command. I think he is entirely unfit to have a responsible command . . . [my son] says it would be dangerous for Wilson to come into the camp" (Office of Adjutant General, Volunteer Branch, 1861 Letter File, NA, G-80). Colonel Wilson made several applications to the War Department as late as 1866 to become recognized and paid for his services with the Mechanics' Fusiliers, but each time he was unequivocally turned down.
20. Thomas M. Eddy, *Patriotism of Illinois* (Chicago: Clarke & Co., 1865), 2:72–73.
21. In a memorandum written after the war was over, Asst. Adj. Gen. Thomas M. Vincent called the regiment a "mob, raised under false pretenses" and mustered out "in consequence of its demoralized condition" (Office of Adjutant General, Volunteer Branch, 1861 Letter File, NA, G-80). According to Sherman's official military record, "This regiment was raised to service as 'Mechanics' Fusiliers,' but there being no law under which it could be recognized as such, the Field and Staff was mustered into and out of the U.S. service on the same day, as Infantry, in compliance with instructions from the A. G. O. dated Jan'y 18, '62." U.S. War Department, *Official Register of the Volunteer Forces of the U.S. Army for the Years 1861–1865,* 7:309.

22. Only this second 56th Illinois appears in the official records. U.S. War Department, *Official Army Register of the Volunteer Forces of the U.S. Army for the Years 1861–65*, 6:309–10. The Mechanics' Fusiliers appears to have vanished completely from official notice.

23. Francis T. Sherman, "Autobiography" (1899, typescript in Papers of J. Frank Aldrich, Chicago Historical Society Library).

24. William H. Newlin et al., eds., *A History of the 73rd Regiment of Illinois Infantry Volunteers* (Chicago: Privately published, 1890), 69. This regiment shared guard duty for a brief period with the 12th Illinois Cavalry.

25. Jordan enlisted in the Confederate army on June 5, 1861, at Jackson, Tenn. He was wounded and captured soon thereafter at Hamburg. Ky., and remained in Camp Douglas and other Union prisons until paroled on May 1, 1865.

26. Jackson had been sent to the Shenandoah valley to threaten a raid on Washington and so to draw Union troops away from McClellan's army, which was approaching Richmond. In this effort Jackson had driven Banks's Union troops out of the towns of Front Royal and Winchester, and down the valley to Martinsburg in what is now West Virginia. Jackson's success had the hoped-for result; it led Union strategists to believe that he was planning to raid the capitol city, and to send substantial Union reinforcements from the Richmond area, who soon forced Jackson to withdraw. Allan Nevins, *The War for the Union* (New York: Scribner's, 1959), 2:123.

27. Ruth Scarborough, *Belle Boyd: Siren of the South* (Macon, Ga.: Mercer Univ. Press, 1983), 68.

28. Belle Boyd, *Belle Boyd in Camp and Prison* (New York: Blelock & Co., 1865), 148.

29. Ibid., 166.

30. A handwritten copy of this report was included in Papers of Francis T. Sherman, Chicago Historical Society Library.

31. The date of an officer's commission determined his seniority and thus was important in the assignment of command. See ch. 3.

32. The "Copperheads" derived their name from the poisonous snake. The term was first used in Ohio in 1861. See ch. 5, n. 12.

33. Pierce, *History of Chicago*, 2:506.

2. The 88th Illinois Goes to War

1. Gen. William T. Sherman's "nervous breakdown" is discussed in Charles E. Vetter, *Sherman* (Gretna, La.: Pelican Publishing Co., 1992), 91–102; and in Lloyd Lewis, *Sherman: Fighting Prophet* (New York: Harcourt Brace, 1932), 182–92 and 202–203.

2. Wilbur Thomas, *General George H. Thomas* (New York: Exposition Press, 1964), 236–46.

3. In a referendum held soon after Tennessee formally seceded, the whole state voted by a margin of 2-1/2 to 1 to cast its lot with the Confederacy. The eastern counties, however, voted 3 to 1 to remain with the Union. At that time, the East Tennesseeans

tried to break away from the rest of the state and join the Union, but they were blocked by Confederate troops sent to occupy the area. In September 1861, Unionists under the leadership of Rev. William B. Carter made an offer to President Lincoln to assist a northern invasion by burning bridges and otherwise obstructing the Confederate forces. Lincoln accepted the offer, and the invasion was scheduled to be carried out in November by a division of Gen. W. T. Sherman's Army of the Ohio.

In October, Sherman canceled the invasion, but the news did not get through to the East Tennessee Unionists. They went ahead with the bridge burnings, but, without the support of Union troops, they were left exposed to Confederate retaliation. Lincoln knew that he had let them down, so, when he received reports of atrocities committed by the Rebel army against East Tennessee Unionists, he gave a high priority to driving the Confederates out of East Tennessee as soon as possible. Stanley F. Horn, ed., *Tennessee's War* (Nashville: Tennessee Civil War Centennial Commission, 1965), 117; Noel Fisher, "The Leniency Shown Them Has Been Unavailing: The Confederate Occupation of Eastern Tennessee," *Civil War History* 40, no. 4 (1994): 275–91. Individual accounts of the conflict in East Tennessee, from the Confederate viewpoint, can be found in Daniel E. Sutherland, ed., *A Very Violent Rebel* (Knoxville: Univ. of Tennessee Press, 1996), and Willene B. Clark, ed., *Valleys of the Shadow* (Knoxville: Univ. of Tennessee Press, 1994).

4. Buell's view has had substantial support from Civil War historians. For example, Ludwell Johnson, "Civil War Military History: A Few Revisions in Need of Revising," *Civil War History* 17 (1971): 123, states that Lincoln's plan showed a "total disregard for logistical realities."

5. Kentucky, birthplace of both Abraham Lincoln and Jefferson Davis and neutral at the beginning of the war, had decided to remain in the Union. Even so, Kentucky harbored much sympathy for the South, and the Confederacy thought that the state might yet secede if Rebel troops controlled it. To that end, in mid-August, Gen. Kirby Smith invaded Kentucky from Knoxville, defeated a Union force at Richmond, and reached as far north as Lexington, only 60 miles from the Ohio River. The Kentuckians, however, did not show much support for the Confederacy, and Kirby Smith's invasion went no farther. When it became clear that Smith was not headed for Cincinnati, the Union command worried that he might be planning to rejoin Gen. Braxton Bragg's main Army of Tennessee for an attack on Louisville. General Buell, therefore, postponed plans to head east and marched from Nashville to Louisville (Thomas, *General Thomas,* 240).

6. Francis, *Private Soldier,* 46.

7. Thomas, *General Thomas,* 243–45.

8. Most regimental officers in the Union army, who were responsible for training enlisted men, were themselves inexperienced. Senior officers in volunteer regiments were appointed by state governments and often had little, if any, military training; regular army officers remained with their regular army units. This policy not only deprived volunteer regiments of trained and experienced leadership, but also made regular

officers resent volunteer officers, since the pace of promotion in the regular units was slower than among the volunteers. The Confederacy made better use of its West Point graduates, "seeding" them throughout its army.

9. "Our arms were of the meanest kind, even for that period—old smoothbore flint-lock muskets changed to the more modern style for percussion caps. They were heavy and dreadful kickers" (Francis, *Private Soldier*, 47).

10. Horn, *Tennessee's War*, 128.

11. OR, ser. I, vol. 16, ch. 28, p. 89.

12. According to Van Horne, "During the night, Colonel Daniel McCook's brigade of Sheridan's division had been thrown forward from the center to occupy the heights in front of Doctor's Creek, about two and a half miles from Perryville. After a sharp skirmish Col. McCook succeeded at daylight in gaining the heights, and secured some pools of water in the bed of the stream . . . for the thirsty troops. About two hours after the heights had been occupied, the enemy in considerable force advanced through the woods . . . and endeavored to regain the position . . . after a severe conflict in which both sides lost heavily, the enemy was forced across the river." Thomas B. Van Horne, *History of the Army of the Cumberland* (Cincinnati, Oh.: Robert Clarke & Co., 1875), 1:186.

13. Horn, *Tennessee's War*, 182. Accounts of the peculiar battle of Perryville also can be found in Thomas, *General Thomas*, 242–49, and Nevins, *War for the Union*, 2:286–87. See also critical accounts by Capt. Marcus Woodcock, in Kenneth W. Noe, ed., *A Southern Boy in Blue* (Knoxville: Univ. of Tennessee Press, 1996), 103–105; and by Francis F. McKinney, in his *Education in Violence* (Detroit: Wayne State Univ. Press, 1961), 102–6.

14. Chaplain Bennett of the 36th Illinois Volunteer Infantry was not as impressed. He wrote that, when the more experienced 36th regiment fell back to replenish its ammunition, it passed through the 88th, "a new regiment and under fire for the first time. The retrograde movement of the 36th through their line was construed by some as a retreat, and created a ripple of excitement nearly approaching a panic. A half dozen or more files broke for the rear . . . and the men wavered as if on the point of flying . . . Observing this, Colonel Sherman and the regimental field officers were instantly at the spot exerting their influence as well as authority . . . and by threats and example the officers succeeded in restoring order." Bennett concedes that the 88th then "fought like tigers until the battle ended." Lyman G. Bennett, *History of the 36th Regiment of Illinois Volunteer Infantry During the War of the Great Rebellion* (Aurora, Ill.: Knickerbocker and Holder, 1876), 267.

15. OR, ser. I, vol. 16, pt. 1, pp. 1081–85.

16. According to Van Horne, *Army of the Cumberland*, 195, "Though Gen. Bragg had withdrawn his army, Gen. Buell still believed that he would deliver battle, and that [Gen. Kirby] Smith's army had joined him for that purpose. He therefore determined to await the arrival of Gen. Sill's division, which he had ordered forward from Frankfurt."

17. After the battle at Corinth, a few days before Perryville, Union troops under Rosecrans, Ord, and McPherson chased Confederate troops under Van Dorn as

far as Ripley. Mark M. Boatner, *The Civil War Dictionary* (New York: David McKay Co., 1966), 177.

18. Bruce Catton, *This Hallowed Ground* (New York: Doubleday, 1956, Pocket Books ed.), 213. Chaplain Bennett, in his *History of the 36th Illinois,* wrote, "General Gilbert had no just conception of the peculiar treatment necessary to control the American volunteer, and when he began to treat him in ways that implied equality with the dregs of society so often swept into a regular army, he woke a spirit of opposition" (297). See also ch. 3, n. 1.

19. Unfortunately for him, Rosecrans did not inspire equal confidence in his superiors. He tended to be irritable and impulsive, and given to tactless outbursts and angry indiscretions. By the time he took command of the Army of the Cumberland, he had alienated Secretary of War Stanton, General McClellan, and, most damaging of all, General Grant. William C. Lamers, *The Edge of Glory* (New York: Harcourt Brace, 1961), 85. However, Rosecrans had commanded the Army of the Mississippi with distinction under Grant, and he had the support of both President Lincoln and General-in-Chief Halleck. Since McClellan's star was setting and Grant's had not yet risen, and since everybody else also seemed to alienate Secretary Stanton, Rosecrans got the job.

20. Francis, *Private Soldier,* 75.

21. Ibid., 82.

22. Ibid., 90.

23. Ibid., 86. Colonel Sherman was very intolerant of stealing (see ch. 11, n. 24).

24. Philip H. Sheridan, *Memoirs of P. H. Sheridan* (New York: Charles R. Webster & Co., 1888), 1:252–53.

25. Another deterrent to the appointment of general officers in the Civil War was attrition; as brigades lost men through enemy action, disease, resignation, and desertion, their numbers often fell below the minimum required to justify a commander of the rank of brigadier general. At such times, the brigade's general probably would be reassigned to another, adequately manned brigade, to replace a colonel who had been in command temporarily. After the carnage at Stones River, where all the brigade commanders in Sheridan's division were killed, Colonel Sherman was given command of a brigade, but soon thereafter lost it to someone with greater seniority. On other occasions, he was given command of a brigade for a short while but then was superseded by a general from another part of the army, one who might have had a great deal less combat experience than Sherman but who outranked him. Colonel Sherman appears to have recognized from the start, however, that his command of the foraging expedition near Nashville was temporary; he probably viewed it realistically, as no more than a measure of General Sheridan's confidence in him.

3. Battle of Stones River

1. Horn, *Tennessee's War,* 125–29.

2. Rosecrans had reorganized his army so that Sheridan's division was now in General Alexander McCook's Corps.

3. Gen. Jefferson C. Davis, a Union general and no kin to the Confederate president, had shot and killed Gen. William Nelson, his then commanding officer, on Sept. 29, 1862, after a bitter argument which culminated in Nelson's calling Davis a liar. He was not tried at court martial, perhaps because he had strong political connections; a little over five weeks after the shooting, he was given command of a division.

4. McKinney, *Education in Violence,* 187–96.

5. Sheridan, *Memoirs,* 1:216–35.

6. Roy Morris, Jr., *The Life and Wars of General Philip H. Sheridan* (New York: Crown Publishing, 1992), 111. See also Lamers, *Edge of Glory,* 249.

7. Colonel Sherman's commission was dated August 15, 1862. There was a precedent for changing such dates, and the precedent was close to home. General Rosecrans was made major general of volunteers on September 17, 1862; but when President Lincoln wanted to appoint him to command the Army of the Cumberland, he backdated the commission to March 21, 1862, and so gave seniority to Rosecrans over General Thomas. Lamers, *Edge of Glory,* 175–76.

8. An indecipherable diagram at the foot of the page is crossed off with the words, "This diagram is not to be used. Refer to the one in pencil [which is lost]." The quality of Colonel Sherman's map making did not equal that of his penmanship.

9. Private Francis did not share Colonel Sherman's rosy view of his regiment's behavior. Earlier in the battle, the private had become separated from the regiment; later he reported "seeing the Eighty-eighth in one disorderly mass near the cotton press, and the Colonel was wildly gesticulating as if endeavoring to have the regiment rally and form into line; but I also saw that he failed altogether, and the men hastily retreated in a demoralized manner to the woods in the rear . . . that is the last I saw of the Eighty-eighth." Private Francis was taken prisoner soon thereafter. Francis, *Private Soldier,* 115.

10. The last half of this letter concerns Chicago politics and is printed in ch. 4.

11. The heavy casualties suffered by the 88th Illinois at Stones River had brought its numbers below half its original force and made it too small to justify having a colonel as its commanding officer. This rule was not always strictly followed.

12. Frederick Tuttle was vice-president of the Chicago Mercantile Association, which "cooperated with the Chicago Board of Trade in all patriotic objectives," presumably including the sponsorship and organization of regiments. Andreas, *History of Chicago,* 2:348.

4. Chicago Politics

1. Cook wrote that "Francis C. Sherman, a rather negative character, at the beginning of the war was an avowed War Democrat, and his son, Francis T., a very resolute character, led a regiment into the field. . . . as time went on the elder became less outspoken for the war; and the fact that he permitted himself to lead a party dominated by the peace-at-any-price element, made his position, to say the least, an equivocal one. In this, however, he only reflected the average of his party which, through loyalty to a name and dislike of its opponents, permitted a determined

minority to place it in a position pregnant with disaster to the cause of the Union." Frederick F. Cook, *Bygone Days in Chicago* (Chicago: A. C. McClurg, 1910), 60.

2. Newspapers began to be published early in Chicago's history, and by 1853, the twenty-year-old city had seven daily newspapers (a hundred years later, with a population one hundred times larger, it had only two newspapers). In 1861, the *Chicago Daily Tribune* had become the strongest Chicago paper, with a circulation of almost 16,500. The antislavery *Tribune* had helped launch the new Republican party in the 1850s and had taken over several of its opposition competitors. The *Daily Chicago Times* emerged in the late fifties and by the beginning of the Civil War had become the main newspaper supporting the Democratic party. As was the fashion of the day, both the *Tribune* and the *Times* were uninhibited in their editorial criticism of the other's politics. Pierce, *History of Chicago,* 2:412–14.

3. The first part of this letter, which describes military activities, is printed in ch. 5.

4. Absentee ballots were sanctioned in a few states but not in Illinois until the presidential election of November 1864. Since the troops were thought to be politically Republican, Democrats opposed and Republicans favored absentee voting. On election day, 1862, "Democrats claimed that [Republican Governor] Yates was allowing Republican soldiers at Camp Butler to go home while [Democratic] troops from Southern Illinois were being kept out of their districts." Bruce Tap, "Race, Rhetoric, and Emancipation: The Election of 1862 in Illinois," *Civil War History* 39, no. 2 (1993): 113.

5. Frederick Tuttle was the Chicago Mercantile Association official mentioned in ch. 3.

6. See ch. 5 for the rest of the March 8 letter.

7. See ch. 5 for the rest of the March 15 letter.

8. The owner of the *Chicago Times,* Wilbur F. Storey, was a persistent and outspoken critic of the Lincoln administration and its management of the war. Although Storey was not hanged as a traitor, Gov. Richard Yates and others called for his paper's suppression. When the paper went so far as to denounce Vallandigham's arrest, Maj. Gen. Ambrose E. Burnside ordered its suppression, and, on June 3, 1863, Union soldiers took over its offices. The suppression lasted only two days, however, in the face of strong demonstrations against the abrogation of free speech and a free press. Craig D. Tenney, "To Suppress or Not to Suppress: Abraham Lincoln and the Chicago Times," *Civil War History* 27, no. 3 (1981): 248–59. See also Pierce, *History of Chicago,* 2:415–16.

9. Unsigned editorial, *Chicago Daily Tribune,* Apr. 21, 1863.

10. Ibid., Apr. 19, 1863.

11. Ibid., Apr. 20, 1863.

12. Ibid., Apr. 21, 1863.

13. Ibid., Apr. 22, 1863.

14. Orrin G. Rose was elected (as a Democrat) to the Board of Commissioners of Public Works. The *Chicago Tribune* stated, on Oct. 26, 1863, that Rose had been "guilty of bribery" in the past and was "no more fitted than a horse" for service on the Board of Public Works.

15. The antislavery Colonel Sherman might not have thought the platform so "good" if

a proposed amendment had not been withdrawn. With the amendment, the platform would have supported "government as it was, the constitution as it is, and the niggers as they were." Tap, "Race, Rhetoric, and Emancipation," 114. Colonel Sherman's antislavery sentiments were not shared by all of his command. Private Francis reported that "there were some—a wonderfully small minority—in our army who were almost seditiously inclined; officers [not named] resigned their commissions rather than be engaged in the forced emancipation of the negroes." Francis, *Private Soldier,* 60.

16. Colonel Sherman apparently continued to be "as good a Democrat as ever"; he was reputed to have supported McClellan in the 1864 election (ch. 11, n. 24), and he ran as a Democrat for the Illinois Legislature in the 1870s.

17. The rest of the letters of May 1 and 7 concern military matters and are included in the next chapter.

18. Pierce, *History of Chicago,* 2:279.

19. Agent William Taylor, whose veracity has been seriously questioned, reported to Provost Marshal Col. John P. Sanderson on July 12, 1864, about a trip he had taken from St. Louis to Chicago, masquerading as a southern sympathizer in order to investigate the Order of American Knights (successors of the Knights of the Golden Circle). He stated that, at Chicago, he had interviewed Mayor Sherman, who told him about the order's political activities in the city and said that the group would elect McClellan president "by fair or foul means." Sherman also said that the order thought that Lincoln might use the army to assure his reelection, and that if he did, "it would be a just cause on their part to rise and turn him out." Although Taylor, in reporting this conversation, did not make it clear whether Sherman was a member of the order or simply an informant, he later included Sherman in a partial list of members (OR, sec. II, vol. 7, p. 746). The validity of Sanderson's reports has been seriously questioned, and Klement says that "Sanderson's tall tales about the American Knights were devised largely as propaganda to influence the 1864 election results." Frank L. Klement, *Dark Lanterns* (Chicago: Univ. of Chicago Press, 1960), 90.

5. A Quiet Spring in Camp

1. The Jordans, in all likelihood, were the parents of Pvt. J. D. Jordan, CSA (see ch. 1, n. 24).

2. Sheridan did not always share information about his plans with his subordinates.

3. "'Our armies swore terribly in Flanders,' cried my Uncle Toby,—but nothing to this.'" Laurence Sterne, *Tristram Shandy,* bk. 3, ch. 11.

4. This was not the better known battle at Spring Hill a year later, between Union troops under Gen. John M. Schofield and Confederates under Gen. Nathan B. Forrest.

5. In his memoirs, Sheridan stated that he was directed to participate in "some operations" against Gen. Earl Van Dorn at Spring Hill. "Knowing that my line of march would carry me through a region where forage was plentiful," Sheridan recalled, "I took along a large train of empty wagons, which I determined to fill

with corn and send back to Murfreesboro." Sheridan, *Memoirs,* 1:256. Either the orders did not indicate urgency or, possibly, Sheridan's leisurely pace reflected his resistance (also seen at Perryville and Missionary Ridge) to following orders which to him did not make sense. As Morris says, "The botched campaign did not reflect badly on Sheridan—it had not been his idea in the first place" (Morris, *Life and Wars of Sheridan,* 116).

6. The remainder of this letter, concerning political matters, is printed in ch. 4.

7. Horn, *Tennessee's War,* 160. Coburn actually may have been a scapegoat for General Gilbert, whose orders he was following. Coburn had advised Gilbert that he was "meeting the enemy in strong force," but Gilbert did not rescind the orders, so Coburn continued to advance. Van Horne, *Army of the Cumberland,* 291.

8. Ellen Sherman was in the reviewing party, along with Mrs. Rosecrans and Mrs. McCook.

9. Bennett priced the gifts at between $1,200 and $1,400, and reported that the "presentation speech was made by Colonel Sherman." Bennett, *History of the 36th Illinois,* 424.

10. This incident is described in Nevins, *War for the Union,* 2:325.

11. Colonel Sherman eventually had a try at farming. Just after his discharge from the army, he unsuccessfully managed a sugar plantation near New Orleans (see ch. 14).

12. The leader of the Copperheads, Clement L. Vallandigham, had been arrested early in 1863 for treason on a questionable order by Gen. Ambrose E. Burnside. He was tried by court-martial and found guilty, but Lincoln commuted his prison sentence to banishment, and on May 25, 1863, he was escorted somewhat unceremoniously through the Union lines near Murfreesboro to the Confederacy. The Confederates, however, were as unhappy to have him as the Union was glad to get rid of him; at the first opportunity, he was sent off to Canada on a blockade-runner. Frank L. Klement, *The Limits of Dissent* (Lexington: University Press of Kentucky, 1970), 191–212. Colonel Sherman's father, in his 1862 campaign for mayor, had been called by the opposition *Chicago Daily Tribune* "the tail to Vallandigham's kite."

13. Colonel Sherman was wrong; the Union army had more men, although the Confederates had more cavalry. Lamers, *Edge of Glory,* 249.

6. Tullahoma Campaign

1. The Tullahoma campaign is described in Lamers, *Edge of Glory,* 275–91. Lincoln called "the flanking of Bragg at Shelbyville, Tullahoma, and Chattanooga the most splendid piece of strategy I know of" (ibid., 290).

2. This was the First Brigade, which included the 88th Illinois Infantry.

3. Sheridan, *Memoirs,* 1:267–70.

4. Stella S. Coatsworth, *The Loyal People of the Northwest* (Chicago: Church, Goodman, and Donnelly, 1869).

5. The nature of Ellen's "spinal affliction" is not known. Apparently it was not too severe, since she joined her husband a week later in Bridgeport.

7. Defeat and Reorganization

1. Early in the fighting at Chickamauga, a gap had developed in the Union lines, just at the point where Longstreet's Confederate troops attacked. Longstreet's troops were reinforcements from the Army of Northern Virginia; they gave Bragg more men than Rosecrans, who had been trying desperately—without success—to get the War Department to send him reinforcements. Although the Confederate sweep was finally slowed by Thomas, the "Rock of Chickamauga," Rosecrans wired Halleck that night, "We have met with a serious disaster" (OR, sec. I, vol. 30, ch. 42, pp. 142–43). Actually, the disaster was not as serious as it appeared at first. The Army of the Cumberland was not destroyed, thanks to Thomas, and in fact Confederate casualties exceeded those of the Union. Nonetheless, the debacle was a major psychological setback for the North and effectively ended Rosecrans's military career.

2. Although Sheridan's division fought well for most of the battle, Sheridan has been criticized for not being as aggressive at the end of the battle as he usually was (Morris, *Life and Wars of Sheridan*, 133–36). However, Sheridan's losses—over 1,500 officers and men out of a force of 4,000—had been severe; they paralleled those at Stones River. Under those circumstances, aggressiveness may not have been possible. Sheridan later complained, "I had been obliged to fight my command under the most disadvantageous circumstances, disconnected, without supports, without even opportunity to form in line of battle, and at one time contending against four divisions of the enemy" (Sheridan, *Memoirs*, 1:287).

3. At Chickamauga, Bragg had about 70,000 men against Rosecrans's 57,000—one of the few major battles of the Civil War in which the Confederates were not outnumbered.

4. Colonel Sherman overlooked the stunning defeat at Chickamauga a few days previously. He habitually overlooked or played down bad news; in this case, it may have been easier for him to deny the defeat because he was on leave and did not participate in that battle.

5. Bragg used his cavalry advantage to restrict the flow of Union supplies, in an attempt to force the Union army out of Chattanooga. The raid to which Colonel Sherman refers took place at Anderson's Crossroads, near Jasper, in which Wheeler's Confederate cavalry destroyed an enormous, ten-mile-long train of supplies and ammunition and then proceeded to capture and demolish a large quantity of stores at McMinnville. Rosecrans continued to have inadequate cavalry to contain the Rebel raids. Lamers, *Edge of Glory*, 374–76.

6. General Steedman was touchy about the spelling of his name. When he was injured at Chickamauga and thought that he might die, he "instructed a staff officer to see to it that his name was spelled correctly in obituaries—Steedman not Steadman." Not a man to be taken lightly, "he was of great size and strength with an aggressive temperament." Boatner, *Civil War Dictionary*, 794. Colonel Sherman understandably was bitter about being replaced, but he was a bit unfair to Gen-

eral Steedman. The latter fought gallantly at Chickamauga, where his brigade lost one-fifth of its strength in twenty minutes.

7. Actually, General Steedman had served in the Ohio Legislature, not the U.S. Congress.

8. Colonel Sherman probably was being facetious; his brother George was eighteen at the time.

9. President Davis indeed had visited the Confederate troops at Chattanooga, in early October, to straighten out dissension in Bragg's command. Davis apparently offered Bragg's job to Longstreet, who turned it down and recommended Johnston, but Davis had no confidence in Johnston, and Bragg ended up holding his command, at least for the time being. James M. McPherson, *Battle Cry of Freedom* (New York, Oxford Univ. Press, 1988), 677. President Davis's respect for Bragg dated back to the Mexican War, when Bragg, then a captain, came to the rescue of the beleaguered Mississippi troops of then Colonel Davis at the Battle of Buena Vista. Grady McWhiney, *Braxton Bragg and the Confederate Defeat* (New York: Columbia Univ. Press, 1969), 1:83–85. Historian W. C. Davis termed Bragg "the pathetic Braxton Bragg, consumed by his own fears and paranoias, unable to face responsibility for his acts." W. C. Davis, review of J. L. McDonough, *Stones River: Bloody Battle in Tennessee* (Knoxville: Univ. of Tennessee Press, 1980), in *Civil War History* 28 (1982): 89–90.

10. See ch. 5, n. 12.

11. It would have been a most unusual army in which the enlisted man "never grumbles or growls"; this is doubtless another example of Colonel Sherman's ignoring or denying evidence that did not reflect creditably upon his troops.

12. Richard S. Merrick was an outspoken Chicago Peace Democrat.

13. Mr. Titsworth was probably the father of Lt. Sylvester Titsworth of the 88th Illinois.

14. In September, Gen. Ambrose Burnside had marched to Knoxville; and the city, then held by a smaller Confederate force under Gen. Simon B. Buckner, had surrendered. In mid-November, President Davis had encouraged Bragg to dispatch Longstreet with 15,000 men to recapture Knoxville, even though the absence of Longstreet's troops severely weakened Bragg's forces as the Battle of Missionary Ridge approached.

15. Charles A. Dana, *Recollections of the Civil War* (New York: Appleton, 1898), 123.

16. Actually Rosecrans appears to have had about 57,000 troops and Bragg 70,000.

17. The business Colonel Sherman mentions probably is the building materials business he entered in 1851.

8. Missionary Ridge

1. Sheridan, *Memoirs*, 1:309.

2. The unexpected success of the assault on Missionary Ridge was due to several factors. (1) Bragg and Breckinridge, convinced that Grant would not attack the center, spread their forces in the center too thin. (2) The Army of the Cumberland

was determined to make up for its defeat at Chickamauga. (3) The Union troops chased the Confederates in the rifle pits so closely that the men on the ridge had to hold their fire for fear of hitting their own men. (4) The pitch of the ridge was so steep that Confederate cannon could not be trained on the attackers. See Peter Cozzens, *The Shipwreck of Their Hopes* (Urbana: Univ. of Illinois Press, 1994).

3. Wiley Sword, *Mountains Touched with Fire* (New York: St. Martin's Press, 1995), 300.

4. OR, ser. I, vol. 31, pt. 2, ch. 43, pp. 230–31.

5. Ibid., 194–96.

6. The first commander of the 22nd Indiana was the fiery Col. (later Gen.) Jefferson C. Davis; Colonel Gooding succeeded Davis when Davis became a brigade commander. Colonel Sherman assigned Gooding to command the third line in his brigade for the assault on Missionary Ridge. In his battle report, he commends the other three line commanders and the other eight regimental commanders but does not mention Gooding in either commendation. Sherman was very careful about such matters, and two omissions can hardly be attributed to oversight. What may have occurred between the two officers is unknown; the 22nd Indiana, however, "was notorious for its controversial behavior" (personal communication from C. Autry, Indiana Historical Society). Gooding resigned two months later (Feb. 7, 1864); and on Apr. 18, 1864, Sheridan transferred the 22nd Indiana to the 14th Army Corps, moving the 28th Kentucky to Sherman's command in its place (OR, ser. I, vol. 32, pt. 3, pp. 408–9).

7. Lieutenant Colonel Chandler had succeeded Colonel Sherman as commanding officer of the 88th Illinois regiment when Sherman became brigade commander.

8. Colonel Jacquess was a clergyman and a lawyer, and twice he had been a college president. He was commissioned as a regimental chaplain but found that role too confining, so he recruited a regiment from church congregations. During a lull in the fighting, he got Lincoln's permission to act as an unofficial envoy to the Confederacy and spent several hours in Richmond with President Davis, trying to convince him to end the war. His 14-year-old son Willie, a drummer boy in the regiment, was captured at Chickamauga but escaped and finished the war under his father's command. Newlin, *History of the 73rd Illinois,* 534–39.

9. Apparently Colonel Harker at first contested Colonel Sherman's claim to have been first over the ridge, but in his later report he said that "my right and Colonel Sherman's left interlocked, so to speak, as we approached the summit . . . [and the first ones there were] a few brave men of my own and Colonel Sherman's command" (Newlin, *History of the 73rd Illinois,* 277). Sheridan wrote in 1886 that he was "not prepared to say which regiment first planted its flag on the hostile works at the summit of Missionary Ridge" (quoted in ibid., 274). Bennett, *History of the 36th Illinois,* 529–30, states, "Perhaps it can never be ascertained exactly what flag was first over the parapet, so nearly together did many of the regiments struggle on to the ridge; but of our part of the line, our [36th Illinois] color-bearer says that the 22nd Indiana was first, while he was second, and the 88th we know was close by." Taylor wrote, "This I can declare: John Cheevers, of the 88th Illinois, planted

his flag by Bragg's headquarters." Benjamin F. Taylor, *Mission Ridge and Lookout Mountain, with Pictures of Life in Camp and Field* (New York: D. Appleton & Co., 1872), 124.

10. Cozzens, *Shipwreck*, 278.
11. Ibid., 307
12. Grant is quoted in Sheridan, *Memoirs,* 1:321.
13. Sheridan, *Memoirs,* 1:316.

9. A Series of Blunders

1. William T. Sherman, *Memoirs of General William T. Sherman,* (New York: D. Appleton and Co., 1891), 1:365.
2. Marcus Woodcock, of the 9th Kentucky Volunteer Infantry, followed essentially the same route through East Tennessee. His more detailed reminiscences of this campaign are in Noe, *Southern Boy,* 243–49.
3. William Marvell, *Burnside* (Chapel Hill: University of North Carolina Press, 1991), 323–33, describes the overall Knoxville campaign, as does W. T. Sherman, *Memoirs,* 393–94.
4. "On General Sherman's arrival at Knoxville, he found a large drove of cattle in a pen, General Burnside comfortably quartered in a mansion, and a fine dinner, including roast turkey, set upon the table" (Bennett, *History of the 36th Regiment*). Although the general may have had turkey, the lower ranks were hungry. Ellen Renshaw House, a Knoxville lady with strong Confederate sympathies, told how Burnside's soldiers came to her house at that time, begging for something to eat (Sutherland, *Very Violent Rebel,* 58–59).
5. There was more mopping up than Granger and the long sequence of other leaders of this expedition had expected, as Longstreet kept reappearing and nipping at their heels. The Union forces, meanwhile, lacked consistent direction and made little, if any, progress. Sheridan described the operations in East Tennessee after Gen. W. T. Sherman's departure for Chattanooga as a "series of blunders and useless marches lasting through the entire winter; a state of affairs doubtless due, in the main, to the fact that the command of the troops was so frequently changed" (Sheridan, *Memoirs,* 1:335–36).
6. Ellen House wrote on December 1 that "the city is completely ruined, scarcely a fence standing. The sidewalks are like a stable yard, and the stench is horrible" (Sutherland, *Very Violent Rebel,* 57).
7. The "big scare" probably was Longstreet's threat to destroy Gen. John G. Parke's force, once Gen. W. T. Sherman returned to Chattanooga. Parke retreated to Blaine's Crossroads, where he was reinforced by Granger (including Sheridan's division), and Longstreet backed off.
8. According to Cozzens, *Shipwreck,* 306, it was Harker's, not Sherman's, brigade which captured the shiny new cannon.
9. Sheridan, *Memoirs,* 1:330.

10. Unfortunately, this recommendation has been lost. A later recommendation by Sheridan is included in ch. 14.

11. To the *Chicago Evening Journal,* Benjamin Franklin Taylor wrote a somewhat lyrical (e.g., "nobler than Caesar's rent mantle are they all") series of letters about the Battle of Missionary Ridge. The letters later were published: Taylor, *Mission Ridge.*

12. Did Colonel Sherman pad his figures? In his diary, he recorded this march as 16, not 23, miles. In 1995, however, on modern roads, my speedometer clocked this trip at 18.5 miles. Plodding along in the cold, it must have seemed to him like 23.

13. Sheridan, *Memoirs,* 1:328.

14. Temple observed that "it is admitted by both Grant and Sherman that an error was committed in not retaining Sherman's army to aid in driving Longstreet beyond the state." Oliver P. Temple, *East Tennessee and the Civil War* (Cincinnati, Oh.: Robert Clarke Co., 1899), 512.

15. No one seemed to want to take responsibility for the East Tennessee operation. General Foster had replaced General Burnside, who had taken over command of the Union forces in the Knoxville area temporarily when Gen. W. T. Sherman left for Chattanooga in November. When a fall from a horse opened an old wound and disabled Foster, Gen. John G. Parke, who had been General Burnside's chief of staff, took on the command in the field. Parke soon passed it on to Gen. Gordon Granger, the 4th Corps commander, who left to join Parke in Knoxville at the start of the Dandridge expedition, so the command ended up, for the time being, with Sheridan. When an engagement appeared imminent, Sheridan, in his usual blunt manner, insisted that Parke and Granger return to the site of action. Although Foster retained titular command, there was no continuity of actual command and no consistency of direction; without consistent leadership, morale was low, and supplies were not provided.

16. General Foster indeed had been injured by a fall from his horse.

17. General Schofield had spent a month in the spring of 1863 in the Army of the Cumberland under Rosecrans but then had been transferred to command of the Department of Missouri. In February 1864, Schofield relieved Foster, and Rosecrans replaced him in Missouri. Schofield was well thought of in the army; W. T. Sherman is reputed to have said on one occasion that he had even more ability than Thomas. Henry Hitchcock, *Marching with Sherman* (New Haven, Conn.: Yale Univ. Press, 1927), 101.

18. Colonel Sherman probably meant Capt. William B. McCreery.

19. In most cases, the three years' service for which veteran regiments had signed up had been completed, and the army mounted an intensive campaign to encourage reenlistment. A generous bounty ($400) was offered, as well as a month's furlough. Presumably it was from this furlough that Colonel Sherman expected the men to return. Their absence delayed the start of the campaign into Georgia, originally scheduled for March, until May 7.

20. On March 10, four days after this letter was written, U. S. Grant became general-in-chief of the Armies of the United States. Colonel Sherman's emphasized pun

on Grant's name suggests that he may have had an inkling of Grant's imminent promotion.

21. Rev. William H. Ryder was pastor of St. Paul's Universalist Church, where the Shermans were members.

22. Sheridan, *Memoirs*, 1:340.

23. Hicken Victor, *Illinois in the Civil War* (Urbana: Univ. of Illinois Press, 1966), 257.

10. Invasion of North Georgia

1. Different views of Johnston's generalship can be found in: Stephen Davis, "A Reappraisal of the Generalship of John Bell Hood in the Battles for Atlanta," in *The Campaign for Atlanta*, ed. Theodore P. Savas and David A. Woodberry (Campbell, Calif.: Savas Woodberry Publications, 1994), 54–55; Stephen E. Woodworth, *Jefferson Davis and His Generals* (Lawrence: Univ. Press of Kansas, 1990), 117; Richard M. McMurry, "Joseph E. Johnston's Atlanta Campaign," in *The Campaign for Atlanta*, ed. Theodore P. Savas and David A. Woodberry (Campbell, Calif.: Savas Woodberry Publications, 1994), 244; and Frank E. Vandiver, "Introduction to Joseph E. Johnston," in *Narrative of Military Operations*, by Joseph E. Johnston (Bloomington: Indiana Univ. Press, 1959), xxvii.

2. Colonel Sherman's orders of May 4, 1864, read: "The general commanding [Newton] directs that Colonel Sherman occupy Rocky Face Ridge with his command, maintaining a sufficient force in his front to repel an assault. The remainder he will distribute along the ridge at the most accessible point north until near the gorge. Orders must be given to commanding officers of regiments to assist each other in case of an attack. He will picket along his eastern front, posting reserves at accessible points. He will also post a strong picket on the western slope of the ridge, connecting with General Wood's pickets." OR, ser. I, vol. 38, pt. 4, ch. 1, pp. 144–45.

3. General Newton reported that the summit of Rocky Face was a sharp ridge, "never wider than the room occupied by four men abreast, often obstructed so that the men had to go in single file." OR, ser. I, vol. 38, pt. 1, ch. 50, p. 290.

4. See also Jeffrey S. Dean, "The Battle of Pickett's Mill," in *The Campaign for Atlanta*, ed. Theodore P. Savas and David A. Woodberry (Campbell, Calif.: Savas Woodberry Publications, 1994), 344–48.

5. Resaca was the first major engagement of the North Georgia campaign. The Union armies, although outnumbering the Confederates by almost two to one, and although forcing their enemy to retreat, failed to deliver the mortal blow that General Sherman had hoped for. Newton's division arrived on May 14, in time to relieve Cox's hard-pressed division of the 23rd Corps on the Union left; by May 15, Newton had moved to the far right of the Union line.

6. Albert Castel, *Decision in the West* (Lawrence: Univ. Press of Kansas, 1991), 193.

7. Scaife's account of the same events differs somewhat. He says that Johnston left Gen. Benjamin F. Cheatham's division (not Wheeler's cavalry) behind to cover his retreat from (not to) Adairsville. Moreover, "Col. Francis T. Sherman's brigade. . . . led the

federal advance down the wagon road, but was delayed several hours by Cheatham's stubborn defense. . . . the skirmishers of Sherman's brigade ran into such heavy resistance that they called on Major Arthur MacArthur's 24th Wisconsin regiment [not General Howard] for support." William R. Scaife, "An Overview of the Atlanta Campaign," in *The Campaign for Atlanta*, ed. Theodore P. Savas and David A. Woodberry (Campbell, Calif.: Savas Woodberry Publications, 1994), 280. Major MacArthur, who received the Congressional Medal of Honor for his conduct at Missionary Ridge, was the father of Gen. Douglas MacArthur.

8. General Kimball had been commissioned as colonel in June 1861 and promoted to brigadier general in April 1862. Among other engagements in which he fought were Antietam, Fredericksburg, and Vicksburg.

9. Colonel Sherman does not give the whole story. At the Battle of New Hope Church on May 25, fought in a deluge of rain, Hooker's Corps suffered heavy losses in an unsuccessful attempt to drive the Confederates from their position; "all that evening and far into the night we assaulted Hood's works again and again . . . but in vain." Oliver O. Howard, *Autobiography of Oliver Otis Howard* (New York: Baker & Taylor Co., 1907), 1:546.

10. At the ferocious battle of Pickett's Mill, on May 27, Wood's division was soundly defeated by Confederate troops under the redoubtable Gen. Pat Cleburne. Dean, "Battle of Pickett's Mill," 344–48; and Castel, *Decision in the West*, 233–41.

11. The Confederate attack at the Battle of Dallas on May 28 was no more successful than the Union attacks on May 25 and 27 had been.

12. Actually the Confederate rear guard action at Adairsville appears to have been under the direct command of Maj. Gen. Benjamin F. Cheatham.

13. The remainder of this letter is lost.

14. The first part of this letter is lost.

15. The 88th Illinois regiment originally mustered 972 officers and men.

16. Lieutenant General (also Bishop) Polk practiced both his professions in this campaign; on two occasions while a corps commander, he took time off to baptize his superior officers, Gen. Joseph E. Johnston and Gen. John Bell Hood. Perhaps he should have stayed with the church; Castel, *Decision in the West*, 289, describes him as "at best mediocre, at worst execrable, as a military leader." "A solemn thinker and a heavy eater," he was killed on the crest of Pine Mountain when he moved too slowly out of the line of fire (Lewis, *Sherman: Fighting*, 184, 359).

17. On this day, General Sherman telegraphed General Halleck: "This is the nineteenth day of rain [this month] . . . The roads are impassable and fields and woods become quagmires after a few wagons have crossed." The troops fought, marched, ate, and slept in mud and in trenches knee-deep in water. Castel, *Decision in the West*, 289–90.

18. Vetter, *Sherman*, 208.

19. General McCook led the assault and was fatally wounded as he reached the top of the rebel works. He was one of nine brothers of Gen. Alexander McD. McCook, in whose corps Colonel Sherman served at Stones River. All the McCook brothers fought in the Union army; four were generals. Boatner, *Civil War Dictionary*, 526–27.

20. Colonel Sherman, once uninhibited in his criticism of his superiors, at this time keeps any such concerns to himself. His former division commander, General Newton, was not so restrained; his comment to General Sherman after the battle was: "Well, this is a damned appropriate culmination of one month's blundering" (Castel, *Decision in the West,* 321).

11. Guest of the Confederacy

1. "Case's Ford" does not appear in available records. Colonel Sherman probably meant "Pace's Ford," a ford across the Chattahoochie River near Atlanta.
2. Howard, *Autobiography,* 1:600. General Howard wrote in his report to Headquarters, Army of the Tennessee, "For gallantry, efficiency, unflinching activity, and gentlemanly deportment I commend the different members of my staff, viz.: Colonel Francis T. Sherman, chief of staff (captured while reconnoitering July 7); [and others]" (OR, ser. I, vol. 38, pt. I, ch. 50, p. 204).
3. Sherman, *Memoirs,* 2:67
4. By the summer of 1864, food for armed forces and civilians alike in the Confederacy was in very short supply, and prisoners were low on the priority list.
5. Officers and enlisted men were kept in separate prisons, and the conditions at Camp Oglethorpe in Macon never were as deplorable as at Andersonville, the enlisted men's prison located about 60 miles from Macon. Conditions were bad enough, however. Chaplain Henry S. White described the Macon stockade as "an enclosure of nearly three acres, surrounded by a strong board fence some sixteen feet high." Armed guards walked along a platform four feet from the top; prisoners had to remain behind a twelve-foot deadline. A very small contaminated brook, used for bathing and washing clothes, ran through the enclosure. There was an old stable and a building used to shelter sick prisoners and senior officers; junior officers "couched down wherever they chose to," some with makeshift shelters. Edible food, potable water, soap, firewood, and cooking utensils all were in short supply. Edward D. Jervey, ed., *Prison Life Among the Rebels* (Kent, Oh.: Kent State Univ. Press, 1990), 55–57.
6. Realf was Colonel Sherman's "lithe and agile" aide, who, Sherman wrote to his brother, had "pricked up the skulkers with his Sergeant's sword" at the Battle of Missionary Ridge. Although Realf served with distinction throughout the war, his peacetime career was erratic. He had emigrated from England at nineteen and soon became an impassioned antislavery proponent; for a while in Kansas, he was a member of John Brown's "cabinet." After the war he led a peripatetic existence as a poet and lecturer, interspersed with several short-term marital and religious commitments. His emotional swings suggest what was then called *la folie circulaire* (later manic-depressive disease), and he committed suicide in 1878. He dedicated one sonnet to Gen. William H. Lytle (Colonel Sherman's replacement, who was killed at Chickamauga), but none to Colonel Sherman. See Richard J. Minton, Memoir, in Richard Realf, *Poems by Richard Realf* (New York: Funk and Wagnalls, 1898).
7. The name or rank may be wrong; I find no record of a Confederate General Nelson who was in the Atlanta area at this time.

8. Colonel Sherman's exchange was "brought about by the efforts of his devoted wife who, after repeated failures, first before President Lincoln and then before the Bureau Officer, finally persuaded the Secretary of War that his immediate exchange was for the good of the service." Military Order of the Loyal Legion of the United States, *In memoriam, Companion Brigadier General Francis Trowbridge Sherman* (N.p.: privately printed, 1905).

9. Presumably Isaac N. Arnold, the Republican who had defeated Mayor Sherman in his race for Congress in 1862. Arnold was a friend and later a biographer of Lincoln. See Isaac N. Arnold, *The Life of Abraham Lincoln* (Chicago: A. C. McClurg, 1884).

10. Lieutenant Davis had been taken prisoner at Gettysburg and had escaped from a Federal hospital. Philip N. Racine, ed., *"Unspoiled Heart": The Journal of Charles Mattocks of the 17th Maine* (Knoxville: Univ. of Tennessee Press, 1994), 359.

11. Fellow prisoner John V. Hadley wrote, "Tunneling was a big business here. There were three of them under way at one time, and came near being successful. But the treachery of an Illinois captain revealed the whole scheme . . . It is said that the captain was promised a special exchange" (John V. Hadley, ed., *Seven Months a Prisoner* (Indianapolis, Ind.: J. M. and F. J. Meikel and Co., 1868). Chaplain White commented, "Attempts to escape employed the attention of a large number [of prisoners] and the hope of escape kept many a poor fellow from sinking in despair" (Jervey, *Prison Life*, 67).

12. On July 17, the much more aggressive Gen. John Bell Hood replaced General Johnston in command of the Confederate army in front of Atlanta, and three days later he made an unsuccessful attack on Thomas's Union forces at Peachtree Creek. On July 22, Hood sent Hardee's Corps on a fifteen-mile night march to surprise McPherson's forces near Decatur, east of Atlanta. This attack came close to success and gave the Union army "the most brutal treatment it had received since leaving Chattanooga," inflicting 4,000 casualties and leaving 12 (not 22) guns captured (Stephen Davis, "Reappraisal of the Generalship of John Bell Hood," in Savas and Woodbury, *Campaign for Atlanta*, 76). General McPherson indeed was killed, on June 24, the only Union army commander killed during the war, but Generals Hood and Smith were not killed.

13. A rescue effort indeed had been instituted, but it did not succeed. Colonel Sherman wrote in his autobiography, "The task of carrying out this schedule was assigned to General [George W.] Stoneman, but he made a miserable failure of it, being taken prisoner by the Rebels and confined in the same place as the others." Actually, Stoneman's cavalry was ordered by Gen. W. T. Sherman only to destroy the railroad to Macon. Stoneman requested and received permission to go further, once he had destroyed the railroad, and raid Macon in order to liberate the prisoners at the Macon officers' prison and at the notorious Andersonville stockade. Instead of carrying out the Macon raid after destroying the railroad, Stoneman split his forces and took 2,200 men directly to the vicinity of Andersonville, where they were cut off by Wheeler's cavalry; Stoneman and 700 of his men were captured. Boatner, *Civil War Dictionary*, 801–2.

14. According to Lt. Edmund Ryan, the "old building" was allotted to "generals and other field officers; captains and lieutenants slept out in the open." Colonel Sherman presumably slept under cover. William M. Armstrong, ed., "Cahaba to Charleston: The Prison Odyssey of Lieutenant Edmund E. Ryan," *Civil War History* 8, no. 2 (1962): 218.

15. President Roosevelt's mother, Martha Bulloch Roosevelt, was an unreconstructed southerner; her half-brother, James D. Bulloch, had been a commander and a foreign agent in the Confederate navy.

16. Military Order of the Loyal Legion, *In memoriam, F. T. Sherman*, 5 (unnumbered).

17. Colonel Hoyt was from Pennsylvania, not Ohio; later he became governor of Pennsylvania.

18. Maj. Charles P. Mattocks, of the 17th Maine Regiment, was on the train with Colonel Sherman but did not jump off. He wrote of a "grand project for seizing the train," which the prisoners had planned in advance but which could not be carried out. When the prisoners heard the news of its abandonment, 84 of them jumped off the cars; 76 of these were recaptured. Racine, *Unspoiled Heart*, 190–91. Another prisoner described the Confederates' response: "After the men began to tumble off we stopped at the first telegraph station . . . the officers . . . turned out promptly with their men and dogs, came up the railroad until they found a fresh track which one crew took, the rest going on until they were after them all." Daniel L. Langworthy, *Reminiscences of a Prisoner of War and His Escape* (Minneapolis, Minn.: Byron Printing Co., 1915), 28–29.

19. Fellow prisoner Daniel Langworthy did not agree with Sherman that the move of prisoners to Charleston "to be placed under fire" was to stave off a rescue attempt. Instead, he wrote, "we were brought [to Charleston] in the hope that we might help to protect the city from the continuous cannonading of our troops on Morris Island" (Langworthy, *Prisoner*, 29).

20. There is no record of either the letter of July 31 or the letter that Colonel Sherman sent to Mrs. Sherman on July 9.

21. Francis T. Sherman, Biographical Memoir (typewritten copy, 1899), 9.

22. Glazier described the Charleston jail as "a large octagonal building of four stories, surmounted by a tower forty feet in height. On its right is the large bastile [*sic*] shaped work-house." Compared to the jail, he found the Roper Hospital a "paradise." Willard W. Glazier, *The Capture, the Prison Pen, and the Escape* (Hartford, Conn.: H. E. Goodwin, 1868), 146.

23. Colonel Sherman took his command duties seriously. Maj. Charles P. Mattocks, a fellow prisoner, wrote on August 16, "Today we have a large detail of our officers busy cleaning up the rubbish in the yard and the dirt in the building. Colonel Sherman, the senior officer present, has been requested by the Rebel authorities to manage affairs according to his own views. Everyone seems to take hold of the business with the right spirit." Racine, *Unspoiled Heart*, 181.

24. Major Vickers was one of the officers who escaped with Colonel Sherman from the train bearing them from Macon to Charleston (see diary entry of July 28, 1864).

Apparently the "great indignation amongst [the] officers" against Vickers was not unanimous. In 1868, when Sherman's appointment as postmaster of Chicago was being considered by the Senate, one J. A. Kellogg, who also had been a prisoner, wrote to Sen. T. C. Howe (Republican of Wisconsin), objecting strongly to the appointment. After calling Sherman a "truckling sycophant to the rebels and a tyrant to ourselves," Kellogg claimed that Major Vickers had been given the blanket surreptitiously by the wife of the hospital janitor and should have been protected, not exposed, by Sherman. The latter, Kellogg said, was "a McClellan man, one of the very few who disgraced themselves and the Cause by supporting him." Sen. Lyman Trumbull (Republican of Illinois) had a copy of this letter made and forwarded to Sherman.

This was not the first time that Colonel Sherman appeared rigid and moralistic about stealing (see ch. 2, n. 12). On the other hand, to condone stealing in this case would have reduced his bargaining power in obtaining concessions from the rebel authorities. To be a prisoner in command of prisoners is not an easy role.

25. The Confederate prison authorities objected to prayers for the president of the United States (Jervey, *Prison Life*, 64–65).
26. Major Mattocks wrote that the Roman Catholic Sisters of Mercy "are everywhere personally attending to the trials and suffering of sick and wounded soldiers. It matters not to which army the soldier belongs. That he needs help is enough for these noble women to know." Racine, *Unspoiled Heart*, 203. The Sisters were particularly helpful during the yellow fever epidemic (376).
27. Presumably the money was Confederate, to be used to buy supplementary food—and to be paid back after the war in U.S. currency.
28. By October 1, the yellow fever "was raging fearfully" in Charleston (Glazier, *Capture*, 166).
29. Colonel Montgomery, who commanded the 25th Wisconsin regiment, lost an arm and was captured at Decatur, Ga., on July 14, 1864 (Boatner, *Civil War Dictionary*, 562).
30. Here and in the entry below, Colonel Sherman doubtless meant Charlotte, N.C.
31. Colonel Sherman probably meant Robert Ould, who had been assistant secretary of war in the Confederacy and at this time was the agent for exchange of prisoners.
32. Colonel Walker, captured at Chancellorsville, became commissioner of Indian affairs and later president of Massachusetts Institute of Technology.
33. "Return of Colonel Francis T. Sherman," *Chicago Daily Tribune*, Oct. 15, 1864.

12. Road to Appomattox

1. In April 1864, Sheridan had been given the task of reorganizing the cavalry of the Army of the Potomac. The cavalry's leader, technically, was Gen. George Meade, although General Grant, by then general-in-chief of the Armies of the United States, made his headquarters with the Army of the Potomac and was the one who called the turn. Sheridan fought with the Army of the Potomac until early in August 1864,

when Grant, frustrated by the inability of Union forces to catch up with Gen. Jubal Early's Confederate cavalry, organized a new army, the Army of the Shenandoah, and put Sheridan in charge of the effort to track down Early. In September, Sheridan caught up with Early at Winchester, defeated him, and proceeded to ravage the Shenandoah Valley, the source of a major share of Confederate provisions. On Oct. 19, the Confederates surprised and almost routed the Federals at Cedar Creek, at a time when Sheridan was in Winchester; Sheridan returned on his horse Rienzi to rally his troops and turn potentially ignominious defeat into a major victory (see preface, n. 1).

2. Col. Henry Hescock, from Missouri, had become chief of artillery in Sheridan's division after the Battle of Stones River. He was captured at Chickamauga.

3. At the time, Chicago voted Democratic by a slim margin, but the Republicans controlled Cook County. The Republican state legislature was trying to place the selection of city officials under county jurisdiction.

4. This is the only mention of what appears to have been malaria, which was endemic below the frost line (hence the term "southern fever"). Whether Colonel Sherman acquired the disease in prison or before is not known.

5. In English: "So that no harm might come to University property."

6. Anne Freudenberg and John Casteen, eds., "John Minor's Civil War Diary," *Magazine of Albemarle County History* 22 (1963): 47, 53.

7. Morris, *Life and Wars of Sheridan*, 240.

8. Carl Sandburg, *Abraham Lincoln: The War Years* (New York: Harcourt Brace, 1939), 4:149–54. See also Philip Van D. Stern, *An End to Valor* (Boston: Houghton Mifflin, 1938), 87–98.

9. General Gordon described the Battle of Fort Stedman in John B. Gordon, *Reminiscences of the Civil War* (New York: Scribner's, 1904).

10. Sheridan relieved Warren of his command because of lack of leadership. Fourteen years later, Colonel Sherman testified at a court of inquiry concerning the matter (see ch. 14).

11. Probably Ford's Station.

12. A very detailed account of these battles can be found in Henry E. Tremain, *Last Hours of Sheridan's Cavalry* (New York: Bonnell, Silver & Bowers, 1904).

13. OR, ser. I, vol. 46, pt. 1, ch. 58, pp. 1114–15.

13. *National Tragedy and Personal Disappointment*

1. OR, ser. I, vol. 46, pt. 3, ch. 58, p. 722.

2. In 1865, Mayor Sherman received just over half the number of votes cast for him two years before, losing to theater director John B. Rice by a vote of 11,078 to 5,600. The old campaigner did not give up; he tried once more, in 1867, and again lost to John Rice, this time by 11,904 to 7,971. Pierce, *History of Chicago*, 2:507.

3. Gen. William T. Sherman had met with both Gen. Joseph E. Johnston and Confederate Secretary of War John C. Breckinridge and had worked out an agreement

which "was more like an outright treaty of peace than a simple surrender document" (Catton, *Hallowed Ground*, 484). It guaranteed the rights and franchises of the rebellious southerners and promised recognition of the southern state governments once they were back in the fold. Had his terms been carried out, a lot of the grief of the Reconstruction era might have been avoided, but clearly he had overstepped his authority. No one knows how Lincoln would have viewed Sherman's efforts, but probably he would have greeted them more sympathetically than Secretary Stanton, who came close to accusing Sherman of disloyalty. The repudiation of Sherman's attempt to arrive at an expeditious and humane reconciliation with the South seems to have contributed to the vindictiveness of the eventual Reconstruction (Johnston, *Narrative*, 402–16).

General Johnston provided a detailed account of his negotiations with his old rival, Gen. W. T. Sherman. It described how the two veteran warriors thoughtfully worked out the surrender terms, each seeking what he felt would be best for their reunited country. At the same time, they were aware that Lincoln's assassination, on the day before the negotiations began, probably would render their efforts useless. As Johnston said, the assassination was "the greatest possible calamity to the South" (402).

4. Joseph G. Dawson III, "General Phil Sheridan and Military Reconstruction in Louisiana," *Civil War History* 24, no. 2 (1978): 149.
5. William L. Richter, "General Phil Sheridan: The Historians and Reconstruction," *Civil War History* 33, no. 2 (1987): 131–35.
6. The letter mentioned here is lost.
7. The identities of "Josh," Aunt Jerusha, and Mrs. Branson remain unknown.

14. End of the Quest

1. Richard Yates was elected governor of Illinois in 1860, and Richard J. Oglesby succeeded him in 1864; both were Republicans. In his July 22, 1865, letter to Secretary Stanton in support of Colonel Sherman's promotion, Governor Oglesby wrote, "I cheerfully endorse it and take pleasure in stating to you should such a thing be considered possible now, that no appointment of the character requested for him could be more pleasing to our people. He is undoubtedly entirely worthy of it" (Office of Adjutant General, Volunteer Service Branch, 1865, NA).
2. "Long John" Wentworth was a colorful Chicago politician who served one term in Congress as a Democrat and, later, another term as a Republican. He was twice mayor of Chicago as a Republican. See Don E. Fehrenbacher, *Chicago Giant* (Madison, Wisc.: American History Research Center, 1957).
3. Office of Adjutant General, Volunteer Services Branch, 1865, NA.
4. Ibid.
5. Stanton's discourtesy to the elder Sherman more likely was due to the fact that he was a politician from the opposing party whose son had, with General Grant's help, outflanked the secretary and gained his promotion.

6. Dengue fever "does not appear in the official lists, but it existed at the time [of the Civil War] and was sometimes diagnosed. An influenza-like disease causing quick prostration (also called 'broken-bone fever'), its course was brief, complications few, and mortality virtually nil." Paul E. Steiner, *Disease in the Civil War* (Springfield, Ill.: Charles C Thomas, 1968), 15. Dengue was insect-borne and apparently entered the U.S. by ship, usually from the Caribbean; hence its presence in New Orleans.

7. The cards were stacked against Sherman's making a success of the sugar plantation. He had no farming experience; few field hands wanted to return to the scene of their previous servitude; neither experienced plantation overseers nor efficient refineries were available; and 1866 and 1867 were poor years for the sugar crop. Roger W. Shugg, *Origins of Class Struggle in Louisiana* (University: Louisiana State Univ. Press, 1939), 248–50. The Shermans' son, Francis Cornwall Sherman II, was born in Jefferson Parish, La., on Oct. 31, 1866. Another son, Eaton Goodell Sherman, was born in Chicago on Nov. 27, 1870.

8. H. A. Musham, "The Great Chicago Fire," in *Papers in Illinois History* (Springfield: Illinois State Historical Society, 1941), 49:142–44.

9. Colonel Sherman appears to have had no wartime association with the 57th Illinois Infantry Regiment. His party of four included his future son-in-law (and my grandfather) J. Frank Aldrich.

10. Noah A. Trudeau, *Out of the Storm* (Boston: Little, Brown, 1994), 314. Sherman's testimony and cross-examination, on the 60th day of the Warren court of inquiry, are recorded in the *Supplement to the OR,* sec. I, vol. 9, pp. 855–67.

11. Military Order of the Loyal Legion of the United States, *In memoriam, F. T. Sherman.*

12. Pension records (microfilmed), NA, Pension Bureau #1325890.

13. 59th Cong., Private Bill 2178, Act granting a pension to Eleanor N. Sherman, *Statutes at Large* (Washington, D.C.: Government Printing Office, 1907), vol. 1, pt. 2, p. 2711.

BIBLIOGRAPHY

Books

PRIMARY SOURCES

Bennett, Lyman G. *History of the 36th Regiment of Illinois Volunteer Infantry During the War of the Great Rebellion.* Aurora, Ill.: Knickerbocker and Holder, 1876.

Boyd, Belle. *Belle Boyd in Camp and Prison.* New York: Blelock & Company, 1865.

Clark, Willene B., ed. *Valleys of the Shadow.* Knoxville: University of Tennessee Press, 1994.

Coatsworth, Stella S. *The Loyal People of the Northwest.* Chicago: Church, Goodman, and Donnelly, 1869.

Dana, Charles A. *Recollections of the Civil War.* New York: Appleton, 1898.

Fowler, William. *Memorials of William Fowler.* New York: A. D. F. Randolph & Company, 1875.

Francis, Charles L. *Narrative of a Private Soldier.* Brooklyn, N.Y.: Wm. Jenkins & Company, 1879.

Glazier, Willard W. *The Capture, the Prison Pen, and the Escape.* Hartford, Conn.: H. E. Goodwin, 1868.

Gordon, John B. *Reminiscences of the Civil War.* New York, Scribner's, 1904.

Hadley, John V. *Seven Months a Prisoner.* Indianapolis, Ind.: J. M. and F. J. Meikel & Company, 1868.

Howard, Oliver O. *Autobiography of Oliver Otis Howard.* New York: Baker & Taylor Company, 1907.

Howard, Oliver O. "The Struggle for Atlanta." In *Battles and Leaders of the Civil War.* Vol. 4:293–325. Edited by Clarence C. Buell and Robert U. Johnson. New York, 1884.

Jervey, Edward D., ed. *Prison Life Among the Rebels.* Kent, Ohio: Kent State University Press, 1990.

Johnston, Joseph E. *Narrative of Military Operations.* Bloomington: Indiana University Press, 1959.

Langworthy, Daniel A. *Reminiscences of a Prisoner of War and His Escape.* Minneapolis, Minn.: Byron Printing Company, 1915.

Musham, H. A. "The Great Chicago Fire." In *Papers in Illinois History.* Vol. 49:69–187. Springfield: Illinois State Historical Society, 1941.

Newlin, William H., et al., eds. *A History of the 73rd Regiment of Illinois Infantry Volunteers.* Chicago: Privately Printed, 1890.

Noe, Kenneth W., ed. *A Southern Boy in Blue.* Knoxville: University of Tennessee Press, 1996.

Racine, Philip N., ed. *"Unspoiled Heart": The Journal of Charles Mattocks of the 17th Maine.* Knoxville: University of Tennessee Press, 1994.

Sheridan, Philip H. *Personal Memoirs of P. H. Sheridan.* 2 vols. New York: Charles R. Webster & Company, 1888.

Sherman, Robert T., ed. *Letters from the Gold Rush.* Chicago: Privately published by R. T. Sherman, 1980.

Sherman, William T. *Memoirs of General William T. Sherman.* New York: D. Appleton & Company, 1891.

Sutherland, Daniel E., ed. *A Very Violent Rebel.* Knoxville: University of Tennessee Press, 1996.

Taylor, Benjamin F. *Mission Ridge and Lookout Mountain, with Pictures of Life in Camp and Field.* New York: D. Appleton & Company, 1872.

Tremain, Henry E. *Last Hours of Sheridan's Cavalry.* New York: Bonnell, Silver & Bowers, 1904.

U.S. War Department. *Compiled Service Records of Military Units in Volunteer Organizations, 1861–65.* National Archives, Washington, D.C. [Microfilm Edition].

——. *Official Army Register of the Volunteer Forces of the U.S. Army for the Years 1861–1865.* 9 vols. Gaithersburg, Md.: R. R. Van Sickle Military Books, 1987, 1865.

——. *The War of the Rebellion: A Compilation of the Official Records of the Union and Confederate Armies.* 70 vols. Washington, D.C.: Government Printing Office, 1880–1901.

SECONDARY SOURCES

Alvord, Clarence W., ed. *Centennial History of Illinois.* Springfield: Illinois Centennial Commission, 1920.

Andreas, Alfred T. *History of Chicago.* 4 vols. New York: Arno Press, 1975.

Arnold, Isaac N. *The Life of Abraham Lincoln.* Chicago: A. C. McClurg, 1884.

Boatner, Mark M. *The Civil War Dictionary.* New York: David McKay Company, 1966.

Castel, Albert. *Decision in the West.* Lawrence: University Press of Kansas, 1991.

Catton, Bruce. *This Hallowed Ground.* New York: Doubleday, Pocket Books ed., 1956.

Cook, Frederick F. *Bygone Days in Chicago.* Chicago: A. C. McClurg, 1910.

Cozzens, Peter. *No Better Place to Die.* Urbana: University of Illinois Press, 1990.

Cozzens, Peter. *The Shipwreck of Their Hopes.* Urbana: University of Illinois Press, 1994.

Commager, Henry S., ed. *The Blue and the Gray.* Indianapolis, Ind.: Bobbs-Merrill, 1950.

Dixon, David. *Hero of Beecher Island.* Lincoln: University of Nebraska Press, 1994.

Eddy, Thomas M. *Patriotism of Illinois.* 2 vols. Chicago: Clarke & Company, 1865.

Fehrenbacher, Don E. *Chicago Giant.* Madison, Wisc.: American History Research Center, 1957.

Hergesheimer, Joseph. *Sheridan: A Military Narrative.* Boston: Houghton Mifflin, 1931.

Hicken, Victor, *Illinois in the Civil War.* Urbana: University of Illinois Press, 1966.

Hitchcock, Henry. *Marching with Sherman.* New Haven, Conn.: Yale University Press, 1927.

Horn, Stanley F., ed. *Tennessee's War.* Nashville: Tennessee Civil War Centennial Commission, 1965.

Klement, Frank L. *Dark Lanterns.* Chicago: University of Chicago Press, 1960.

Klement, Frank L. *The Limits of Dissent.* Lexington: University Press of Kentucky, 1970.

Lamers, William C. *The Edge of Glory.* New York: Harcourt Brace, 1961.

Lewis, Lloyd. *Sherman: Fighting Prophet.* New York: Harcourt Brace, 1932.

Marvell, William. *Burnside.* Chapel Hill: University of North Carolina Press, 1991.

McKinney, Francis F. *Education in Violence.* Detroit: Wayne State University Press, 1961.

McPherson, James M. *Battle Cry of Freedom.* New York: Oxford University Press, 1988.

McPherson, James M. *For Cause and Comrades—Why Men Fought in the Civil War.* New York: Oxford University Press, 1997.

McWhiney, Grady. *Braxton Bragg and the Confederate Defeat.* 2 vols. New York: Columbia University Press, 1969.

Military Order of the Loyal Legion of the United States. *In memoriam, Companion Brigadier General Francis Trowbridge Sherman.* N.p.: privately printed, 1905.

Moore, Frank. *Women of the War.* Hartford, Conn.: S. S. Scranton, 1866.

Morris, Roy, Jr. *The Life and Wars of General Philip H. Sheridan.* New York: Crown Publishing, 1992.

Moses, John, and James Kirkland. *History of Chicago, Illinois.* Chicago: Munsell and Co., 1895.

Nevins, Allan. *The War for the Union.* 4 vols. New York: Scribner's, 1959.

Pierce, Bessie. *A History of Chicago.* 2 vols. New York: Knopf, 1940.

Read, Thomas Buchanan. *Sheridan's Ride.* Philadelphia: J. B. Lippincott Co., 1892.

Sandburg, Carl. *Abraham Lincoln: The War Years.* 4 vols. New York: Harcourt Brace, 1939.

Savas, Theodore F., and David A. Woodberry, eds. *The Campaign for Atlanta.* Campbell, Calif.: Savas Woodberry Publications, 1994.

Scarborough, Ruth. *Belle Boyd: Siren of the South.* Macon, Ga.: Mercer University Press, 1983.

Shugg, Roger. *Origins of Class Struggle in Louisiana.* University: Louisiana State University Press, 1939.

Steiner, Paul E. *Disease in the Civil War.* Springfield, Ill.: Charles C Thomas, 1968.

Stern, Philip Van D. *An End to Valor.* Boston: Houghton Mifflin, 1938.

Sword, Wiley. *Mountains Touched with Fire*. New York: St. Martin's Press, 1995.

Temple, Oliver P. *East Tennessee and the Civil War*. Cincinnati, Oh.: Robert Clarke Company, 1899.

Thomas, Wilbur. *General George H. Thomas*. New York: Exposition Press, 1964.

Trudeau, Noah A. *Out of the Storm*. Boston: Little, Brown, 1994.

Upton, George P., and Elias Colbert. *Biographical Sketches of the Leading Men of Chicago*. Chicago: Wilson, St. Clair Company, 1868.

Van Horne, Thomas B. *History of the Army of the Cumberland*. 2 vols. Cincinnati, Oh.: Robert Clarke & Company, 1875.

Vetter, Charles E. *Sherman*. Gretna, La.: Pelican Publishing Company, 1992.

Woodman, James M., ed. *Portrait and Biographical Album of Lake County, Illinois*. Waukegan, Ill.: Lake Publishing Company, 1891.

Woodworth, Stephen E. *Jefferson Davis and His Generals*. Lawrence: University Press of Kansas, 1990.

Newspapers and Periodicals

Chicago Daily Tribune
Chicago Times
Civil War History
Journal of the Illinois State Historical Society
Magazine of Albemarle County [Virginia] History
Papers in Illinois History

Documents

Records of the Adjutant General's Office. National Archives, Washington, D.C., M619, M1064.

Sherman, Francis T. "Autobiography." 1899. Typescript in Papers of J. Frank Aldrich. Chicago Historical Society Library.

INDEX

Quest for a Star was designed and typeset on a Macintosh computer system using PageMaker software. The text and titles are set in Adobe Garamond, the chapter numerals in Chevalier Open, and the ornaments in Zapf Dingbats. This book was designed by Todd Duren, composed by Kimberly Scarbrough, and manufactured by Thomson-Shore, Inc. The recycled paper used in this book is designed for an effective life of at least three hundred years.